Richard H. Blum
and Associates

DRUG DEALERS- TAKING ACTION

Jossey-Bass Publishers
San Francisco • Washington • London • 1973

DRUG DEALERS—TAKING ACTION
Options for International Response
       by Richard H. Blum and Associates

Copyright © 1973 by: Jossey-Bass, Inc., Publishers
                     615 Montgomery Street
                     San Francisco, California 94111

                          and

                     Jossey-Bass Limited
                     3 Henrietta Street
                     London WC2E 8LU

Library of Congress Catalogue Card Number LC 76-187065

International Standard Book Number ISBN 0-87589-166-7

Manufactured in the United States of America

JACKET DESIGN BY WILLI BAUM

FIRST EDITION

Code 7309

The Jossey-Bass
Behavioral Science Series

General Editors

WILLIAM E. HENRY, *University of Chicago*

NEVITT SANFORD, *Wright Institute, Berkeley*

Foreword

The International Research Group on Drug Legislation and Programs is pleased to present under its sponsorship *Drug Dealers—Taking Action,* a companion to several volumes produced by the Group as part of its program. One of these, *Controlling Drugs: An International Handbook for Drug Classification* (R. Blum, D. Bovet, and J. Moore, editors, Jossey-Bass), was prepared for and is published under the auspices of the United Nations Social Defense Research Institute, Rome. Another, on the uses of information in drug legislation, by William Lanouette, presents work sponsored by the Group. A third, on the international organs in the drug control field, will be published in 1974. The Group, through these publications as well as its other work, hopes to provide information and perspectives helpful in improving present international drug activities and useful in planning new legislation and programs designed to reduce problems associated with psychoactive drugs.

However comprehensive may be the work in which the Group and its affiliated members, agencies, and governments en-

gage, considerable areas of uncertainty will remain as to what constitutes the most desirable action to interdict drug problems, especially in developing policies and instruments to cope with the
pervasive and troubling national and international drug traffic. For
this reason, *Drug Dealers—Taking Action* is most welcome, for its
aim is to provide information and suggestions bearing on policy
development in regard to drug traffic and drug traffickers. As the
authors affirm, their findings and suggestions are but illustrations
of the research and thinking that can be helpful in policy making.
We too emphasize the importance of fact finding by objective means
and reflection on those facts to generate action proposals. The
Group, and the individual authors of this volume, would not contend that the substance of this volume is sufficient for the final
establishment of any national or international law or program. They
would suggest that the findings are powerful enough to require their
inclusion in any consideration of revisions in present policy and
policy instruments, at least for the regions in which these studies
have been conducted.

Alertness to the likelihood that policies need to be attuned to
regional realities is a theme found consistently as the work of the
Group progresses. To determine regional realities thus becomes a
compelling requirement. *Drug Dealers—Taking Action* and the
previous work its authors have done on drug dealers and the origins
of illicit drug use (all cited in this volume) offer models to others
who wish to make their decisions rationally. Insofar as such work
shows similarities across national boundaries, the international task
is made simpler, for one may assume that uniform joint endeavors
will be fruitful. As an illustration, the marked similarities between
drug dealers in the London and San Francisco regions (as reported
in the study preliminary to this volume—Blum and Associates,
1972a) suggest that in youthful drug delinquency two Western
nations may face similar phenomena. But that same study showed
some differences as well, ones compatible with what either cultural
anthropologists or lay observers might be expected to see in comparing California with England. Such a demonstration of dissimi-
larity argues for diversity in regional approaches. The task is to find
a structure that maximizes common endeavors addressed to com-

mon problems but that provides for diversity when dissimilar problems exist. *Support* is a key word here, for if the emphasis is on international action—which is the commitment of the Group and its affiliates—then diversity need not mean separateness any more than independent action means lonely endeavors not subject to the interest of or assistance from other nations.

The work reported in *Drug Dealers—Taking Action,* as well as other work, clearly indicates that nations may jointly contribute to one another's separate difficulties; or, said differently, each nation may reflect a different aspect of a common problem. The work reported here on Mexican–United States cannabis traffic and on international heroin traffic (Chapters Three, Four) is illustrative. Perhaps as long as one nation sees its drug problems as distinct from another's or indeed as caused by another, fruitful collaboration will be difficult. Objective study of and reflection upon drug trafficking and traffickers as a genuine international phenomenon make it possible to see how each nation suffers, how each contributes to the problem, how each may redefine its role in the light of broad knowledge, and how cooperatively all may participate to solve multiple local problems and, thereby, a common international one.

Only some of the chapters in *Drug Dealers—Taking Action* are international in scope; for instance, those that examine cannabis and heroin traffic and offer recommendations for the international community, for the pharmaceutical industry, for education in nations facing a drug problem among youth, and for the criminal law in nations with high social costs and low benefits in enforcing criminal sanctions against the widespread use of cannabis. The other work reported here is regional in scope; but, to illustrate its possible extensions, one cannot help but wonder whether the demonstration of the high level of impurities in and false labeling of drugs sold on the illicit market in the United States may not reflect a problem that is present wherever illicit drugs are sold. Similarly, one asks whether drug traffic flourishes only in the prisons in California (described here). Is it the case generally that, as we can infer from the California observations, the nature of prison itself affects the level of traffic inside? Is it only in California that the rate of illicit dealing in juvenile correction centers varies with the type of juvenile held there and, importantly, with the administrative milieu? Are local California police the only ones who say they give priority to arresting the big drug dealers but who, in fact, seem mostly to arrest the readily detected young offenders whose dealing is likely to be less extensive? Is it the case elsewhere besides California that the risk of arrest is, in fact, rather low even if one is a dealer, providing one is a member of social groups that are either very skilled in conducting themselves discreetly or are protected by their status and position? Does intervention medically, legally, or socially follow the same pattern of differential success in altering drug-and-delinquent conduct in many countries and not just in those in which studies reviewed here have been conducted? These are important questions, and they can be answered only if they are asked and answered through fact finding with other groups and in other settings. Many other questions can be asked as well.

The Group and the authors of this volume will be well pleased if their endeavors encourage such inquiry and if, like the thoughtful proposals presented here, realistic proposals for action result from the findings.

Geneva   INTERNATIONAL RESEARCH GROUP
January 1973   ON DRUG LEGISLATION AND PROGRAMS

Published under the auspices of the

International Research Group on Drug Legislation and Programs

Geneva, Switzerland

PARTICIPANTS IN THE WORK OF THE GROUP

(Participants are not responsible for the positions taken by any Group member writing in this volume. The contents of each chapter reflect solely the work and opinions of its author(s).)

DAVID H. ARCHIBALD, *director, Addiction Research Foundation, Toronto*

MAUREEN BAILEY, *scientific staff, United Nations Social Defence Research Institute, Rome*

GUIDO BELSASSO, *general director, Centro Mexicano de Estudios en Farmacodependencia, Mexico City*

BRIT BERGERSEN-LIND, *director of research, Department of Health and Social Affairs, Oslo*

J. P. BERTSCHINGER, *head, Pharmaceutical Section, Public Health Service, Berne*

EVA M. BLUM, *Joint Program in Drugs, Crime and Community Studies, Center for Interdisciplinary Research, Stanford University, California*

RICHARD H. BLUM, *director, Joint Program in Drugs, Crime and Community Studies, Center for Interdisciplinary Research, and consulting professor of psychology, Stanford University, California*

DANIEL BOVET, *director, Laboratorio di Psicobiologia, Rome*

KETTIL BRUUN, *research director, Finnish Foundation for Alcohol Studies, Helsinki*

DALE C. CAMERON, *chief for drug dependence and alcoholism, World Health Organization, Geneva*

H. DANNER, *minister counselor for family affairs and health, Ministry of Health, Bonn*

JOSEPH DITTERT, *secretary, International Narcotics Control Board, Geneva* (*observer only*)

GUISEPPI DI GENNARO, *legal consultant, United Nations Social Defence Research Institute, Rome, and member, Supreme Court of Italy*

HARRY GREENFIELD, *president, International Narcotics Control Board, Geneva, and chairman, Institute for the Study of Drug Dependence, London*

HANS HALBACH, *former director, Division of Pharmacology and Toxicology, World Health Organization, Geneva*

KOKICHI HIGUCHI, *director, Research and Training Institute, Ministry of Justice, Tokyo*

LAWRENCE HOOVER, *special counsel for Bureau of Narcotics and Dangerous Drugs, former U.S. State Department liaison to United Nations Narcotics Commission, Washington, D.C.*

SUSAN IMBACH, *legal adviser, Hoffman La Roche, Basle*

C. R. B. JOYCE, *consultant, Medical Department, Ciba-Geigy, Ltd., Basle*

JOHN KAPLAN, *professor of law, Stanford University, California*

A. M. KHALIFA, *director, National Centre for Social Research and Criminology, Cairo*

PEIDER KÖNZ, *director, United Nations Social Defence Research Institute, Rome*

VLADIMIR KUSEVIC, *former director, Division of Narcotic Drugs, United Nations, Zagreb*

EMIL LANG, *vice-director, Ciba-Geigy, Ltd., Basle*

WILLIAM LANOUETTE, *senior staff member,* National Observer, *Maryland*

ROBERT LIND, *professor of economics, Stanford University, California*

JAMES MOORE, *executive secretary, Commission of Inquiry into the Non-Medical Use of Drugs, Ontario*

SATYANSHU MUKHERJEE, *scientific staff, United Nations Social Defence Research Institute, Rome*

LYNN PAN, *coordinator, International Research Group on Drug Legislation and Programs, Geneva*

INGEMAR REXED, *secretary, Swedish Narcotics Commission, and magistrate, Swedish Appellate Courts, Stockholm*

MAX TAESCHLER, *deputy director, Roche-Sandoz Ltd., Basle*

JARED TINKLENBERG, *professor of psychiatry, Stanford University, California*

JASPER WOODCOCK, *assistant director, Institute for the Study of Drug Dependence, London*

Preface

Many people are concerned about drug use and traffic and about the individuals who sustain it, the drug dealers. The growth of illicit drug use, especially among children and young people, demonstrates that adequate supplies to sustain drug use are available. One must therefore conclude that traditional approaches and institutions designed to prevent dealing cannot be functioning too well. We need to know what is wrong and what we should do.

Little information is available about who is dealing, how they become dealers, and what business practices emerge as a person becomes involved in the dealing life. We sought to provide information bearing on these questions in *The Dream Sellers* (Blum and Associates, 1972a). We also have little information on the etiology of those adolescent or childhood propensities to illicit drug use which, when pursued, lead to psychoactive drug-taking and to becoming a member of drug-taking groups. Our work shows that, at least in the United States, these are the necessary antecedents for becoming a drug dealer. Interest in the origins of youthful drug use as such led us to investigate that etiology. We present those findings in *Horatio Alger's Children* (Blum and Associates, 1972b), which shows how powerful family factors are in accounting for drug risk, at least among some United States groups.

The foregoing studies coupled with the fine work that other investigators have begun in regard to drug traffickers and drug trafficking plus the continuing public concern about drug traffic as such lead one to many questions. What goes on in international drug traffic? How does local drug law enforcement work? What do drug peddlers sell? If offenders are in correctional facilities—either juvenile detention centers or adult prisons—do their drug use and drug-dealing cease? Overall, what can one expect if one tries to intervene to deter drug-dealing of individuals through either treatment or law enforcement? Given the information available on these matters, what action comes to mind? *What ought to be done?*

Probably there is no single or simple answer. Drug use is complex. Drug-dealing occurs on many levels. Intervention efforts vary, as do their rates of success and failure. The costs of intervention also vary, along with local or national opportunities for innovation and evaluation. In consequence one must assume a variety of possible responses, a number of different ways to deal with drug dealing and drug dealers. Here our questions and especially the responses can be only the beginning of what we hope will be intensive future considerations of international cooperation, of individual rehabilitative intervention, of pharmaceutical industry response, of educational endeavor, and of the role of the criminal law and its enforcement. Regrettably we cannot be either more intensive or broader now; the data we present in this and preceding volumes are mostly restricted geographically not just to the United States but to one metropolitan region. For work under the auspices of an international body this is parochialism indeed. Yet research on drug dealing must begin somewhere—a place—and so it has been.

Just as the observations and research findings presented in *Drug Dealers—Taking Action* are limited, so too are the directions for action proposed. With our present knowledge, degree of social change, and kind of social policy, neither adequacy nor certainty can be found. That can only be disappointing to those who feel one must act now, decisively, powerfully, and permanently to interdict national and international drug-dealing. But those who are willing to tolerate uncertainty, to act provisionally, and to plan multiple activities each subject to reflection and evaluation can expect their limited goals to be accomplished.

At the present time, we must take advantage of anxiety and dissension to stimulate basic and practical research; to reexamine traditional approaches to see whether they are working well; to set up innovative programs at community, national, and international levels; and to encourage a multiplicity of interests and efforts at governmental and nongovernmental levels. Over time, there will be increased consensus about what our drug-trafficking problems are, which approaches work best in given situations and with particular drug traffickers, and which costs incurred are acceptable given the benefits gained. This optimism about the future rather than any sense of satisfaction about what our research findings or current proposals offer encourages us to share with others our research beginnings and ensuing provisional proposals.

The support of the Bureau of Narcotics and Dangerous Drugs of the United States Department of Justice under contract J-69-13 is gratefully acknowledged. So too is the assistance of the staff of the Bureau and its fine director, John Ingersoll. Gratitude is also due to President Richard Nixon's Cabinet Committee on International Narcotics Control for their work presented here. The cooperation of the California Department of Corrections and its director, R. K. Procunier; of Police Chiefs Charles Gain, James Zurcher, and Thomas Cahill; and of Sheriff Earl Whitmore is acknowledged with pleasure, as is the assistance of San Mateo County (California) Probation Service Director Lauren Beckley and Juvenile Facility Chaplain Ralph Benson. Other acknowledgements to persons participating in this work, conducted as part of the Joint Program in Drugs, Crime and Community Studies of the Center for Interdisciplinary Research (then the Institute for Public Policy Analysis) at Stanford University, are given in *The Dream Sellers* and in *Horatio Alger's Children*.

The International Research Group on Drug Legislation and Programs, under whose auspices this volume is presented, wishes to acknowledge with thanks the financial support and in-kind contributions of personnel and facilities which have made its work pos-

sible. The group and its programs have benefited from the assistance
of a number of national governments, United Nations agencies, and
scholarly institutions, as well as from the European pharmaceutical
industry, the Drug Abuse Council, and individual scholars.

Stanford, California   RICHARD H. BLUM
January 1973

Contents

Foreword
  *International Research Group on Drug Legislation
  and Programs*   vii

Preface   xiii

Contributors   xxi

1. Problems Associated with Drug-Dealing
    Richard H. Blum   1

                       ONE: TRAFFIC

2. Substances in Illicit Drugs
    Jean Paul Smith   13

3. Marijuana Use, Distribution, and Control
    William H. McGlothlin   31

xvii

4. International Opiate Traffic   62
    *Cabinet Committee on International Narcotics
    Control, 63–76, 86–105
    Andrew Tartaglino and the Staff of the Office
    of Criminal Investigations, Bureau of
    Narcotics and Dangerous Drugs, 76–86*

TWO: POLICING

5. Considerations on Law Enforcement
    Richard H. Blum   106

6. The Narcotics Law in Action: A College Town
    Richard H. Blum, Andrew Gordon   114

7. The Narcotics Law in Action: A Major City
    Richard H. Blum, Terence Egan   139

THREE: AFTER ARREST

8. Juvenile Detention Centers
    Richard H. Blum   162

9. Prisons
    *Nicholas Munson, Ingemar Rexed,
    Robert Packard, Richard H. Blum*   171

FOUR: POLICY

10. Drug-Dealing and the Law
    John Kaplan   201

11. Corrections and Treatment
    Jared Tinklenberg   213

12. Social Response to Drug Problems
    *Richard H. Blum, Sanford Kadish, Milton Luger,
    Arnold J. Mandell, Patricia Wald,
    Norman V. Lourie*   232

Contents

13. Future Research and Policy Action
    Peider Könz   243

14. Responsibilties of the Pharmaceutical Industry:
    A Personal View
    C. R. B. Joyce   251

15. Action in the Schools
    Jasper Woodcock   267

16. Taking Action
    Richard H. Blum   282

    Bibliography   293

    Index   309

Contributors

RICHARD H. BLUM, *director, Joint Program in Drugs, Crime, and Community Studies, Center for Interdisciplinary Research, and Consulting professor of psychology, Stanford University*

TERENCE EGAN, *research assistant and student, Stanford University*

ANDREW GORDON, *research assistant and student, Stanford University*

C. R. B. JOYCE, *consultant, Medical Department, Ciba-Geigy, Ltd., Basle*

SANFORD KADISH, *professor of law, University of California, Berkeley*

JOHN KAPLAN, *professor of law, Stanford University*

PEIDER KÖNZ, *director, United Nations Social Defence Research Institute, Rome*

NORMAN V. LOURIE, *deputy secretary, Commonwealth of Pennsylvania Department of Public Welfare, Harrisburg*

MILTON LUGER, *director, New York State Executive Department, Division of Youth, Albany*

WILLIAM H. MCGLOTHLIN, *research professor of psychology, University of California, Los Angeles*

ARNOLD J. MANDELL, *professor and chairman, Department of Psychiatry, University of California, San Diego*

NICHOLAS MUNSON, *San Francisco Police Department*

ROBERT PACKARD, *research assistant, Stanford University*

INGEMAR REXED, *secretary, Swedish Narcotics Commission, and magistrate, Swedish Appellate Courts*

JEAN PAUL SMITH, *deputy director, Center for Studies of Narcotic and Drug Abuse, National Institute of Mental Health*

ANDREW TARTAGLINO, *deputy director for enforcement, US Bureau of Narcotics and Dangerous Drugs*

JARED TINKLENBERG, *professor of psychiatry, Stanford University, and consultant in psychiatry, California Youth Authority*

PATRICIA WALD, *attorney, Center for Law and Social Policy, Washington, D.C.*

JASPER WOODCOCK, *assistant director, Institute for the Study of Drug Dependence, London*

Drug Dealers–
Taking Action

Options for International Response

UNDER THE AUSPICES OF THE INTERNATIONAL RESEARCH
GROUP ON DRUG LEGISLATION AND PROGRAMS, GENEVA

IN COOPERATION WITH THE UNITED NATIONS SOCIAL
DEFENCE RESEARCH INSTITUTE, ROME

Problems Associated with Drug-Dealing

Richard H. Blum

In *The Dream Sellers* (Blum and Associates, 1972a), we undertook to examine the characteristics and careers of a sample of California drug dealers. We also looked at drug dealers among college, high school, and junior high school students, learning about prevalence and characteristics that set ex-dealers apart from nondealing users and from nonusers. We also examined persons who have access to drugs but who do not, for the most part, deal: college faculty, physicians, pharmaceutical detail men, pharmacists, and narcotics law enforcement officers. From them we learned about group and individual factors that prevent or constrain illicit drug-dealing. To learn about environmental circumstances, including those personal attributes that are associated with settings, we looked at the dealing life in the Haight-Ashbury District of San Francisco, where the flower children first emerged; at the black ghetto of Oakland; at a heroin

1

copping corner; at a mountain commune in California; and at dealers in mod and swinging London. Out of these studies there came a description of drug dealers and the dealing life. This description, when juxtaposed with the characteristics and conditions associated with nondealing even when opportunity is present, provides information and understanding about those—mostly young people—who engage in regular drug traffic.

In *Horatio Alger's Children* (Blum and Associates, 1972b), we examined the characteristics of families that are associated with high and low drug risk. Middle- and upper-class white families, hippie families, working-class black and white families, and lower-class (semiagrarian) Mexican-American families in the San Francisco Bay Area were intensively studied. We were able to identify family features that were associated with both the use of illicit drugs and the dangerous use of tobacco and alcohol (the two phenomena correlate highly). The family study revealed that one characteristic of the high-drug-risk youngsters was acquaintance with drug dealers; youngsters who were not involved in illicit drug use were not acquainted with dealers. The family study did not examine dealing but was limited in its inquiries to more immediate measures for bad drug outcomes for children, as, for example, accidents, illness, and the like. However, we believe that family features that predict illicit use and dangerous outcomes are also predictive of the risk of becoming a youthful drug dealer. It is clear from all our work as well as that of others (Carey, 1968; Goode, 1970; Preble and Casey, 1969) that dealing is one expression of involvement in the drug life. Further, the deeper that involvement—depending on the person's background and the kind of drugs used and sold—the greater the risks of other inimical changes, as, for example, fear, dependency, disenchantment, arrest, violence, and even death.

We now know about some of the conditions that contribute to becoming a drug dealer; we know the steps during childhood, adolescence, and youth that are part of the dealing career; and we know the correlates of the various stages or levels of involvement in the dealing life. We know that the roots of dealing are deep indeed, traceable in many cases to the values, conduct, and characteristics of the parents before a child, the dealer-to-be, is born. Other roots are found in infancy—in the (inferred) interaction between mother and infant, which can be expressed in health or feeding problems in the infant or in the worries of the mother. Later developmental features are also involved, although we can only guess at some of these. We do know that family values and conduct are learned and that parental problems are transmitted. Moreover, the combination of identifiable family features and idiosyncratic characteristics of the child can lead to an early companionship with drug-using peers; to experimentation with drugs; and usually, sequentially, to greater drug use, the sharing and giving of drugs, and then the selling of drugs. Not all those who share or sell illicit drugs become regular dealers; only a minority do so. In this minority of youths with experience as regular dealers, of youth more delinquent than their siblings and peers, most do not go on to become heavily involved in the dealing life. "Going on" is defined by stages measurable in a number of ways—the variety and amounts of drugs used and sold, the relationships between seller and clients, the profits made, the arrests and incarceration experienced, the participation in violence and in organized traffic, and the extent to which the dealer's associates suffer deleterious effects either from drugs or from the hostile and frightened world that can be the dealing environment.

For the moment, let us turn our attention from the developmental, social, and criminal evolution of the dealer, which depends upon his person, his family, his social class, his friends, and his using and dealing acquaintances, to consider those events that are the consequence of plans. By plans we do not mean those of the dealer himself, for the evolution of dealing seems remarkably free from stated intentions as the dealer drifts from one stage to the next. We mean instead the plans of others; that is, society, which, having defined drug use as a bad thing and dealers as sick, criminal, deviant, or otherwise undesirable, intervenes to return the prodigal to the path of righteousness. The most potent of these planned forces, as we infer it from our findings, is arrest or the fear of arrest.

Generally, the risk of arrest increases the longer a person is in the dealing life. A general outcome of this duration-linked risk among street and criminal dealers, as opposed to those dealers protected by a sanctuary (a campus, an esteemed profession), is an exciting, financially rewarding, but also increasingly distasteful life. For those who are making big money, arrests are common but appear to have little impact on deterring business. For others, the plans of society as executed in the operation of the criminal law do make a difference. At this point, we may conclude that intervention has impact and that we can make policy optimistically, knowing that wheels, once set in motion by plans, move events and people.

The conclusion is proper but requires qualification. It is not so easy to identify the direction of effects or their magnitude. Risks are dependent upon features that makers of plans probably did not envision; that is, risk of detection, arrest, and conviction vary according to personal, familial, class, and milieu characteristics that are not supposed to make any difference within the law or to the police. Further, even when the impact of intervention produces results in the desired direction—for example, a dealer tired of the hassle quits—we cannot assume that deterrence was perfect or that society is safe. Some dealers turn to other forms of crime. Others tire of being "paranoid" but retire only when rich. Some who are drug-dependent appear to give up illicit drugs but apparently become skid-row alcoholics instead.

Nevertheless, older criminal dealers are ever mindful of arrest; and, among those in our sample who were quite successful, the majority spoke of quitting someday. On the other hand, among those who were no longer dealing—either because they were in jail or on probation or had otherwise retired—were many who planned to return to the dealing life. Again, such plans depend upon the nature of the person and his environment: middle-class youth in a commune who had quit dealing were not likely to return; former heroin peddlers in a Bible college seemed, we speculated, more vulnerable to reconversions; the probability of resumption of the peddler's trade seemed highest, among those we talked to, for persons in prison. Among those who had never been arrested and who were still dealing, we found more who said that they planned to stay in the business than among those who were still dealing but did have a history of drug arrests. If we classify dealers by arrest histories, those who had never been arrested and those who had experienced only drug arrests were similar in their characteristics; both differed from those dealers who had experienced nondrug arrests (usually along with drug arrests as well). Those who had never experienced a nondrug arrest were "psychedelic" dealers (who handled primarily cannabis and hallucinogens). The others, who were characterized as "criminal" dealers, were more often lower class in origin, were less well educated, were more businesslike and better organized in their drug dealing, used opiates and were addicted, and had begun drug use earlier and more heavily. However, when we compare arrested dealers in both populations—psychedelic and criminal —with their cohorts who had never been arrested to assess arrest impact, we find that arrest interdicts dealing at the same rate for both groups. However, analysis reveals within the criminal group two subgroups; one consists of the persistent dealers—organized and violent—who are not affected by arrest and incarceration; the other is made up of those who "go quickly down the tubes"—who are arrested very early in their careers and do drop out of dealing. Among the psychedelic dealers, we can distinguish the casual or sometime dealer, who appears to be experimenting with the dealing life as part of social involvement in drug groups, and the successful serious dealer, the cool-man-hip-on-a-big-dealing-trip who is both sophisticated and almost immune from arrest.

These differential arrest rates for various dealer groups and differing impacts of arrest within groups bear on the operation and efficacy of the criminal law as such. The importance of these issues increases when we realize the magnitude of illicit dealing in the United States, which occurs in spite of current penalties and programs. Consider that during the course of our work we identified several thousand dealers in the San Francisco Bay Area alone, and we have no reason to believe ours was anything but a small sample. The group for which we have our best estimate of the prevalence of current dealers is the schools; and we found that, among metropolitan-area public high school and college students (and indeed among junior high students as well), about 7 percent of the total student body deal. This figure indicates that, for every 1 million urban/suburban students, perhaps as many as 70,000 are violating our laws on drug trafficking. Obviously, most are not arrested. Who does get arrested then? How *do* police departments operate to enforce narcotics laws?

Some of the questions that occur as we consider the impact of the law bear not on its differential effects but on the immediate consequences for those who are caught and convicted. Detention in prison or a juvenile facility is supposed to correct the offender. Not only our data but also follow-up studies in general (see Chapter Eleven) show that straightening out is a sometime thing because recidivism is common and, for drug offenders, may be as high as 90 percent. What *does* happen in prison? It was beyond our scope to consider this problem generally, but we did ask the very simple question of whether incarceration even deters offenders from using and dealing while in the "joint."

The operation of the criminal law can be examined in terms of what police departments and courts do or what happens inside prison or juvenile facility or what happens after detention. It can also be examined in terms of its milieu effects; that is, the business of criminal processing and labeling and the impact on the lives of those outside the law. This is usually referred to as criminalizing or stigmatizing. Many scholars and critics contend that much of what is seen in the drug scene is an anticulture that develops in consequence of the criminal law because it compels user-dealers to be devious and disaffected. At this time, we have more speculation than facts about these effects, but the correlates of heavy involvement in an illicit life—nondrug crime, violence, hassle, anxiety, and "paranoia"—are evident. We have not set out to solve the chicken-and-egg dilemma; the greater nondrug delinquency of dealers compared with their own siblings, the enjoyment some get out of violating the law and being in a criminal life, and the likely existence of delinquent conduct before the onset of illicit drug involvement, clearly indicate that there is an egg before the chicken. Zacune's (1971) study of the life of immigrant Canadian addicts in England shows how deviling it is to adhere to the simple notion either that some men are born bad while the law does only good or, conversely, that bad law ruins good men. In this volume, contributors address themselves to this issue.

It is often suggested that treatment would correct illicit drug use and the dealing that follows upon it, as well as prevent the unhappy effects that accrue from criminalizing drug users. Proposed treatment methods are usually medical-psychological but encompass a variety of other approaches as well. We have elsewhere (Blum and Blum, 1967) considered the varieties of treatment, problems in their application and evaluation, and the likely outcomes for one form of drug dependence, alcoholism. Many scientists and clinicians labor in the treatment vineyard. As shown in *The Dream Sellers* (Blum and Associates, 1972a, Chapter 17), rates of volunteering for and remaining in treatment (mostly methadone maintenance) varied with the role the addict had in the buying-selling structure of a copping community; for example, those who already had straight jobs did much better (staying in treatment) than did big dealers and street dealers. Even dealers who go into treatment may continue to sell drugs. It was further observed that heroin sellers and buyers differed considerably in terms of their psychopathology, these differences being closely linked to the level of their trafficking. Furthermore, although the psychiatrist might think of a big dealer as "sick," heroin-using peers considered him a model of adjustment, that is, a big success. The big dealer stood high on his copping corner, but to him the prestige of being a patient was meager—this might in part account for his staying in the life. Observations in an Oakland ghetto (Sutter, 1972) confirm the rewards and gratifications attendant upon making it big in the tough and exciting world of drugs and crime.

In this volume, we approach treatment by review and commentary, seeking to sum up what we know and where we stand with regard to individual intervention among dealers—or those most like them. We consider the various treatment forms, comparing these to penal-correctional endeavors and to nature's own way, maturation. The question of treatment efficacy looms large; and, as we shall see, if we want to be practical in devising policy, we must accept that neither good thoughts alone nor confidence in the measures at hand offers solace. Success is possible, but it is by no means to be uniformly expected.

Many of the dealers in our study called for the repeal of criminal laws pertaining to drug traffic, especially in marijuana. At the same time, these dealers were likely to lament the impurities in drugs and the variability in potency; they pleaded for regulation of contents and truth in labeling. Likewise, dealing advocates of free enterprise complained about inflated drug prices and some called for price controls in the drug market. There is paradox here, the more so if one demands freedom and restraint simultaneously and universally. If we become specific, asking what actions are responsive to what types of control, we can—as some dealers did and as contributors to this volume do—lay the groundwork for the intricacies of realistic policy. As long as the drug market is simultaneously totally prohibited by the letter of the law and almost totally uncontrolled by law in fact, the regulation of contents and potency is impossible. Dealers and users are facing, in their marketplace, the same problems that were faced early in this century for legitimate products and led in the United States to the Pure Food and Drug Act. The data presented in this volume make it clear that unless some control is exercised over purity and potency, whatever else happens, there will be discomfort, disease, and death in association with illicit drug use.

Whatever advances in public health and safety have been made as a function of the control of legitimate drug production, the constraints on distribution, and the requirements for packaging and labeling, present regulations have not solved all the problems of safety associated with legitimate psychoactive-compound production and use. To the contrary, a number of unresolved issues affect the development, marketing, and control of approved substances, whether these are over-the-counter or prescribed pharmaceuticals. Basic problems here include standards for the classification of drugs for the purposes of control, standards for research that provides information on drug safety and methods, and standards for estimating costs and benefits and dangers. Related to these are important questions about responsibility for security of pharmaceuticals that are legitimately distributed and marketed and the proper orientation of the pharmaceutical industry itself relative to invention and production of mind- or mood-altering substances. As our contributors note, these matters will not be resolved easily; however, some powerful proposals are set forth.

Commerce in legitimate drugs is international. Drugs discovered in one nation become drugs used dangerously in another. Drugs used safely in one culture are associated with problems of crime or public health in another. Laws that appear to work well in one country can, if thoughtlessly exported or copied, create unnecessary agricultural, religious, fiscal, police, or public health burdens on another country. A body of international law pertaining to psychoactive drugs is accumulating; these laws become mandatory for nations that ratify or accede to the agreements containing them, thus making international law rather than national law sovereign. In consequence of these and other international developments, methods for the control of substances are made universal: United States federal agents work abroad with the police of many countries; Scandinavian epidemics of stimulants used by children lead to pressures on many nations for the control of stimulants; Egyptian worries about khat use by their soldiers returning from Yemen stimulate concern over khat use internationally; Soviet morality, which judges cannabis and opium harshly, joins with other Western morality in attempts to induce Asian nations to seek to alter the folk medical habits of their people, who may have used these substances for milennia without ill effect.

The problems of drug abuse are international. (We use the term *drug abuse* here to signify disapproval of some conduct that occurs in connection with psychoactive drug use.) Of the dealers in our intensive sample of Californians, 29 percent had engaged in international trafficking; they ventured, in order of preference, to Mexico, mid-Asia (Nepal, Afghanistan, India, Pakistan), the Far East (Hong Kong, Bangkok, Singapore, Laos), the Near East (Turkey, Lebanon), Europe, Canada, and Africa (Morocco, Tunisia, Nigeria). The dealers in our English sample also traveled, but they prefer mid-Asia and then Africa. Young English dealers commerce on a smaller scale than their North American counterparts, but they buy similar drugs, except that they traffick in hashish rather than marijuana.

The fact that nearly one-third of the California dealers engage in international traffic suggests that the dimensions of trafficking far exceed any model based on the notion of a few cohesive systems or syndicates that control and engage in such commerce. When generalized, the data imply that worldwide tens of thousands of mostly young drug users are trafficking. We do not know whether their contribution to illicit drug flow constitutes a primary source for all substances or for only the psychedelics or whether it is only supplemental to the widely publicized but poorly documented syndicated traffic.

Other international drug problems are evident. Alcoholic spirits are introduced into Nepal with Western technology and local urbanization; worries about local alcoholism arise. German hippies visit Afghanistan; upper-class Afghans fear their children will begin to use hashish. American psychedelic dealers establish a market in Denmark. French and English dealers complain that the Americans are taking over their territory and introducing violence as part of an Al Capone type of business practices. The United States government complains that Mexico, Turkey, and France are not doing their part to stamp out heroin traffic. Iran returns to opium production and heroin manufacture, complaining that by abiding by the United Nations Single Convention she has suffered an immense increase in heroin addiction and a loss of gold to Turkish and Afghan smugglers. Denmark accuses Lebanon of not cracking down on heroin traders, and Lebanon feels that the United States has insisted on the Lebanese solving the American hashish problem without regard to economic consequences for Lebanon, which denies any internal hashish use. Vietnamese and Thai generals are accused of being criminal traffickers more than military allies of the United States. Laotians use American agricultural aid to augment opium harvests. McCoy's book (1972)' on heroin traffic in Southeast Asia becomes a cause célèbre by implicating not only Asian high officials but United States government agencies as well. Charge and countercharge fly, but one thing remains substantiated: Drugs are an important international business and, in countries where all big business is concentrated at the top, it is more than possible that high officials are realizing profits if not actually running the show. Clearly drug traffic *is* an international problem, but the definition of the problem varies markedly depending on where one is sitting.

Interest in drug policy requires that knowledge and perspective be international. Whether we consider legitimate production or illicit traffic, the whole world requires our attention. Contributors to this volume, many of them active in international affairs in the drug arena, recognize this. Several present information on international drug traffic, others consider directions for research and subsequent international collaboration. Still other contributors who focus primarily on the United States, whether on the role of the criminal law or that of the government, take heed too of international realities.

In *Students and Drugs* (Blum and Associates, 1969b), we had shown that large numbers of students in California colleges and high schools were experimenting with drugs and that a goodly minority were using illicit substances with some regularity. By 1972, a rough-and-ready estimate was that three-quarters of high school and college students had at least tried illicit drugs and about two-fifths were periodic if not regular users. In *The Dream Sellers* (Blum and Associates, 1972a) we reported that most dealers became involved in drugs and in dealing in their adolescent years and, by 1972, that use and dealing were common in junior high school as well (ages 11 to 13). Recall that an average 7 percent of students from junior high through college in our metropolitan region had commerced in drugs. Rates of use and dealing vary with such things as residence, age, urbanism, family income, religion, and politics. Dealing itself shows a correlation with school performance in most settings studied, for example, dealers compared with nondealing users are more likely to perform poorly academically and to be more uncertain about their careers. We infer from their heavier drug use that they are also more likely to be among the group at high risk of dropping out of school even while in school, as, for example, by passing out in class. This is the group that also will pass out doses of drugs to others on campus and in class, and, of course, will drop out of school for longer periods as well.

For these reasons, citizens and school personnel cannot but have an interest in children's drug use and in dealers in particular. They cannot help but wish to consider the possible role of education as either a preventive or a remedial endeavor. Yet the decision to engage in drug education is not and should not be easily made. Its implications and complexities are considered by one of the contributors to this volume who asks, "What should the schools do?"

All of us who have joined together to work on this volume are bound by an interest in understanding the traffic in psychoactive drugs. We share a faith as well as a desire that wise planning can reduce human distress, that policy can be formulated with an eye to efficient application so that demonstrable benefits are achieved at least cost, and that diverse interests nationally and internationally can be mediated, if not harmonized, as we seek, first, to learn what is involved in drug dealing and in intervention and, second, to introduce changes linked to specific goals. There is agreement on the complexity of drug dealing and its immersion in moral, legal, political, economic, social, psychological, medical, and educational issues. There is some question about the desirability of intervention, and there is humility with regard to the capabilities of human beings to intervene in the lives of others to bring about constructive change. There is consensus on the priority of realism, which means having facts, knowing costs, and being aware that all programs have unanticipated outcomes, some of which can be worse than the problems they were instituted to remedy. There is concurrence about the particular importance of the criminal law, which is, at this time, a vehicle with very costly national and international side effects in its applications to drug control. The paradox of institutions is recognized; there is the striking incongruity between what they are established to do and what the personnel who operate them actually do. Obstinacy is also admitted: humans change with reluctance; institutions with greater reluctance; and laws with perhaps most reluctance. However, obstinacy has an anticharge—spontaneous change. The problem lies in predicting that change, in understanding what brings it about, and in seeking to guide it.

All such agreements can be mobilized in the search for understanding and workable solutions. As for disagreement—when it is recognized, its origins understood, its implications respectfully entertained, and the energy mobilized by its presence is channeled, it too can be put to use. We hope that the reader will join us both in agreement and in disagreement to seek and test answers to our question: "What ought we do about drug-dealing?"

2

Substances in Illicit Drugs

Jean Paul Smith

The actual contents of illicit drugs is a subject—and an issue—that has been neglected by the major professional groups attempting to control drug abuse. Scientists, enforcement officials, and health specialists often speak about drugs of abuse as if they were invariably pharmacologically known and pure substances. Largely by default, discussion of actual contents has become dominated by rumor, exaggerated claims, and benign ignorance. While legitimate drugs—especially over-the-counter preparations—are sold in far greater quantities to the public on much the same basis, the presence of additives, contaminants, and impurities in illicit drugs constitutes a health risk that goes beyond economic wastage.

The purpose of our discussion here is to present several of the issues related to the question of contents and the importance of these issues to research, law enforcement, treatment, and educational approaches to the prevention and reduction of drug abuse. Further, the limited information now available about actual contents is presented for hallucinogens, alcohol, marijuana, and heroin. Claims made about the contents of "street drugs" are compared with laboratory findings in order to separate pharmaceutical fact from fancy and fraud.

Nature of the Issue

The meaning and significance of the question of contents depends upon the impact that this information has on people. To label some contents as drugs and others as contaminants, adulterants, or impurities prejudges the issue unless a specific target group agrees in some measure with these designations. Varying concentrations of active ingredients—levels of purity—are equally as important as impurities. Very pure heroin for example, may cause an overdose when used by an addict with a "small habit." Yet warning the addict community that dangerously high concentrations of heroin are being sold on the street may be counterproductive if addicts desire the *uncut* drug. A warning to the nonuser may serve as an invitation to an addict.

Although we are discussing the question of impurities in drugs from both the pharmacological and psychosocial points of view, we recognize that there is a complex interaction involving the drugs, the body's biochemical processing of them, and the person's pattern or frequency of use. For some drugs, and we include alcohol here, the contaminants in one or two doses, if not present in large quantity, may not affect health. With ingestion over a period of time, however, the body may not break down or excrete chemicals as rapidly as they build up. Lead found in moonshine whiskey illustrates how frequency of use may be more important than the contaminant found in a single dose. Epidemiology and pharmacology cannot be pursued as independent lines of inquiry if our ultimate concern is the well-being of the individual.

Student Opinions

In order to provide information on the importance of this issue, questions were posed to students in a psychology class in a large Western private university in early 1970. Two questions were

asked of these students. The first began with a statement of a hypothetical situation:

*One of the persons who lives in the same house that you do
has recently picked up a batch of new stuff (drugs). He does not
tell you where he gets it or how it was made but you know it was
made in a private lab by chemists, several guys operating on their
own. This acquaintance comes by your room and asks you if you
would like some of the new batch that his friends have just cooked
up.*

The question itself was: "What degree of confidence do you have
that, when this person from your house says it is LSD, mescaline,
speed, THC, or STP, the drug is really what he says it is and is
relatively pure and free of contaminants?" Responses were entered
on a five-point scale ranging from "Extremely Confident" to "Extremely Skeptical" with "Not Sure—Either Way" as an inter-
mediate-indeterminate category.

Results for the 76 students were grouped in three categories
as described in Table 2-1. More than half of the responses indicate
that the students would be skeptical of the contents. One-third were
unsure and one-tenth expressed confidence in the drugs. The ab-

Table 2–1

CONFIDENCE OF STUDENTS IN PURITY OF DRUG SAMPLES

	Confident	*Unsure*	*Skeptical*
Speed	12	26	38
LSD	9	25	42
Mescaline	8	27	41
THC	5	28	43
STP	6	28	42
Total	40	134	206
Percent of Total Responses	11%	35%	54%

sence of significant variation among the drug classes raises several questions. These students may not be knowledgeable about production of illicit drugs; for example, they may be unaware that no real tetrahydrocannabinol (THC) from underground labs has been found even though many street drugs are sold as "synthetic marijuana" or THC. Equally plausible is the hypothesis that the question elicits a global reaction to the issue, which obscures opinions about individual drugs. Responses might also have been different if the hypothetical situation were defined in a more vivid, personal fashion.

The second question directly probed these students' reaction to the importance of the contents issue. It was worded in the following manner: "How important is it to you that the stuff he has *really* is what he says it is and only that, not some other kind of drug with possible unknown ingredients?" Responses were obtained on a five-point scale ranging from "Totally Irrelevant" to "Extremely Important" with a separate, intermediate category of "Not Sure— Either Way." Of the 76 students, 57 (75 percent) of them said that knowing the contents of drugs is extremely or moderately important. Twenty-one percent said that they were not sure either way and only 4 percent said that the issue is irrelevant to them.

Results for both questions should be considered tentative since reliability and validity of the questions are unknown. Since an overwhelming majority of the student body at this university has used illicit drugs on one or more occasions, we assume that among our subjects were experimenters, users, and a few "heads." If so, users and nonusers generally appear to agree that the question of unknown ingredients of drugs, possibly impurities or adulterants, is a central concern.

Counterfeiting Drugs

Counterfeiting is the illicit production or alteration of drugs that are facsimiles of authentic products. Detection of counterfeits, which for psychoactive drugs means primarily amphetamines and barbiturates, is a responsibility of state and federal law enforcement agencies. For the most part, however, it is the drug companies that conduct active surveillance of their products to protect their market position and the reputation of their products.

Counterfeit drugs are offered (sometimes at reduced prices) to socially sanctioned drug dealers, namely, pharmacists and physicians. They may also be sold directly to illicit dealers who spread them through whatever channels they have. To our knowledge, no systematic studies of counterfeits have been done to attempt to trace them through the various levels of distribution or to determine what factors make entry into a counterfeiting operation seem more desirable from the illicit operator's point of view.

In their discussion of the identification of counterfeit drugs, Eisenberg and Tillson (1966) say: "Counterfeit or imitation drug products are detected by their deviations from the genuine product in one or more diagnostic physical or chemical properties. They may be further identified if reference samples traced to their manufacturing source are available for comparison."

Both the form and contents of drugs are used in detecting phony products. For tablets, the surface is examined to determine the presence of characteristic marks left by punch presses and measures of suspected samples are compared to authentics by "measuring diameter, thickness, weight, shape, color, bevel, surface, and monogram. In addition, the examiners evaluate the tablet's groove mark for its silhouette, width, depth, and angle" ("How the FDA Traces Counterfeit Drugs," 1964, page 34). In 1968, federal responsibility for detecting counterfeits was assigned to the Bureau of Narcotics and Dangerous Drugs, Department of Justice.

Detecting counterfeits in capsule form is more difficult since the containers—the gelatin capsules themselves—are available from retail outlets without restriction. Authenticity of contents of either capsules or tablets may be determined by several methods, among which is the comparison of the optical properties of the suspected drug with known optical properties of authentic specimens obtained from the producing company.

Even if counterfeits contain the same chemicals as the authentics, they may not be reliable because they may dissolve at a far different or more variable rate. Extremely rapid dissolving obviously results in overdosing; when tablets break apart too slowly, blood levels remain too low to bring about the intended effect.

Although counterfeiting by definition requires an authentic drug for comparison, illicit manufacturers may also have their products imitated. After Augustus Owsley Stanley III, known as the acid king, produced very large quantities of illicit LSD of high quality and reliable composition, imitators soon appeared, capitalizing on Stanley's reputation by claiming their drugs were "Owsley's Acid."

Effects

The major means that society has to prevent and reduce use of and dealing in illicit drugs are research, education and information, law enforcement, treatment, and rehabilitation. All these approaches are affected by both theoretical and practical problems of varying concentration and impure contents of drugs.

Research. The presence of unknown or undesirable ingredients in drugs has complicated scientific research. For marijuana, in contrast to other drugs, research before the 1960s was hampered by the lack of an adequate explanation of the chemical structure of the active constituents. The true structure of important tetrahydrocannabinols was clarified in the mid-1960s so that suitable methods for detection and quantification could be applied (*Marihuana and Health,* 1972).

In 1969, a material called marijuana extract distillate (M. E.D.) was prepared from seized marijuana before the National Institute of Mental Health began to grow its own product to supply researchers. Unfortunately, the M.E.D. contained a large percentage of fatty acids not usually present in the plant. Speaking specifically about marijuana, the Secretary's report comments about a condition that applies to other drugs as well: "an almost limitless number of compounds are available as possible contaminants ranging from deliberately added adulterants to inadvertent pollution by herbicidal action" (*Marihuana and Health,* 1971, page 17).

Varying potency and contaminants affect research on hallucinogenics. While the question of LSD and chromosome damage has not been settled, it is clear that persons who believe they have taken "LSD," which they obtained from street sources, may not have taken the drug at all, as will be discussed below. Relying on patients' knowledge of actual contents is risky; relying on their recall to establish a pattern of use in the past is even more fraught with error.

After reviewing the methodological problems of major reports of chromosome damage supposedly due to LSD, Dishotsky and colleagues (1970) say: "We believe that the original sample populations were inadequately described as LSD users. In fact most subjects were multiple-drug users, abusers, or addicts exposed to toxic substances of unknown composition and potency. Given the unreliability of self-report and the unpredictable composition of illicit drugs, it is unlikely that all investigators could have sampled comparable drug abuse populations."

Respondents' lack of adequate knowledge about the contents of the drugs implies that self-reports of use on surveys, polls, and questionnaires are open to question. Surveys measure opinions or beliefs about drugs that a respondent has taken, not necessarily what he has in fact used.

The drug class involved is extremely important. It has been estimated that about 90 percent of the stimulants and depressants on the illicit market originate from legitimate sources. If counterfeiting and cutting (diluting and repacking) are not major illicit activities, then, for diverted drugs, mislabeling of contents is not sufficient to invalidate research findings. For drugs produced in clandestine labs or those smuggled into this country in relatively pure form and cut to give bulk and to increase profits, it is more likely that additives or adulterants reduce the accuracy of research findings. Hallucinogenics, opiates, and certain forms of stimulants —methamphetamines—are the drugs that are most likely to be inaccurately reported if our surmises are sound.

Users and dealers often claim this problem is unimportant because they take a dose of the drug to determine what effect it has on them in order to avoid being cheated. To the degree that drug effects are determined by psychological set of the user and the milieu or physical setting in which the drug is taken, on-the-spot self-testing (street bioassay) of compounds is not free from error. Even if some experienced users can determine contents by the effects of certain drugs on themselves, the vast majority of users and dealers have not had sufficient experience to discern these effects reliably. We conclude that it is far more sound to make allowance in any research for unknown contents, mistaken claims, and dummy or placebo compounds.

Enforcement. Chemical profiles of pure and impure drugs

may be used to trace samples of drugs acquired by undercover narcotics agents in street buys. If unusual chemicals are present, specimens from different sources may be compared to trace a possible common source—whether an illegal manufacturing lab or a reprocessing center. This technique can be used not only with adulterants and unusual diluents, but also with derivatives found in such drugs as the opiates. For example, the presence of monoacetyl morphines and the proportions in which they exist make it possible to track some opiates through a chain of distributors just as a tracer drug would. According to Lerner and Mills (1963), cutting of heroin by addition of lactose or quinine does not impair the chemist's ability to identify these key derivatives.

The question of impurities appears to have been neglected in recent legislative discussions and enactments for controlling distribution and use of drugs. By and large, drug laws have not dealt with the issue of increased risks to health of contaminants in illicit drugs. Possession or peddling of LSD laced with arsenic or strychnine carries the same penalty as simple possession or illicit distribution. No added liability is present to make a dealer wary of his product or even face loss of reputation in the drug subculture although hazard to health—the reason for controlling drugs in the first place—may be significantly increased by impurities. The rationale behind strict regulation of purity of drugs from the legitimate drug industry should also, in our opinion, apply to illicit drug makers.

Treatment. Contaminants and unknown ingredients complicate the treatment process. Resulting diagnostic problems are common in hospital emergency rooms. Allergic or shock reaction to drugs is common after administration of a wide range of chemicals, and overdose and sudden unexplained reactions may occur with potent chemicals. Intravenous administration places a person especially at risk since contamination of needles and drug solutions in syringes is widespread. Viral hepatitis, bacterial endocarditis, pneumonia, bacteremia, and skin infections are common among users who share their paraphernalia.

Quinine was first added to heroin apparently in the 1930s as a diluent to increase its bulk and provide a bitter taste, masking the absence of concentrated heroin while at the same time preventing malarial reactions. Since 1943, no deaths due to malaria have been reported among heroin addicts in New York City (Baden, 1968), but this benefit has not been without its price. According to Cherubin (1967), addition of quinine to heroin increases the possibility of tetanus among "skin popping" addicts. Quinine apparently facilitates the growth of the tetanus organism by producing an oxygen-free condition (Talbott, 1968). Female Negro addicts have been especially susceptible to this progressive disease in the Harlem area of New York City (Cherubin, 1967).

Treatment of medical problems sometimes requires the use of blood for transfusions with a major source of supply being commercial blood banks. Many donors to these banks are rejected as possible transmitters of diseases such as infectious hepatitis, and screening procedures to detect drugs or contaminants in urine specimens may assist in this process. Coumbis, Albano, and Lyons (1970) screened 50 donors at a commercial blood bank and found that, in spite of the screening procedures, 15 of the 50 had over-the-counter (OTC), prescription drugs, and adulterants in their urine. On qualitative testing, they found salicylates, quinine, nicotine, morphine, and barbiturates, the order indicating the relative frequency, with 7 donors showing salicylates and 1 showing barbiturates. Detecting 4 probable heroin addicts among their 50 donors, they observe:

Morphine absolutely and quinine relatively are significant findings. Morphine unless prescribed is an indication of narcotic (heroin) abuse. A simple heroin injection with a positive urine morphine recovery could more than likely indicate addiction. When quinine is found in association with morphine it is virtually pathognomic of a drug abuse inasmuch as quinine is still the most common adulterant in the heroin sample. Quinine by itself may simply indicate that the person has been drinking beverages containing quinine compounds, such as tonic water.

Education. The use of the impurity issue to give clout to educational efforts is welcomed by those who have employed traditional health education with questionable results. Although a belated response, much time and effort is now being poured into "respect for drugs" to persuade people, mostly young people, not to experiment with or use controlled drugs. Considering the impurity issue, we should be more concerned with teaching "drug skepticism"—a questioning, disbelieving attitude suspending naïve faith in the contents of illicit drugs and, in our opinion, OTC preparations as well.

Educators and mass media personnel should be cautious in their use of the contaminants issue and should not invoke it without supporting evidence. Exaggerated claims and a new mythology about contaminants will only set back or undercut honest efforts to inform people about drug contents and effects. The fact that many young people appear to be more willing to accept this type of information makes it more important to proceed cautiously.

Information about Drugs

In this section, issues and information on hallucinogenics, heroin, marijuana, and alcohol are presented. Few empirical studies have been done to date, and more are needed for obvious reasons.

Sources of illicit drugs are diversion from legitimate channels, importation, or manufacture in clandestine labs. Importation (with subsequent cutting and repacking) and unsanitary conditions in underground labs are prime sources of adulteration. The more layers or levels illicit drugs move through, the more they are exposed to additives not wanted by or harmful to the user.

Hallucinogens. Although the importance of adulterants in hallucinogenic drugs has been discussed by many people since at least 1960, the first empirical study was conducted by Marshman and Gibbins (1970) in Toronto. Using two different sampling periods, January to August 1969 and December 1969 to February 1970, they found differences between purported and actual contents of street drugs. Some of these differences, however, could have been due to sampling bias. Comparing alleged and actual composition, they say: "Of the 519 samples for which the alleged composition was stated, 65 percent were found to contain the drug said to be present. If cannabis preparations are excluded this value declines to approximately 59 percent. . . . The proportion of alleged LSD samples which were subsequently found to contain this drug increased from 68.4 percent to 84.0 percent between the two sampling periods."

Mescaline proved to be the most frequently mislabeled hallucinogenic. Of 58 samples examined, none were in fact mescaline. Approximately one-half $(N = 27)$ were LSD. Roughly one-tenth were impure LSD $(N = 7)$. The remainder were mixtures resulting from unsuccessful attempts at synthesis $(N = 8)$, no drug at all $(N = 6)$ or LSD plus phencyclidine $(N = 5)$.

In January 1970, Cheek and coworkers (1970) published the analyses of 36 samples collected by investigators at the New Jersey Neuropsychiatric Institute in Princeton. Their results are summarized: "Most of the samples said to be LSD were actually LSD, none of the samples said to be mescaline, psilocybin, or THC were those substances. Four of the samples said to be mescaline were actually STP (2,5-dimethoxy-4 methylamphetamine). There was a wide variation in the amounts of LSD and STP in the samples. The amounts of LSD ranged from 50 to 283 micrograms (median 100 micrograms)."

With the advent of large rock festivals, tribal gatherings, and protest marches, rapid distribution of drugs with unknown contents has increased. The attempt to keep out "bad drugs" and prevent adverse reactions by informal and on-the-spot field testing of drugs —the "underground FDA"—is a fascinating recognition of the problem and is consistent with the students' opinions mentioned earlier. The accuracy of these field tests is unknown but even the attempt of users to protect themselves against pushers with adulterated drugs may have a beneficial effect.

Before conclusions are drawn about the flow of impure drugs into a community, systematic sampling is needed to obtain drugs from several different sources, including users, addicts, parents, seizures by police and narcotics officers, and specimens of body tissues from post mortems by medical examiners' offices.

We hypothesize from the limited evidence available that drug deceptions are a function of not only illicit dealers but also the community setting, perceptions by users of both real and falsely labeled drugs, and the availability of specific drugs. In neutralized language, these inaccuracies represent a "labeling shift." Our hypothesis is that, in settings where illegal drug use is relatively recent and experimental or "naïve" in nature, potent hallucinogenic drugs (for example, LSD, STP) will tend to be sold as weaker, less potent drugs (for example, STP sold as mescaline). Conversely, in communities with relatively well-established or experienced drug-using elements, weak drugs with little psychoactivity are likely to be peddled as stronger drugs (for example, aspirin sold as amphetamines).

Alcohol. Increasing the concentration of alcohol by the process of distillation has brought to alcoholic beverages additional sources of impurity not readily detected by tongue or eye.

The contents issue with alcohol appears to have received most intense discussion in the 1920s, that being a time when social policy on the drug was most unsettled. Perhaps concern over the adulteration and mislabeling of drugs, outside of medical and pharmaceutical contexts at least, is a correlate of the lack of consensus on social policy. Highlighting harmful content, derivatives, and additives may serve to express in a semidirect fashion powerful negative opinions about drugs, access to them, or their availability.

Moonshine liquor is a nostalgic remnant of the past, deeply embedded in recollections of a rural, quiet, nonurbanized time in our history. The prospect of taking a slug from a jug of "corn likker" still brings a gleam to the eyes of many men who grew up at a time when friends or members of their family were either "making it or running it." Illicit hooch dealing of previous decades has become a conversation piece of the present. As the older generation looks back on its rum-running, past illegal activities have now become opportunities for braggadocio.

Preparation of bootleg liquor under such romantic names as "white lightning" or "mountain dew" has declined in popularity in recent times. (These names out of the past have been appropriated by legitimate vendors to sell their products; Mountain Dew is now the trade name of a soft drink.) The U.S. District Court for Eastern Kentucky, for example, reports that only about one-tenth as many moonshine cases are heard today in comparison with two decades ago.

Concerning the actual contents of liquor, Lythgoe (1928) summarized the results of a study of the contaminants found in samples of illicit liquor in Massachusetts. Of the samples of prohibition liquor, 67 percent were adulterated with water. For the two-year period of 1926 and 1927, more than 17,000 samples were analyzed and only 23 were found to contain methanol (wood alcohol). One isolated sample responsible for a death was, however, 28 percent methanol.

Miles (1935) noted that moonshine whiskey contained fusel oils and acetaldehyde, both very harmful substances. Some moonshiners distilled denatured alcohol to make "synthetic hooch," unsuccessfully trying to remove all of the poisonous wood alcohol. In one study cited by Miles, 6 samples of illicit liquor of 100 contained small amounts of methyl alcohol.

Citing previous studies, Weeks (1942) notes that in England as well as the United States, people drink their bootleg liquor without knowing how concentrated it is, a problem frequently found with other illicit drugs. In one large sample, very high concentrations of ethyl alcohol (80 percent for one, 60 percent for another) were found.

Many impurities possibly leading to serious health consequences have been reported in moonshine liquor: copper, lead, fusel oils, and acetaldehydes. Many ingredients previously thought to be harmful are not. In its discussion of this issue, a report of the National Institute of Mental Health, *Alcohol and Alcoholism* (1969), states:

> *The notion that all "congeners" are toxic, unhealthy, or otherwise undesirable is invalid since some of the nonalcoholic substances—such as the salts, sugars, amino acids, and vitamins—are nutritionally useful.*
>
> *Certain of these components of alcoholic beverages—especially some of the higher alcohols known as fusel oils—are relatively more toxic than ethyl alcohol. But these usually occur in such low concentrations that they pose no clinically significant hazard. Contrary to popular belief that fusel oils occur primarily in new, raw or unaged whiskey, and similar spirits, and cause most of the objectionable taste and aroma of such beverages, chemical analysis has shown that their concentration actually increases with aging.*

The presence of contaminants such as lead in whiskey from illegal stills has led to clinically significant poisoning. To complicate the picture for clinicians, the symptoms caused by excessive use of ethyl alcohol can mask symptoms that are due to lead salts in moonshine. Diagnosis of lead encephalopathy may be difficult if the physician suspects only excessive intake of alcohol. According to Crutcher (1967), lethargy, convulsion and semistupor, and coma are common to both lead encephalopathy and acute alcoholism. Diagnosis of lead poisoning is possible if proper blood tests are carried out.

Marijuana. As suggested by Waller (1971), the plant *cannabis sativa L.* appears to have two major variants, a drug type and a hemp type. The drug type contains higher proportions of delta-9 tetrahydrocannabinol (THC), the principal active ingredient, and cannabinol (CBN), while the hemp or fiber type contains less of these in relation to cannabidiol (CBD). According to Doorenbos (1971), high THC content of samples appears to be correlated with type of plant (fiber or drug), method of cultivation and harvesting, and most important, the degree of manicuring to select those parts of the plant that contain the most delta-9 THC. Of less importance in determining potency is the sex of the plant, climatic condition of the region, and generation, up to the third generation at least.

Indigenous marijuana is primarily the fiber type with low concentration of delta-9 THC, averaging somewhat less than 1 percent for more than 100 samples taken from Minnesota, Iowa, and Illinois.

Plants grown in this country from seed obtained elsewhere yield more variable concentrations, ranging in delta-9 THC from 0.02 percent for stems, roots, and seeds to 11.4 percent found in the leaves surrounding the flowers themselves. Highly manicured samples from drug-type plants may be higher in delta-9 THC than hashish, the concentrated resin of the plant.

Discussion of potency is especially important since most survey research attempting to determine how often marijuana is used has neglected actual content of the drug. Relating the reported adverse effects of marijuana to variations in potency and loss of delta-9 THC during administration is necessary if self-reports of adverse effects are attributed to the drug. Concerning smoked marijuana, it was estimated in 1971 that half of the delta-9 THC in a marijuana cigarette is destroyed or lost before the smoke reaches the lungs. More recent research indicates that absorption of THC can vary widely, depending upon many variables. For this reason, survey and comparative studies should proceed with caution when making assumptions about absorbed marijuana.

After searching the world literature, McGlothlin (1970)' related estimates of daily use to estimated THC content for various marijuana preparations in different regions of the world. With 24 samples taken from five countries (Egypt, India, Morocco, Africa, and the United States), he estimates that median daily doses range from 5 milligrams of THC in one sample from the United States to 150 milligrams in a sample of ganga or charas from India. He also reports that tobacco is often mixed with cannabis preparations for smoking (for example, two-thirds tobacco and one-third kif in Morocco); and, in the case of heavy users, datura (containing scopolamine and atropine) is the most frequent additive other than tobacco.

A report by the Bureau of Narcotics and Dangerous Drugs Laboratory Operations Division states that during the fourth quarter of fiscal year 1970, a total of 1645 exhibits of suspected marijuana were analyzed. Qualitative analysis showed negative results for 12 percent of the total, or 191 exhibits. Even with the use of a large number of specimens, the false positive claim rate fluctuated; 14 percent for the first quarter, 16 percent for the second quarter, and 7 percent for the third quarter. (Marihuana and Health, 1971.)

Substances most commonly used to cut or adulterate marijuana are plant material of similar color and texture, the degree of required similarity being limited only by the audacity of the giver-seller and the naïveté of the receiver-user. Oregano, tea, catnip, parsley, and others are frequently found.

The Marshman and Gibbins (1969) study, cited earlier, discussed marijuana and hashish as well as hallucinogens. Of the samples alleged to be hashish, 100 percent were hashish. Of those purported to be marijuana, 67 percent contained marijuana. They state:

In regard to the 36 samples alleged to be marijuana, with a high cannabinoid content, "good grass," as it would be called on the street, some were marijuana cut with other substances and some contained no marijuana at all. Some of it appeared literally to be lawn clippings; some of it looked like hay and smelled like hay. Our figure of 64 percent for samples that "contained marijuana" includes all the samples that contained any marijuana at all. It is clear that a sizable portion of what is sold and smoked is not marijuana but other substances, sometimes of unknown origin.

Heroin. Since heroin is not used in medical practice in this country, all of it is illegal except when procured by recognized investigators for approved research projects. Smuggled into the country, it crosses the borders in relatively pure form compared to street or dosage units. Less bulk makes it easier to conceal. Inside the country, it may be diluted with any combination of several substances to give it bulk, to disguise the diluents or toxic additives, or to give it a crystalline appearance or bitter taste. Commonly used substances are quinine, dextrose, mannitol, mannite, and lactose.

Packaging into dosage units may follow a variety of techniques, such as using small glassine bags, the method of choice in New York City or No. 5 gelatin capsules, often found in the Washington, D.C., area.

The sale of cutting and packaging materials is itself big business. In recent congressional hearings, it was asserted that those pharmacists who sell these paraphernalia may make from 400 to 500 percent profit and remain immune from prosecution in almost all states (Pepper, 1970b). One small drug store in Harlem over a three-year period legally sold more than 47 million glassine bags, 40,000 ounces of quinine, 25 million empty capsules, and 4 tons of mannitol, all most likely used in preparing heroin for illicit distribution (Pepper, 1970a).

In the early 1960s, the Office of the Chief Medical Examiner of the city of New York reported on a sample of 216 specimens confiscated by the Police Department ("Analysis of Drug Samples . . . ," 1964; Fulton, 1965). All were thought to be heroin; only samples of 30 grains or more were studied. Three of the samples contained neither heroin nor any other drug but were in fact baking soda and starch. Three other specimens were aspirin or APC; four were marijuana and three were methadone—all sold and confiscated as heroin. Thirty-five of the specimens had heroin only with no adulterants; 130 had heroin with quinine and various combinations of mannitol and lactose as diluents. Procaine (trade name Novocaine), methapyrilene, and caffeine were found in 11 specimens.

No apparent differences among these groups exist when median values of percentage of heroin is inspected. The range of medians for all 216 specimens is from 4 to 31 percent heroin. This figure is somewhat misleading since the range of content of individually tested specimens is from zero to 77 percent pure heroin.

At approximately the same period covered by the New York City study, the early 1960s, experience in the southwestern region of the country showed heroin to be more concentrated but still highly variable in percent of pure material (personal communication, January 1971). The Chief of the California State Bureau of Narcotic Enforcement (Storer, 1964) testified in 1964 that:

Both quantitative and qualitative analyses are made, as a matter of routine, in all of our larger drug seizures. Samples of one-half ounce or more, will almost invariably test from a low of 15 percent to the highest we have seen in recent years, a sample of 169 grams which tested 94 percent heroin. The average heroin content of the larger samples will exceed 30 percent purity.

A typical small seizure of 1-grain bindles or capsules will assay from 3 to 9 or 10 percent. The addict who is the ultimate consumer seldom has access to uncut heroin.

Thus it appears that the higher one goes in the chain of illicit distribution, the more pure the drug is likely to be. Selecting only drugs from large seizures most likely yields specimens with high concentration.

Using data attained from over a million surgery and autopsy case files of the Armed Forces Institute of Pathology, Froede and Stahl (1971) describe 174 cases of death due to narcotics from 1918 to 1970.

In 155 of the cases, the cause is given as due to drugs, or more specifically a drug overdose or hypersensitivity. . . . It is interesting to note that of the six deaths attributed to homicide, two were the result of the injection of an admixture of cyanide and opiates. It is in this kind of case that the veracity of the "hot shot," homicidal administration of a deliberate overdose or poison, can no longer be doubted.

Fatal narcotism occurred more frequently in lower ranks of the military with the lowest three enlisted grades accounting for the greatest number of cases. Elaborating on fatal narcotism, Helpern (1970) recently stated:

In some fatal acute cases, the rapidity and type of reaction do not suggest simple overdosage but rather an overwhelming shocklike reaction due to sensitivity to the injected material.

The possible admixture of poisonous substances like nicotine and cyanide must also be kept in mind and considered another reason for careful, complete toxicological analysis in fatal cases.

Further information is needed to be able to establish a more complete picture of the causal factors involved in fatal narcotism and the frequency with which morbidity and mortality occur compared to the extent of heroin use in this country and abroad.

3

Marijuana Use, Distribution, and Control

William H. McGlothlin

In this chapter, we will examine the available information on marijuana use, distribution, economics, and control. We will also consider the use patterns, along with alternative control policies, that may become evident in the United States within the next few years.

Prevalence and Patterns of Use

In the past few years, numerous surveys have been conducted on the prevalence of marijuana use—especially in high schools and colleges. Berg (1970) has summarized the statistics from 69 sources. Table 3-1 shows the percentages of those who have ever used marijuana, as determined by national surveys conducted during the period 1970 to 1972; results from a 1970 survey of New York State are also shown.

Table 3–1

SURVEY RESULTS ON PREVALENCE OF MARIJUANA USE; 1970 TO 1972

Sample	Year	*Percentage of marijuana users* Total	Male	Female
General population				
Age 18–75 (national)[1]	1970–71	4	6	3
Age 18 and over (national)[2]	1971	15	21	10
Age 18 and over (national)[3]	1972	11	16	7
Age 14 and over (New York State)[4]	1970	10	—	—
College				
National[5]	1971	44	—	—
National[6]	1971	51	58	43
New York State[4]	1970	48	54	38
Secondary schools				
Age 12–17 (national)[7]	1971	15	17	14
Age 12–17 (national)[2]	1971	14	14	14
High school (New York State)[4]	1970	23	26	20

SOURCES: [1]Parry, 1971; [2]Commission on Marihuana, 1972; [3]Gallup Poll, *Los Angeles Times,* Feb. 10, 1972; [4]Chambers, 1971; [5]Groves and others, 1971; [6]*Gallup Opinion Index,* Report No. 80, February 1972; [7]Josephson and others, 1971.

These data indicate that, in the general population, males are about twice as likely to have tried marijuana as are females. The male-female ratio is about 3:2 for college students, and it is somewhat closer at the high school level. Two surveys have shown that the percentage of college students who have used marijuana is nearly twice that for the same age group (18 to 24) of nonstudents (Chambers, 1971; Parry, 1971), although this difference is probably decreasing as marijuana use becomes more widespread. Usage is still low among the older age groups; the 1970 New York State survey found that those who had ever used the drug constituted 4 percent for the 35 to 49 age group and 2 percent for those 50 and over; the 1972 Gallup survey reported 7 percent for the 30 to 49 age group and 2 percent for those 50 and over. The survey of the Commission on Marihuana and Drug Abuse, however, reported 6 percent for those 50 and over.

The values presented in Table 3-2 represent a best estimate of the number of persons who had used marijuana one or more times by mid-1972. They are based on a composite of the various survey results projected to the 1972 time period. Since data on student usage are much more extensive than those for nonstudents, these estimates are treated separately from the remainder of the population. In summary, we estimate that as of mid-1972 about 22 million persons in the United States had used marijuana, that is, about 14 percent of the population age 11 and over.

Frequency. Until recently, most survey results were reported only as percentages "having-ever-used" or in vague terms such as *occasionally, frequently,* and *regularly.* Table 3-3 provides limited data on frequencies of use. In the early 1970s, apparently about one-third of all persons who had ever tried marijuana were using it one or more times per week. More males than females have tried marijuana, and males are also more likely to use the drug frequently. The proportion of females who have ever used the drug who fall in the range of three or more times per week, is about one-half that for males (Hochman and Brill, 1971; McGlothlin and others, 1970b). In schools where marijuana usage has existed for several years and prevalence is high, the proportion of frequent users tends to be relatively high; for example, San Mateo County high schools in California. Schools that exhibit low prevalence of use typically show that 50 percent or more of those who have ever used marijuana are experimenters (fewer than ten times) (McGlothlin, 1971). Limited data on usage among persons over 35 also show that a high proportion of those who have used the drug are in the experimenter class (Chambers, 1971).

Table 3-4 provides frequency-of-use estimates that are consistent with the data shown in Table 3-3. Estimates are made by sex, by student and nonstudent status, and by two age categories in

Table 3-2

Estimate of Persons in United States Who Had Used Marijuana One or More Times by Mid-1972

	Percent			Number		
	Total	Male	Female	Total	Male	Female
Grades 6–8	7	8	6	770,000	450,000	320,000
Grades 9–12	28	32	25	4,130,000	2,330,000	1,800,000
College	54	62	41	4,110,000	2,920,000	1,190,000
Age 18–24 (nonstudent)	30	39	20	4,990,000	3,350,000	1,640,000
Age 25–34 (nonstudent)	15	19	10	3,340,000	2,250,000	1,090,000
Age 35 and over (nonstudent)	6	9	3	5,040,000	3,360,000	1,680,000
Total, age 11 and over	14.2	18.9	9.5	22,380,000	14,660,000	7,720,000

Table 3–3

FREQUENCY OF MARIJUANA USE AS REPORTED IN
SURVEYS CONDUCTED IN 1970 AND 1971

Sample	Year	Users: one or more times, percent	Users in upper ranges	
			Frequency	Percent
General population				
Age 18 and over			1–6 times/wk	9[a]
(national)[1]	1971	15	daily	3[a]
Age 14 and over				
(New York State)[2]	1970	10	≧ 6 times/mo	34
College				
National[3]	1971	44	≧ 2 times/mo	22
National[4]	1971	51	≧ 25 times/mo	10
New York State[2]	1970	48	≧ 6 times/mo	34
			male	36
			female	29
Secondary schools				
Age 12–17 (national)[5]	1971	15	> 60 times	20
Age 12–17 (national)[1]	1971	14	1–6 times/wk	13[b]
			daily	5[b]
High school	1970	23	≧ 6 times/mo	38
(New York State)[2]			male	43
			female	31
San Mateo County	1971	54[c]	≧ 1 time/wk	47
high school seniors[6]			male	55
			female	38

SOURCES: [1]Commission on Marihuana, 1972; [2]Chambers, 1971;
[3]Groves and others, 1972; [4]*Gallup Opinion Index,* Report No. 80,
February 1972; [5]Josephson and others, 1971; [6]San Mateo County
School Study.
[a]Of those indicating use, 30 percent did not reply as to frequency.
[b]Of those indicating use, 12 percent did not reply as to frequency.
[c]Used during preceding 12 months.

the nonstudent group. In the early 1970s, the frequency-of-use data
were reasonably plentiful for the student population, but were scarce
for other groups. In particular, the 18 to 34 nonstudent group was
estimated to have a relatively high proportion in the daily-use category because of the subculture characterized by heavy drug use,

which is largely contained in this segment. However, since no data were available on the size of this subculture, this estimate could be substantially in error.

In summary, of the estimated 22 million persons in the United States who had used marijuana one or more times by mid-1972, we further estimated that 48 percent had stopped using the drug or had used it fewer than ten times; that 37 percent were currently using marijuana one to eight times per month; and that 15 percent were using on a basis of three or more times per week. Of those who used the drug three or more times per week, an estimated 80 percent were males.

Amount. Information on the amount of marijuana consumed per use is essential—both from the standpoint of assessing the impact on the user and for estimating the volume and economics of the marijuana market. In this country, marijuana is normally smoked in the form of cigarettes, so the natural unit of measure is the number of cigarettes per use or per day. Certain exceptions exist. Marijuana may be smoked in a pipe, but probably no more than 10 percent is used in this manner (Haines and Green, 1970); it is also occasionally taken orally, but the amount consumed in this manner is negligible (Haines and Green, 1970). Finally, use in the form of hashish is increasing and probably represents 15 to 20 percent of the total at present. Although survey data generally do not distinguish between marijuana and hashish use, seizure data provide the basis for an estimate. In 1971, federal agencies seized 100,627 kilograms of marijuana and 3,526 kilograms of hashish (Bureau of Narcotics, 1971). Assuming that hashish is approximately five times as potent as marijuana by weight (Lerner and Zeffert, 1968; Mechoulam, 1970), the hashish seizures would be equivalent to 17,630 kilograms of marijuana, or about 15 percent of the total seizures. Hashish use is increasing and has been projected to represent 20 percent of the total use by mid-1972. For the purposes of this subsection, total use will be estimated in terms of marijuana cigarettes and then 20 percent will be subtracted as representing use in the form of hashish.

Studies that report the amount of marijuana smoked per occasion indicate that the majority of users consume no more than one cigarette. One study found that 50 percent reported using one

Table 3-4

Estimates of Frequency of Use in the United States Among Persons Who Have Used Marijuana One or More Times, Mid-1972

Frequency of marijuana use

Group	> 1 time/mo[a] %	Number	1-4 times/mo %	Number	1-2 times/wk %	Number	3-6 times/wk %	Number	Daily %	Number	Total %	Number
Students												
Male	40	2,280,000	20	1,140,000	21	1,197,000	13	741,000	6	342,000	100	5,700,000
Female	50	1,655,000	22	728,000	19	629,000	7	232,000	2	66,000	100	3,310,000
Nonstudents (18–34)												
Male	45	2,520,000	20	1,120,000	14	784,000	13	728,000	8	448,000	100	5,600,000
Female	55	1,502,000	22	600,000	13	355,000	7	191,000	3	82,000	100	2,730,000
Nonstudents (35 and over)												
Male	50	1,680,000	20	672,000	19	638,000	8	269,000	3	101,000	100	3,360,000
Female	60	1,008,000	20	336,000	15	252,000	4	67,000	1	17,000	100	1,680,000
Total	48	10,645,000	20	4,596,000	17	3,855,000	10	2,228,000	5	1,056,000	100	22,380,000
Male	44	6,480,000	20	2,932,000	18	2,619,000	12	1,738,000	6	891,000	100	14,660,000
Female	54	4,165,000	22	1,664,000	16	1,236,000	6	490,000	2	165,000	100	7,720,000

[a]Includes persons who have stopped using marijuana and/or have used a total of less than ten times.

cigarette or less and 10 percent more than three cigarettes (Nisbet and Vakil, 1971). Another interview study of fairly regular users (median two times per week) found that the large majority smoked one-half to one cigarette "to get high," but that 76 percent reported they normally smoked an additional amount subsequent to achieving this effect (Haines and Green, 1970). A third study of an older sample (mean age 44) of persons who had typically used marijuana for many years found that 63 percent used no more than one cigarette per occasion, while 26 percent stated that they normally smoked three to five (McGlothlin and others, 1970a). The potency of available marijuana varies widely and contributes to the variability in amount consumed. The delta-9 tetrahydrocannabinol (THC) content varies from 0.1 to 5.0 percent in the dried material exclusive of stems and seeds. Mexican-grown marijuana sold in the United States averages about 1 percent THC (R. T. Jones, 1971; Lerner and Zeffert, 1968); domestic marijuana contains only 0.1 to 0.5 percent THC (Phillips and others, 1970).

Experimental data provide further evidence on the effective marijuana dose level. When given as a single administration, smoked doses of 2 milligrams of THC, or its marijuana equivalent, are sufficient to produce a mild euphoria in experienced users; 7 milligrams produce some perceptual and time-sense changes; and 15 milligrams produce a relatively high level of intoxication (Isbell and others, 1967; Weil and others, 1968). Assuming that marijuana contains 1.0 percent THC and that a cigarette weighs 0.5 gram, these doses are equivalent to about one-half, one and one-half, and three cigarettes respectively. Marijuana users do not necessarily smoke it in a single dose, however, and larger amounts would be required to maintain these effects over a period of several hours.

Table 3-5 presents an estimate of the mean amount of marijuana smoked per user per occasion as a function of frequency of use. More precisely, it is the mean amount smoked during the days on which any marijuana is consumed. The estimated amount used increases with frequency of use. This is partially a reflection of the fact that frequent users are more likely to smoke at intervals during a longer period of intoxication, or at more than one time during the day. No estimate of amount used is made for the category of Table

Table 3-5

ESTIMATED NUMBER OF MARIJUANA CIGARETTES (OR EQUIVALENT)
CONSUMED AS A FUNCTION OF FREQUENCY OF USE

| Frequency of use | Number of persons | Mean number cigarettes smoked per person | | Annual consumption | |
		Per occasion	Per month	Number of cigarettes	Percent
Daily	1,056,000	3.0	90	1,140,000,000	43
3–6 times week	2,228,000	2.0	36	962,000,000	37
1–2 times week	3,855,000	1.5	9	416,000,000	16
2–4 times month	4,596,000	1.0	2	110,000,000	4
Total	11,735,000			2,628,000,000	100

3-4 showing those who use less than one time per month, since this group consists primarily of the experimenters or persons who have stopped using marijuana. Their contribution to the total amount of marijuana consumed is negligible.

Table 3-5 also shows the total estimated annual consumption of marijuana cigarettes, that is, number of users times number of cigarettes used per month times 12. Hashish use and smoking by pipe are included in terms of cigarette equivalents. Note that 1 million marijuana users account for 43 percent of the estimated 2.6 billion marijuana cigarettes consumed. A comparable relationship exists with respect to alcohol.

Market

Annual National Consumption. Assuming an average cigarette weight of 0.5 gram,[1] the gross weight of the 2628 million ciga-

[1] Data from 54 seizures in the Los Angeles area showed the average net weight per cigarette to be 0.61 gram, with a range of 0.25 to 1.12 grams

rettes smoked annually is 1,314,000 kilograms of dried, cleaned marijuana. As discussed previously, the amount of hashish consumed is assumed to be equivalent to about 20 percent of the total consumption, so we may substract this amount (262,800 kilograms), leaving 1,051,200 kilograms of clean marijuana plus 52,560 kilograms of hashish.[2]

Crude marijuana loses 25 to 30 percent by weight when prepared for smoking, due to the removal of seeds, stems, and excess moisture (Doorenbos, 1971). Assuming a weight ratio of 10:7 for crude to cleaned marijuana, an estimated 1,501,700 kilograms of crude marijuana are required to satisfy the annual consumption.

In larger quantities, marijuana is usually sold in the form of wrapped bricks of compressed material ostensibly weighing 1 kilogram. In actual practice, the bricks typically weigh substantially less than 1 kilogram. Statistics from 35 seizures involving some 5000 bricks revealed an average net weight of 780 grams, with a range of 539 to 995 grams.[3] The number of short kilograms necessary to supply 1,501,700 kilograms of crude marijuana is thus 1,925,250.[4]

Source. Some marijuana is cultivated or collected from low-potency wild growth in the United States, but most is grown outside the country, principally in Mexico.[5] As of 1972, substantial

---

(data provided by William Arnold of the California State Bureau of Narcotics, Los Angeles office, and Paul Kayne of the Los Angeles Sheriff's Crime Laboratory). The mean weight for some 9000 marijuana cigarettes seized by the New York City Police Department in 1969 and 1970 was 0.32 and 0.36 gram respectively (New York City Police Department annual reports, 1969, 1970). Other sources indicate cigarettes used in Eastern states are smaller than those rolled in the West, possibly due to the higher cost of marijuana (see Haines and Green, 1970).

[2] Assumes the potency is five times that of marijuana.

[3] Data supplied by Norman Nordweir (U.S. Customs, Los Angeles Office), Lloyd Sinclair (BNDD, Los Angeles Office), and William Arnold (California State Bureau of Narcotics Enforcement, Los Angeles Office).

[4] An alternative approach to estimating the amount of marijuana consumed is to utilize data on the number of cigarette papers sold, which is available from tax records. After subtracting those used for tobacco cigarettes, this presumably provides an estimate of the number used for marijuana. This approach has been attempted (see McGlothlin, 1971), but the instability of the recent cigarette paper sales data made the results of dubious value.

[5] This subsection is largely based on information obtained in interviews with U.S. Customs, BNDD, California state and local narcotics agen-

quantities originated in Jamaica and to a lesser extent in Central America, Southeast Asia, and other areas; but the primary source was still Mexico. For the present purposes, we assume that 90 percent of the crude marijuana consumed in the United States originates outside the country.

Of the 1,501,700 kilograms of crude marijuana consumed annually in this country, 90 percent (1,351,500 kilograms) originates outside the United States. Adding 130,000 kilograms of marijuana seized,[6] we get the total amount of marijuana grown in foreign countries for the United States market: 1,481,500 kilograms or 1,899,400 short kilograms. The land required to produce this amount is about 7600 acres.[7]

In Mexico, marijuana sells for $6 to $10 per 1-kilogram brick in the fields, and purchases are often of the order of several tons. It is normally trucked to points on the Mexican side of the border, where it sells for $35 to $40 per short kilogram in quantities of 100 kilograms or more. At the $35 price, the estimated annual expenditure for marijuana before importation is $66 million.

Hashish is generally assumed to originate in Lebanon and other Middle Eastern countries. Prices paid at the point of origin are not well established, but it may be bought in several Middle Eastern countries for $35 to $45 per kilogram. Assuming an annual United States consumption of 52,560 kilograms and a price of $40 per kilogram, the current estimated expenditure at the point of origin is $2 million.

Importation. The enormous bulk of the marijuana traffic does not impose severe restrictions on the Mexican side of the

---

cies, and various other persons familiar with the sources and distribution of marijuana and hashish. Some published and unpublished data on prices and seizures were obtained from BNDD and U.S. Customs, and several published descriptions of the retail marijuana market were also utilized.

[6] 1971 BNDD and Customs seizures plus an estimated 30,000 kilograms by California state and local narcotic agencies. The Mexican government also reported seizing 35,000 kilograms of marijuana and the destruction of 390,000 kilograms of dried marijuana in the fields during the period October 1969 to March 1971 (BNDD *Bulletin,* U.S. Department of Justice, May–June, 1971).

[7] Based on the average of 300 pounds of dried cleaned marijuana obtained per acre from experimental cultivation in Mississippi (Doorenbos, 1971).

border. At the point of importation and beyond, the bulk involved imposes a severe limitation and is the major factor shaping the distribution system on the United States side. When one considers that approximately 4 tons of marijuana per day must be smuggled into the United States, typically in lots of no more than 50 to 300 kilograms, and that the bulk of marijuana makes it infeasible to store in quantity on the United States side, the prohibitive complexity of organizing more than a relatively small operation becomes apparent. By comparison, the annual importation of heroin is equivalent to only one or two days of smuggling activity for marijuana by weight, and heroin can be imported and stored in the United States well in advance of its distribution.

Amounts of marijuana smuggled from Mexico vary from 1 or 2 kilograms brought across the border by an individual to as much as 5 tons brought up the coast by boat, as reported in the *Los Angeles Times* of May 5, 1971. The vast majority of smuggling attempts involve amounts on the low end of the scale. In 1971, the mean weight of the 6312 marijuana seizures made by Customs was less than 15 kilograms (Bureau of Narcotics, 1971). About 85 percent of marijuana seized at the United States–Mexican border is intercepted in vehicles. However, some authorities are of the opinion that aircraft and boats are carrying an increasing portion of the traffic—considerably more than is indicated by the percentage of seizures.

Hashish is most frequently smuggled into the United States aboard commercial aircraft. The mean weight for 1757 Customs seizures in 1971 was 1.8 kilograms (Bureau of Narcotics, 1971), although in the early 1970s seizures of 40 to 50 pounds were not infrequent.

Distribution. On entry into the United States, marijuana sells for $75 to $90 per short kilogram in lots of 100 or more bricks at points near the Mexican border. Virtually all warehousing of large quantities of marijuana is done outside the United States. Normally, the buyer for a given lot of 100 kilograms or more is known before importation, and dispersal or transshipment takes place immediately after delivery.

Typically, although an individual who buys in 100-kilogram lots would not sell in quantities of less than 5 or 10 kilograms, he may frequently be willing to sell much larger quantities for lower profits, particularly to another known wholesaler, a transaction that involves little risk. In general, the price is dependent on the size of transaction, extent of risk, and distance from the border. The quality of the marijuana and the actual weight of the "kilogram" bricks are also factors, especially in smaller transactions. Finally, the price varies with availability, and there is some seasonal fluctuation corresponding to the time of harvest in Mexico. In the spring of 1972, marijuana was in short supply; and the price per single short kilogram in California was $300 to $400, or about double the price for 1971. For the present purposes, such prices are assumed to be atypical, and calculations are based on the 1971 prices, that is, $150 to $200 per single short kilogram in California and other border states and $225 to $275 in most other areas of the country.

Assuming an annual consumption of 1,925,250 short kilograms of marijuana (including Mexican, domestic, and other origin), the annual expenditures in the United States as a function of lot size are estimated as shown in Table 3-6.

Table 3–6

ESTIMATED ANNUAL UNITED STATES EXPENDITURES
FOR MARIJUANA, 1972

Level, lot size	Price per short kilogram	Annual expenditure
100 kilograms and up	$ 85	$163,600,000
10–15 kilograms	150	288,800,000
1 kilogram	250	481,300,000

Hashish sells for $600 to $1000 per pound. Apparently, there is little regional variation in price, although it generally sells for less in areas where there is a relatively large market or where it is in competition with low-priced marijuana, for example, San Francisco and Los Angeles. No information was available on price for multipound lots. Assuming the annual consumption at 52,560 kilograms, or 115,900 pounds, and a price structure similar to that for marijuana, the annual expenditures for hashish are estimated as shown in Table 3-7.

Table 3–7

ESTIMATED ANNUAL UNITED STATES EXPENDITURES
FOR HASHISH, 1972

Level	Price per pound	Annual expenditure
10 pounds and up	$500	$57,950,000
1 pound	800	92,700,000

The standard retail unit for marijuana is an ounce or "lid" of uncleaned material. Generally, the "ounce" is short by about the same proportion as the brick; that is, it averages around 22 grams instead of the full 28.3 grams. Marijuana is also sold in 1-pound, ½-pound and ¼-pound quantities. The 1972 price per short ounce in California and the Southwest was $10 to $15; in most other areas, a short ounce sold for $20 to $25, and prices in Chicago and Ohio were quoted as high as $35 to $40. Marijuana may also be retailed in "nickel bags," containing 3 to 5 grams and selling for $5. Occasionally, the smaller quantities are sold in loose cleaned (manicured) form or as cigarettes. The addition of adulterants such as oregano is not uncommon in this form.

Hashish retails for $5 to $10 per gram, but it is often sold to the ultimate consumer in 1-ounce quantities at prices ranging from $70 to $125.

Several authors have described the distribution of marijuana at the retail level (Anonymous, 1969; Carey, 1968; Goode, 1969, 1970; Mandel, 1967). The majority of persons who use the drug several times per week technically have also sold marijuana, although it may be no more than sharing a purchase with friends at no profit. One survey reported that 85 percent of persons who use it three or more times per week fall in this category (Goode, 1970). Others casually sell to a few close acquaintances to earn enough for their own supply and a small amount of money. Others retail marijuana as a full-time occupation. Still others move further up the ladder, buying in quantities of 5 to 10 kilograms, selling some as single bricks and retailing the remainder in ounces or fractions of a pound.

Retail expenditures. In order to estimate the retail expenditures for marijuana, it is necessary to assume the size of the purchase made by the ultimate consumer. As would be expected, heavier users are more likely to buy larger amounts in a single purchase. The buying of ¼ pound up to 1 pound, or even a kilogram, for sharing among a group of users is not uncommon. In one study of fairly heavy users, 17 percent stated they purchased a kilogram at a time about one-half of the time (Hochman and Brill, 1971). The size of purchase is also influenced by the economic status of the buyer and the price of marijuana; for example, purchases of less than an ounce are relatively uncommon in California where the ounce price is $10 to $15, but in the East a cost of $25 per ounce reportedly results in more frequent purchases of smaller quantities, especially among lower socioeconomic groups. The retail expenditures for marijuana and hashish are estimated in Table 3-8, account being taken of the variability in purchase sizes as a function of frequency of use. The number of users and percentage of total consumption by frequency of use are taken from Table 3-5. The national average price of marijuana is assumed to be $250 per short kilogram and $20 per short ounce, or $700 for a short kilogram bought in short-ounce units. The more frequent users are assumed to obtain their supplies at less than $20 per short ounce, by purchasing in larger quantities, by sharing in group purchases, or by obtaining lower prices through familiarity with dealers. The average price paid by those who use daily and those who use three to six times per week is estimated to be $450 and $575 per short kilogram respectively. Of those persons who use the drug two times per week or less, half are assumed to buy at $20 per short ounce and half in smaller units equivalent to $30 per short ounce, for an average of $875 per short kilogram.

Similar assumptions were made for hashish purchases. Retail prices for hashish were assumed to be $8 per gram and $90 per ounce. Three-fourths of the daily users and one-half of those who use three to six times per week were estimated to obtain hashish at

Table 3-8

Estimate of Retail Expenditures for Marijuana and Hashish

	Frequency of use			
	Daily	3–6 times/wk	≦ 2 times/wk	Total
Number of users	1,056,000	2,228,000	8,451,000	11,735,000
Annual consumption:				
Proportion of total consumption	43%	37%	20%	100%
Marijuana	827,850 kg[a]	712,350 kg[a]	385,050 kg[a]	1,925,250 kg[a]
Hashish	49,840 lb	42,880 lb	23,180 lb	115,900 lb
Retail cost:				
Marijuana	$ 450/kg[a]	$ 575/kg[a]	$ 875/kg[a]	$ 581/kg[b]
Hashish	$2,000/lb	$2,500/lb	$3,600/lb	$2,500/lb
Total annual expenditures:				
Marijuana	$372,530,000	$409,600,000	$336,920,000	$1,119,050,000
Hashish	$ 99,680,000	$107,200,000	$ 83,450,000	$ 290,330,000
Total	$472,210,000	$516,800,000	$420,370,000	$1,409,380,000
Individual user expenditures:[b]				
Annual	$447	$232	$50	
Weekly	$ 9	$ 4	$ 1	

[a]Short kilograms.
[b]Average expenditures for all users: annual, $120; weekly, $2.

the ounce price and the remainder at the gram price. All who use the drug two times per week or less were assumed to buy at the gram price.

The estimated annual retail expenditure for marijuana and hashish combined is about $1.4 billion. Average cost per user is about $9 per week for daily users and about $4 per week for those who use three to six times per week.

Subtracting the previously estimated annual expenditure for marijuana at the short-kilogram level ($481 million) and that for hashish at the pound level ($93 million) from the retail expenditure in Table 3-8 leaves a gross retail profit of $835 million. Several authors have concluded that marijuana-hashish dealing at the retail level is a low-profit operation—a dealer serving only about 25 customers and making $200 to $300 per month (Carey, 1968; Goode, 1969; Mandel, 1967). At this rate, the gross retail profit estimated here would be sufficient to employ some 280,000 persons in retail selling. Data are not available for estimating the number of persons involved in the wholesale marijuana-hashish market. If we assume the average gross profit to be $20,000 per year per person, then the gross wholesale profit subsequent to purchase on the United States side of the border ($353 million) would result in some 17,500 persons being employed at the wholesale level.[8] Figure 3-1 provides a summary of the estimated use, distribution, and economics of the marijuana-hashish market for mid-1972.

Enforcement

Seizures. In 1971, the U.S. Bureau of Customs and the federal Bureau of Narcotics and Dangerous Drugs (BNDD) seized 91,400 kilograms and 9,200 kilograms of marijuana, respectively (Bureau of Narcotics, 1971). The corresponding hashish seizures were 3,100 kilograms and 400 kilograms. California state and local seizures in 1970 accounted for an additional 26,000 kilograms of marijuana (Bureau of Criminal Statistics, 1970b). Data on seizures by other state and local agencies are generally not available but are

---

[8] Since both wholesale and retail dealers often sell other drugs in addition to marijuana, the total number of persons involved is likely to be substantially larger than the numbers estimated here.

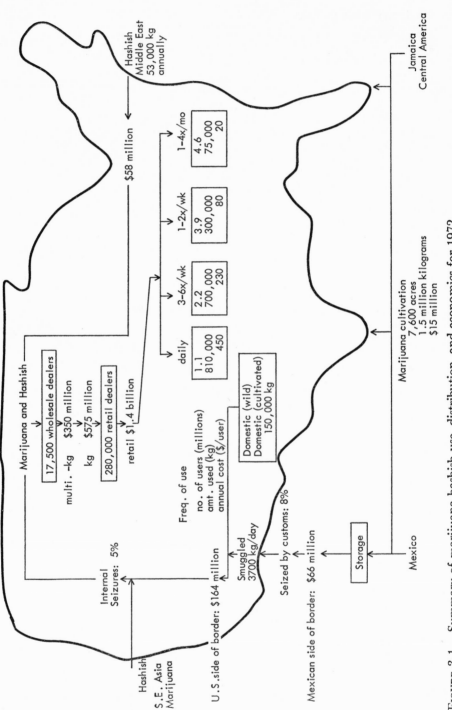

FIGURE 3-1. Summary of marijuana-hashish use, distribution, and economics for 1972.

known to be relatively small in comparison to those for California
[(McGlothlin, 1971). The marijuana seizures by Customs (1971),
BNDD (1971), and California (1970) represent 8 percent of the
estimated 1972 consumption. Assuming that the 1971 consumption
was no more than 75 percent of that for 1972, and that state and
local agencies other than those of California seized an additional
20,000 kilograms, the total 1971 marijuana seizures represented
about 13 percent of the 1971 attempted importation.

Arrests. Statistics from the 1970 *Uniform Crime Reports*
show 157,000 arrests for marijuana or 45 percent of the total 346,-
000 drug arrests (Federal Bureau of Investigation, 1971). The
1970 adult and juvenile marijuana arrests in California totaled
69,000 (Bureau of Criminal Statistics, 1970b). For 1969, 34 percent of the 55,000 California marijuana arrests were of persons age
18 to 20, which yields an arrest rate of 1.8 per 100 (Bureau of
Criminal Statistics, 1969). Of marijuana arrests for persons 18 and
over, 86 percent were males, for an arrest rate of 3.0 per 100 in the
18 to 20 age group. In San Mateo County, California, 50 percent
of senior high school males reported marijuana use during 1969
'(San Mateo County School Study, 1968 through 1972). Assuming
the statewide average for marijuana use at about 80 percent of that
for San Mateo County, the arrest rate for males age 18 to 20 who
used marijuana one or more times in 1969 is estimated to be 7.4
per 100. If we further assume that virtually all the arrests are among
the 60 percent who used marijuana on more than an experimental
basis (ten or more times), the arrest rate for this group of males
age 18 to 20 is 12 per 100.

The number of California arrests for sale or transportation
of marijuana in 1969 was 7800 (Bureau of Criminal Statistics,
1969). If we assume that the number of persons involved in wholesale and retail selling in California during 1969 was 30,000, the
arrest rate was 26 per 100.[9]

In summary, the risk of arrest for use or sale of marijuana is
quite substantial, at least in California. The penalties imposed by
the courts are also significant. Of the 37,700 adult (18 and over)'

---

[9] Assumes the number of persons involved in wholesale and retail
selling in 1969 was 50 percent of the 300,000 estimated for 1972 and that 20
percent of the total were in California.

nonfederal arrestees in 1969, 21 percent were convicted on felony charges. Incarceration rates were relatively low—0.6 percent of the total arrested received prison sentences, and 8 percent received jail sentences; however, the additional implications of felony convictions are severe. The cost of processing the California adult and juvenile marijuana arrests for 1969 has been estimated to be $43 million, or about $780 per arrest (McGlothlin, 1971).

Future Use

Current trends. Figure 3-2 presents some trend indicators of marijuana use and control between 1967 and 1971. Obviously the seizure and arrest data may reflect variations in enforcement emphasis as well as changes in usage.

As the percentage of students who have ever used marijuana approaches or exceeds the 50 percent mark, increasing interest focuses on trends in the proportion of such students who continue use. A comparison of the Gallup college surveys for 1970 and 1971 indicates continuing use may be nearing a plateau (Gallup Opinion Index, 1972). On the other hand, the San Mateo County secondary school data show a definite increase over the same period, in the proportion of students who use marijuana one or more times per week (San Mateo County School Study, 1968 through 1972). This survey showed a tendency toward leveling out of use from 1969 to 1970, but the sharp rise resumed in 1971. Interview studies have provided additional data on the question of duration of use. One 1970 college survey found that, of those persons who had been initiated to marijuana more than three years before and who had used it on more than an experimental basis (ten or more times), 37 percent had currently either stopped or were using infrequently, and 32 percent and 31 percent reported current usage at several times per month and several times per week, respectively (Hochman and Brill, 1971). Another 1970 college study found that 77 percent of those who had been initiated to marijuana four or five years previously were still using to some degree (Lipp, 1971).

In summary, the currently available (1972) trend data on marijuana usage leave unanswered the question of whether it is likely to be a transient or a permanent phenomenon. The number of persons who have ever used marijuana in continuing to increase,

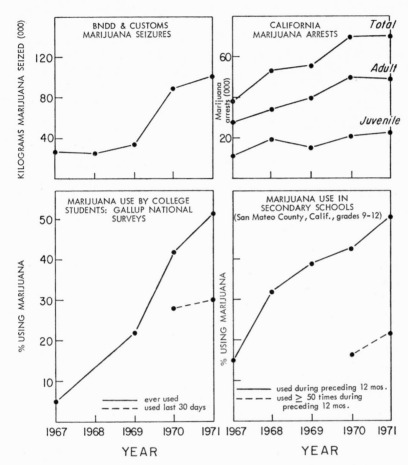

FIGURE 3-2. Marijuana trend indicators: use and control.

probably at a rate of 25 to 30 percent per year. In addition, there is no evidence as yet that the number of persons who discontinue after a significant period of usage are exceeding the number who are initiating such behavior. On the other hand, the behavior has many of the characteristics of a fad or temporary style: its very rapid acceptance by that segment of the population most susceptible to fads; the fact that it has been enthusiastically propagandized via music, a pseudophilosophy, and the popular media; the fact that its use is, in part, an antiestablishment reaction stemming from factors other than the properties of the drug itself. In addition, the appearance of Western-style (Occidental) marijuana use among university students in most countries throughout the world has more the flavor of adoption of styles of music or hair length than a lasting behavior.

The contrary view holds that since cannabis (marijuana) is the second most widely used intoxicant in the world, it clearly is a drug that may prove attractive to large numbers of people on a continuing basis. Once a drug with these features is introduced into a culture on a widespread basis, it seems quite likely to be retained by some portion of the population. Blum has noted that in the history of drug use there are few instances in which a drug achieved widespread acceptance in a culture and was subsequently discarded (Blum and Associates, 1969a).

Insights from Other Cannabis-using Cultures. Cross-cultural generalizations are hazardous; however, a brief examination of the prevalence and patterns of cannabis use in cultures where it has existed for centuries may be helpful in forecasting the future use in the United States. For instance, what proportion of the population elects to use the drug under conditions of acceptance in countries with a long history of use? In Nepal, which is reportedly the only country in the world that imposes no restrictions on cannabis use, approximately 4000 acres are officially cultivated and taxed, and additional amounts of hashish are harvested from wild growth for commercial purposes (McGlothlin, 1971). In spite of the fact that cannabis is legal, readily available, and inexpensive, Nepalese use is very limited and virtually all the crop is illicitly exported to India and Pakistan.

In India and Pakistan, charas (hashish) was prohibited in 1945, but other preparations of cannabis (bhang and ganja) are still legal in selected states. Daily users probably number 2 million to 3 million, or about 4 per 1000 on a per capita basis (McGlothin, 1971). However, since use is restricted to lower-class males and is concentrated in certain states, daily users may constitute as high as 5 percent of the relevant population in some areas.

In Morocco, occasional and regular cannabis users were estimated to represent 10 percent of the population before prohibition of the drug in 1954 (Roland and Teste, 1958). Since use was primarily restricted to males, this was about 25 percent of the adult male population. Other estimates of regular use have run as high as 50 percent of the native male population in some areas of South Africa (South Africa Drug Report, 1952) and 40 to 50 percent of the male population in Jamaica (*Marihuana and Health*, 1972).

In summary, in very few areas in the world does the prevalence of cannabis use approach that for alcohol in the Western culture. Usage is largely restricted to lower-class males, and daily use seldom exceeds 5 to 10 percent among this group. By comparison, it is estimated that 2.5 percent of United States males age 14 to 34 are currently (1972) using marijuana daily and that an additional 4.6 percent are using it three to six times per week (Table 3-4).

Probably the most significant comparison between the use of marijuana in the United States and that in other cultures concerns the amount consumed. In Table 3-5, the typical American dosage is estimated at one to three marijuana cigarettes, or 5 to 15 milligrams of THC, per day. The maximum amount consumed by heavy users is of the order of ten cigarettes, or 50 milligrams of THC, per day. By contrast, the *average* amount consumed by daily users in India, Egypt, and Morocco is estimated to contain 45 to 60 milligrams of THC, and the maximum is around 200 milligrams (McGlothlin, 1971). Some studies have indicated usage equivalent to more than 700 milligrams of THC (Chopra and Chopra, 1939). In Greece, chronic hashish users serving as experimental subjects are routinely given smoked-THC doses of 150 milligrams, whereas 15 milligrams is normally the maximum dose administered to experimental subjects in this country. The one- to three-cigarette dosage of the early 1970s is also low in comparison with the six to ten cigarettes per day estimated for regular users in the 1940s (Charen and Perelman, 1946; Mayor's Committee, 1964). It is also low in comparison with the amounts used in the early 1970s by American soldiers in Vietnam and Germany. One study of heavy hashish users among the United States military forces in Germany found an average use of more than 3 grams per day, that is, the equivalent of 30 marijuana cigarettes per day (Tennant and others, 1971).

In summary, most of the current marijuana smokers in the United States are best described as playing at cannabis use in comparison with users in other cultures. It seems likely that the average amount of THC consumed by continuing users in this country will increase in the next few years, although probably not to the level observed in other cultures. Additional experience, the availability of more potent preparations, and the development of tolerance among frequent users will tend to increase the average amount consumed. In addition, it would not be surprising if some individuals daily consume 200 milligrams of THC or more in the form of hashish or other concentrated preparations, an amount greatly in excess of that previously observed in this country. Experience in other countries indicates that the use of these very large amounts occurs in about the same proportion of users as does alcoholism in the United States, that is, about 5 to 10 percent of the total number of users.

Predicted Use in 1976. Table 3-9 compares higher and lower predictions of marijuana-hashish usage for 1976 with the estimate for 1972. The predicted use of larger quantities of THC in the form of marijuana or other preparations is reflected in the 1976 estimates. It is estimated that daily users and those who use the drugs three to six times per week will be using five and three marijuana cigarettes, or equivalent, respectively, in comparison with three and two cigarettes assumed in Table 3-5 for 1972. Although the lower estimate for 1976 assumes a somewhat smaller population of users than that for 1972, the predicted larger amounts per user result in an increase in total consumption. The estimated retail expenditures are calculated on the same basis as those in Table 3-8.

Alternative Control Policies

Marijuana control policies have been discussed at length in previous documents (Kaplan, 1970; Brill, 1971–1972). The present section will be primarily limited to an examination of the major alternative policies in the context of the quantitative estimates of use, distribution, and enforcement effectiveness developed in the previous sections.

Several features characterize the current (1972) marijuana-hashish market as summarized in Figure 3-1. First, in the case of marijuana, the fact that 99 units of inert substance must be handled for every one unit of the active drug means that large amounts of

Table 3-9

Estimated Marijuana-Hashish Usage and Expenditures for 1972 and 1976

	1972 estimate	1976 prediction	
		Minimum	Maximum
Number of users:			
Daily	1,100,000	800,000	2,500,000
3–6 times/week	2,200,000	2,000,000	3,500,000
1–2 times/week	3,900,000	3,000,000	6,000,000
1–4 times/month	4,600,000	3,000,000	10,000,000
Total	11,800,000	8,800,000	22,000,000
Annual national consumption of crude marijuana or equivalent	1,900,000 kg	2,300,000 kg	5,400,000 kg
Wholesale expenditures	$ 600,000,000[a]	$ 700,000,000[a]	$1,700,000,000[a]
Retail expenditures	$1,400,000,000[b]	$1,600,000,000[b]	$3,700,000,000[b]

[a] 1972 prices at 1-kilogram level.
[b] 1972 prices.

bulky material must be transported—an estimated 4 tons are smuggled into the United States daily. Second, distribution within the United States involves numerous independent operations with little evidence of central organization. This is probably closely related to the difficulty of smuggling and storing large quantities of the drug. Third, the market involves a large number of users who make a relatively small amount of money by retail selling. Fourth, the monetary cost of marijuana use to the individual is relatively low, that is, $0.50 to $9 per week, depending on the frequency of use.

The effectiveness of the present marijuana control system may be measured (1) in terms of enforcement statistics, for example, drug seizures and arrests for sale and use; (2) indirectly in terms of availability and price of the drug; and (3) directly in terms of extent and type of use. An overall evaluation should also consider the costs of control, monetarily, as well as in terms of unintended side effects such as alienation of youth or diversion to more dangerous drug use. With regard to the more quantitative measures, and based on California statistics, we estimate that the current marijuana control system results in seizure of 13 percent of the marijuana and hashish intended for sale, in the arrest of 26 percent of those who are regularly involved in selling and in the arrest of up to 3 percent of those who use marijuana one or more times during the year (Bureau of Criminal Statistics, 1970a).

The present control system has had only limited success in restricting the availability of marijuana and hashish. Availability is not sufficiently open that purchases can be easily made by persons who are not involved in the drug subculture, but regular users generally have little difficulty obtaining the drug (Haines and Green, 1970). Periodic shortages occur, but they appear to be mostly related to seasonal fluctuations in harvesting, rapid increases in demand, and variations in supply related to the situation of storage being largely outside the United States. The price of marijuana increased by about 50 percent from 1969 to 1972, but this increase was not a limiting factor for most users. With respect to controlling the extent of marijuana use, the present policies have obviously been unsuccessful in preventing the rapid increases over the past few years.

With respect to possible policy changes, there are three primary alternatives: (1) increase criminal sanctions for both use and sale; (2) decrease or eliminate penalties against use and continue or increase efforts to eliminate the supply; and (3) regulate the sale of marijuana in the manner of alcohol controls.

The adoption of the first alternative in terms of penalties as well as arrests would undoubtedly increase the level of deterrence. It seems equally clear that society would be unwilling to incur the costs of such an approach. The current trend toward decreasing or eliminating penalties at the user level is essentially being forced by the realities of the widespread usage. This leaves the second and third alternatives as feasible policy changes.

Suppress Supply. The immediate question with regard to alternative 2 concerns the ability to suppress the supply of marijuana and hashish. The increased pressure against smuggling by Customs in 1969, 1970, and 1971 clearly resulted in a sharp increase in seizures (see Figure 3-2). The current estimated seizure rate of 13 percent is substantial when interpreted in terms of risk of arrest. While no attempt was made in the present study to estimate the results of additional enforcement efforts, such a policy can reasonably be expected to further increase both seizures and arrests. On the other hand, there is no indication as yet that the present level of enforcement is capable of severely restricting the availability of marijuana.

Efforts are also being made to eliminate the sources of marijuana in Mexico (McGlothlin and others, 1970b). Information necessary for evaluation of the progress of this effort is not available, but clearly this approach to cannabis control on a worldwide basis would be more difficult to implement than the current attempt to suppress the sources of opium. Cannabis grows wild in many portions of the world and may be cultivated with relatively little effort in any temperate or tropical climate. It requires no processing in the crude form, and relatively little for the more concentrated preparations.

Increase Smuggling Controls. The major difficulty in smuggling marijuana is the excessive bulk. The estimated 3700-kilogram amount smuggled into the United States daily contains only about 37 kilograms of THC. Further significant increases above the already high marijuana seizure rate will likely result in efforts to decrease the risks of detection by means of reductions of bulk. The most obvious countermeasure would be the gradual replacement of the marijuana market with hashish from the Middle East, smuggled into the United States either directly or by way of Mexico or Canada. Hashish is estimated to contain 5 percent THC compared with 1 percent for marijuana, and is also a solid; for equivalent amounts of THC, hashish requires far less space than does the leafy marijuana. As mentioned earlier, the increased smuggling of hashish is already evident—the ratio of hashish to marijuana seizures in 1971 was double that for 1970. Very little technical skill is required for converting hashish to an extract containing up to 20 percent THC; this method has already been employed on a small scale and seems likely to be used increasingly. In general, any method that permits importation in a more concentrated and compact form will increase the ease of concealment for smuggling and will reduce information leaks by permitting more centralized operations.

Another result of increased enforcement effectiveness would be an increase in the price paid for marijuana and hashish. One of the announced objectives of Operation Intercept in 1969 was to place the price of marijuana beyond the reach of the adolescent. The price in the United States increased by about 50 percent from 1969 to 1972; however, the relative costs of comparable levels of intoxication achieved by use of marijuana and alcohol are probably still of the order of 1:2 or 2:3. This result of Operation Intercept would indicate that the price of marijuana might rise by 50 to 100 percent if the risks of importation and distribution are again substantially increased. It is interesting that the price of hashish is about $1 per gram in Holland and Denmark, which have relatively permissive policies; about $3 per gram in Norway, which stresses enforcement; and $8 per gram in the United States ($3 per gram in ounce quantities).

Limitations on marijuana supply should also be considered in the context of availability of other drugs. For instance, during the period when the price of marijuana increased by 50 percent, the widespread availability of LSD resulted in its wholesale price dropping to one-fifth its former level. Marijuana shortages apparently result in increases in the use of other drugs (McGlothlin and others, 1970b). Alcohol and hallucinogens are the most frequent substitutes, but there is also some increase in sedative, stimulant, and opiate use, especially among those who are heavily involved in the drug subculture. Finally, increased domestic cultivation of marijuana is another possible reaction to heightened controls against importation. Marijuana plants may be grown indoors as well as outside. Should sanctions be dropped at the user level, cultivation for personal use might pose a difficult legal problem.

Contribution to Criminal Behavior. A control policy that attempts to deal severely with the seller and deals leniently or not at all with the user will inevitably encounter difficulty in differentiating between the two categories. A major disadvantage of maintaining marijuana in the illicit drug category is the encouragement of large numbers of young persons to become involved in retail selling. It is especially easy to begin selling marijuana on a casual basis and quickly become seriously enmeshed in a highly criminogenic subculture. As previously discussed in the section on the marijuana market, the majority of regular users have technically sold the drug at some time—280,000 persons are currently estimated to earn all or a significant portion of their income by retail selling. Applying the same formula of $250 per month for the retail dealer to the 1976 upper estimate of $2 billion in gross retail profits would result in some 670,000 persons employed in the retail selling of marijuana.

In addition to encouraging young marijuana users to adopt the dangerous and unproductive life of retail selling, the large wholesale profits are attractive to organized crime—a development that is considered more likely if the more concentrated preparations replace marijuana. The present estimated wholesale market of $600 million per year (1-kilogram level) is predicted to increase to $700 million to $1.7 billion by 1976. With additional pressure against smuggling and distribution, price increases might raise these market values by 50 to 100 percent.

Regulate Sale. Legal distribution of marijuana would provide the usual advantages of licensing, including control of conditions of sale, especially those relating to the age of the purchaser. Other controls employed in some countries are the limiting of the amount purchased and the issuing of permits for use.

Another advantage of regulated sale is the imposition of quality and potency control. As discussed earlier, increased pressure against sales and smuggling seems likely to result in a shift to more potent forms. While the availability of the more potent preparations of cannabis does not necessarily result in the consumption of larger amounts of the active ingredient, there is general agreement that excessive use is more prevalent under such conditions. Some countries have initiated controls that allow consumption of low-potency materials but prohibit the more concentrated forms (Krisnamoorthy, 1969). Regulated sale would also prevent adulteration. This has not been an appreciable problem thus far because of the lack of an economic incentive, but if extracts come into use it is likely they would often be mixed with other active adulterants.

Another major advantage of legal sales is the removal of large numbers of youth from the criminogenic retail sales occupation. It would also reduce the cost of enforcement, disassociate marijuana from other drug sales, and encourage a credible approach to education.

Finally, if sales of marijuana were regularized in the same manner as sales of alcohol, the profits that now go into criminal channels could presumably be converted to tax revenues. If we assume the same tax percentage for marijuana as alcohol (approximately 30 percent), the current estimated $1.4 billion retail expenditure for marijuana and hashish would yield around $420 million in taxes per year, or about 8 percent of the current alcohol tax revenue. The 1976 lower and upper estimates of retail sales would result in tax revenues of $480 million and $1.1 billion or 9 to 22 percent of the current alcohol revenues. The current retail price of marijuana could probably be doubled and still be competitive with alcohol and, since marijuana is easy to grow and process, the tax percentage could be substantially higher than 30 percent of the total price. Thus, it is reasonable to predict that tax revenue could be nearly $1 billion at present, and possibly as much as $2 billion within five years, or some 40 percent of the alcohol revenue.

Future Policies. We have examined some of the implications of various marijuana control policies in the context of estimates of current and future use and distribution. In summary, the current prevalence of marijuana use is high and is likely to continue to increase, at least for two or three years. Among younger age groups, the present policies do not effectively deter use, particularly in certain areas of the country. The reaction of policy makers to the failure of deterrents and to the cost of criminal sanctions has been to reduce penalties against the user, while continuing or increasing pressure against distribution. It is reasonably certain that this trend will continue in the immediate future, possibly including dropping other than token sanctions against the user. Additional pressure against smuggling and sale of marijuana should further increase seizures and prices, although as yet there is no evidence that this approach is capable of severely restricting availability. A likely countermeasure is the shifting to hashish or other concentrated preparations in order to reduce the risks associated with smuggling. A major cost of a policy aimed at suppressing supply is the criminalizing of large numbers of young persons involved in retail sales. A policy of legalization would eliminate this problem, encourage a credible educational approach, produce a substantial tax revenue, and provide control of potency and other controls related to legal sale. On the other hand, legalization would very likely produce greater prevalence of use, whereas strong efforts against the supply of marijuana, together with token sanctions against use, would indicate social disapproval and discourage its use, at least among some portions of the population.

The major uncertainty concerns the future trends in marijuana usage related to factors other than control policies. If the demand for marijuana continues at the present or higher level and efforts to suppress the supply are unsuccessful, then a policy of continued prohibition would have most of the disadvantages of legalization and none of the advantages. On the other hand, the current epidemic use of marijuana among the middle class is too new to allow confident predictions as to whether or not it will be a permanent phenomenon. Early legalization would provide official, and perhaps irreversible, sanction to a potentially harmful behavior that might otherwise have been primarily a transient phenomenon.

4

International Opiate Traffic

Cabinet Committee
on International Narcotics Control

Andrew Tartaglino and the Staff
of the Office of Criminal Investigations,
Bureau of Narcotics and Dangerous Drugs

Of all the drugs about which Americans are concerned, heroin stands foremost. Although its use is not common at this time (BNDD estimates between 500,000 and 600,000 users), the characteristics of heroin addiction are such as to generate considerable apprehension in the public. People fear either that their own children may become involved with heroin use or that their family may be the victim of a crime perpetrated by a heroin user. Because of this apprehension enforcement efforts directed against heroin traffic

have the greatest priority, and, internationally, collaborative efforts have taken their strongest form in this area.

In order to provide a picture of international heroin traffic and to identify some of the organizations in whose hands the options for international response lie, we have drawn on two excellent sources of information, the Cabinet Committee on International Narcotics Control and the Office of Criminal Investigations of the BNDD. *This chapter consists of two interwoven documents, beginning with the* World Opium Survey *of the Cabinet Committee, then moving to a description by Andrew Tartaglino and his* BNDD OCI *staff of the international narcotics traffic system originating in the Mideast, and then returning to the Cabinet Committee* World Opium Survey *for a description of additional networks, prices, and multilateral drug control efforts. We are in debt to the authors of both documents for the fine descriptive material they have prepared. For an additional report on the Southeast Asia network refer to McCoy (1972).*

R. H. B.

Essentially there are two separate and distinct major markets for opium—the licit and the illicit market. In 1971 the licit market probably accounted for 1500 metric tons of world production of opium and the illicit market for at least an additional 1000 tons. The licit market is geared to world demand for opium for use in manufacturing pharmaceuticals. International prices in this market are determined generally by the interplay of supply and demand forces, and trading is usually carried out between large pharmaceutical firms on the one hand and government agencies who supply the opium on the other. These agencies purchase the raw opium from farmers who are licensed by the government to plant a specified acreage to the crop. Payment to farmers growing licit opium poppies generally is governed by the world market price as well as the quality of the product. International movement of licit opium from producing areas to points of processing is accomplished under strict security controls.

The illicit market for opium is much more complex. In contrast to the licit market, all phases of activity are illegal, and the trade in illicit opium is a highly covert operation. Another important difference, moreover, is that illicit trade in opium involves numerous differentiated products and markets. In many areas, for example, opium and its derivatives are consumed locally as well as processed into morphine base and heroin for other consuming markets. By and large, however, most opium consumption tends to be centered in the regions where it is produced. By comparison the international market in illicit opium is geared around the trafficking of heroin for consumption mainly in the United States and Western Europe and involves only a fraction of world consumption of opium.

Licit Opium Market

Both production and consumption of licit opium have been on the rise since the mid-1960s. In 1971, licit production amounted to approximately 1500 tons, an increase of at least 25 percent from the previous year (see Table 1). The increase primarily reflected higher production levels in India and the resumption of large-scale production by Iran. Indeed, after a 14-year prohibition on production ending in 1969, Iran now ranks as the world's third largest producer of licit opium. India, however, still far outranks any other country, with output reaching 943 tons in 1971, or about two-thirds of the total. Other major producers include the Soviet Union (200 tons) and Turkey (150 tons). To judge from likely medical requirements, the People's Republic of China probably produces some 100 tons a year of licit opium. Much smaller amounts are produced by such countries as Pakistan, Yugoslavia, and Bulgaria.

Most licit opium is used to manufacture medicinal opiates. About 90 percent goes for morphine production, which has been increasing fairly steadily and now runs about 160 to 170 tons annually, compared with 100 tons in the early 1960s. About 95 percent of this morphine is now converted into other substances, chiefly codeine. So far, no satisfactory synthetic substitute for codeine which is wholly acceptable to the medical profession has been found, and the only alternative to raw opium as a source of morphine is the processing of poppy straw. Indeed, poppy straw has become an increasingly important source of morphine over the past decade; about 30,000 tons are currently processed annually for the manufacture of morphine. About 65 percent of total licit morphine production, however, still comes from raw opium.

The major purchasers of licit opium are pharmaceutical firms in Western Europe and North America. Their chief supplier is India, which is rapidly taking on a near-monopoly position as the world's only significant exporter of licit opium (see Table 2). By the end of the 1960s, India was accounting for about 85 percent of total world exports of opium. This figure will undoubtedly increase sharply in the near future because of Turkey's decision to end licit opium production after the 1972 crop is harvested. Except for India, Turkey is the only other significant exporter of raw opium, and in 1971 the two countries probably accounted for close to 99 percent of total world exports. World export of poppy straw was about 14,000 tons in 1969, about 90 percent of which came from Turkey.

Despite increased production of licit opium in 1971 and probable further increases in supply in 1972, world market prices have risen dramatically since 1970 (see Table 3). Indeed, India and Turkey plan 33 percent and 45 percent increases, respectively, in export prices of opium from the 1972 crop. This will put prices at almost double their mid-1960s level and at their highest in at least two decades. The Turkish price increase no doubt reflects an attempt to maximize returns from the 1972 crop, which will mark the end of Turkish licit production. Although Indian opium is generally lower in quality than Turkish, Indian price increases probably reflect the near-monopoly position held by that country in the licit opium market. Other factors tending to boost prices are the worldwide inflation and the international effort to eliminate opium poppy production. This last factor has created uncertainty and apprehension among legitimate buyers of opium as to future sources of supply and tends to reinforce the trend toward higher prices.

In addition to medicinal requirements, licit opium is also used to provide maintenance dosages for registered addicts in government treatment programs. Among the countries producing licit opium, India, Pakistan, and Iran have such programs. Only Iran's program, however, represents a serious effort. India, for example, dispenses only about 3 tons of opium annually to registered addicts, which represents only a small fraction of total consumption

Table 1

WORLD LICIT PRODUCTION OF OPIUM, BY COUNTRY

Metric Tons

Crop Year[a]	Total[b]	India	Turkey	USSR	Iran	Other[c]
1950	739	179	147	86	307	21
1951	832	410	284	94	21	23
1952	849	272	370	104	83	19
1953	1,007	489	255	92	145	26
1954	609	341	56	103	92	18
1955	660	281	176	109	61	33
1956	643	270	220	105	—	48
1957	589	377	40	147	—	24
1958	775	511	144	93	—	27
1959	909	593	149	132	—	35
1960	1,253	711	323	169	—	50
1961	1,037	709	157	120	—	51
1962	1,203	755	284	148	—	15
1963	993	538	263	172	—	20
1964	787	501	73	188	—	25
1965	754	486	77	177	—	14
1966	671	339	126	201	—	5
1967	662	368	104	181	—	8
1968	815	585	111	116	—	3
1969	1,219	868	117	217	8	9
1970	1,157	794	51	227	78	7
1971	1,449+	943	150	200	156	N.A.

Note: Data for 1950–1969 are from International Narcotics Control Board reports; data for 1970–1971 are estimated. Data for India, Turkey, and Iran refer to opium containing 10 percent moisture. The USSR and most other countries have not provided information to the United Nations on the moisture content of their opium.

[a] Ending July 30 of the stated year.

[b] Because of rounding, components may not add to the totals shown.

[c] Including Yugoslavia (40 tons in 1960, reduced to 1 ton in 1970), Japan (4 tons or less annually), Pakistan (12 tons annually), Bulgaria (7 tons in 1952, reduced to little or none in recent years). Data on licit production in China and North Vietnam are not available.

Table 2

WORLD LICIT OPIUM EXPORTS, BY COUNTRY

Calendar Year	Total	India	Turkey	Iran	Others
1950	755	234	265	246	10
1951	810	358	173	267	12
1952	537	163	167	200	7
1953	393	168	169	41	15
1954	540	263	211	56	10
1955	600	199	296	100	5
1956	668	266	274	106	22
1957	652	361	205	71	15
1958	800	493	207	98	2
1959	767	593	170	—	4
1960	733	626	103	—	4
1961	725	658	64	—	3
1962	530	375	116	—	39
1963	619	472	147	—	—
1964	663	473	190	—	—
1965	683	426	257	—	—
1966	834	531	303	—	—
1967	573	419	151	—	3
1968	647	532	111	—	4
1969	721	602	118	—	1
1970	885	808	77	—	—

Note: Data for 1950–1969 are from International Narcotics Control Board reports; data for 1970 are estimated.

by Indian addicts and users. Moreover, in both India and Pakistan the maintenance dosage programs have been declining for years. In 1951, India dispensed 151 tons under its program, while the Pakistani program is now dispensing less than half the amount it did in 1957. This decline in part reflects the fact that government prices for opium sold to addicts are well above black market prices in these countries. In contrast to India and Pakistan, Iran may dispense around 155 tons of opium in 1972 under its treatment program, which began in late 1969. Iran had an estimated 90,000 registered users at the outset of 1972 and the number possibly will increase to an average of about 105,000 for the year as a whole. Even this,

Table 3

INDIAN OPIUM EXPORT PRICES

Crop Year^a	US $ per Kilogram
1952	15.50
1953	13.00
1954	12.60
1955	12.40
1956	12.10
1957	12.40
1958	14.10
1959	14.80
1960	15.50
1961	15.50
1962	15.50
1963	13.95
1964	13.00
1965	13.00
1966	12.00
1967	11.50
1968	11.75
1969	13.50
1970	15.00
1971	18.00
1972	24.00

Note: With 10 percent morphine content.
[a] Ending June 30 of stated year.

however, is only about one-fourth of the probable addict and user population in Iran, and, as in other victim countries, most addicts are supplied essentially by the illicit market.

Illicit Market

The concerted effort by the United States government and other governments to exploit the accumulated knowledge of specialists in narcotics enforcement as well as the development of new sources of information is resulting in increases in information on the illicit traffic in narcotics. Nonetheless, the information still is not sufficient to allow accurate measurement of worldwide production, consumption, and flows of illicit opium and its derivatives. Although many countries report such information as seizures of narcotics and arrests of traffickers, few have good estimates of domestic illicit production or of the size and characteristics of their user and addict populations. The rough approximations that follow are based on estimates and judgments of police and health officials throughout the world as well as on reports of observers in various countries where illicit production and trafficking are known to exist. Because of the clandestine nature of the traffic, the estimates on the size of the market should be viewed as minimum estimates.

An assessment of the available information indicates that at least 1000 tons of illicit opium were produced in 1971 (see Table 4). A minimum of 700 tons was produced in the hill region of Burma, Thailand, and Laos, which constitutes the largest single area of production of illicit opium. At least another 220 tons were

Table 4

ESTIMATED ILLICIT OPIUM OUTPUT, BY MAJOR PRODUCERS, 1971

Country	Metric Tons
India	100
Afghanistan	100
Turkey	35 to 80
Pakistan	20 to 160
Burma, Thailand, and Laos	700
Mexico	10 to 20
Other[a]	20 to 50
Total	990 to 1,210[b]

[a] Mainly Eastern Europe.
[b] Additional amounts probably are produced in Latin America, North Africa, and the Far East.

produced illicitly in India, Pakistan, and Afghanistan. Illicit Turkish production has been estimated at at least 35 tons in 1971. Lesser amounts of illicit opium were produced in Mexico, Yugoslavia, and Bulgaria. In addition, an unknown amount of opium is being produced in South America and probably in scattered parts of North Africa. Persistent reports of expanded poppy cultivation in the highlands of Latin America suggest that production in this area is rising.

Only a small share of this illicit production represents diversion of opium from licit cultivation. Rather, most of it comes from regions where opium cultivation is prohibited by law but where the government lacks the political control to enforce the prohibition. The most notable example of this is production from the Burma, Thailand, Laos region—the Golden Triangle. The same is true of tribal areas of Afghanistan and Pakistan, which account for a major share of illicit output in those two countries. Nevertheless, in some countries, legal production does provide a cover for illicit opium growing. Virtually all of Turkey's illicit output, for example, represents diversions from areas where poppy cultivation is legal. With the end of licit poppy growing, illicit supplies can be expected eventually to dry up unless growers are willing and able to flout the prohibition. As in Turkey, a substantial share of India's illicit production reflects diversions from legal production.

Most illicit opium produced in the world is consumed by addicts and users within or close to the areas of production and does not enter the international market. The largest consuming region is Southeast Asia, which absorbs perhaps 600 of the 700 tons produced in Burma, Thailand, and Laos. A substantial share of illicit output from the Golden Triangle is consumed by hill tribes themselves. Many if not most of these consumers are probably more appropriately classified as opium users rather than addicts. They tend to use opium for medicinal purposes as well as for social and religious purposes and for the most part probably do not consume regular amounts from day to day or week to week. To the extent that this is so, the tribal growers could be induced to sell part of what they normally consume if offered enough of a price incentive.

In addition to satisfying their own needs, production from the tribal areas also meets the illicit opium requirements of the rest of Southeast Asia. The chief ultimate customers are the large communities of opium and heroin smokers which exist in most big cities of Southeast Asia. A large number of heroin and opium addicts, for example, are known to live in Thailand's urban areas and in Hong Kong; the user and addict population in Hong Kong alone could well run up to 150,000 persons. These two markets alone probably require on the order of 300 tons of raw opium equivalent annually. Much smaller amounts are needed by the user and addict population in places such as Singapore, Malaysia, the Philippines, and Macao, where opium needs are essentially met out of production from the Golden Triangle.

China has historically been associated with the opium problem both as a classic example of a "victim" country and as a center for opium growing. Nevertheless, it seems clear that the government of the People's Republic of China has effectively remedied the domestic problem of opium use and maintains stringent controls over licit opium cultivation within its borders. There is no reliable evidence that China has either engaged in or sanctioned the illicit export of opium and its derivatives nor are there any indications of PRC participation in the opium traffic of Southeast Asia and adjacent markets.

As in Southeast Asia, most illicit production in the Indian subcontinent and the Middle East is consumed in the general region where it is produced. Probably almost all of India's illicit output— at least 100 tons in 1971—is channeled into the domestic black market, and on a net basis India is probably neither a large importer nor an exporter. Most illicit production from Afghanistan and Pakistan apparently goes to Iran, where, despite the rapidly expanding addict treatment program, illicit imports still run anywhere from 100 tons to 300 tons annually. Almost all of these imports come from Afghanistan and Pakistan, although some illicit supplies still come from Turkey. Small amounts of illicit opium produced in the region probably find their way to North Africa as well.

At present there are no means of estimating with any confidence how much of total world illicit production of opium is available for, or is actually converted into, heroin for the international market. A rough approximation based on rather tenuous estimates of production and consumption in local markets is that a minimum of 200 tons of illicit production in 1971 probably was available for the international heroin market. In addition, there were undoubtedly substantial illicit stocks available for the international markets.

These include stocks of raw opium held by growers as well as stocks of processed opium, morphine base, and heroin held by processors and traffickers. Indeed, chances are good that stocks in Southeast Asia rose in 1971 because little of the opium available in that region was converted to heroin after mid-year. However, most of the opium entering the international market from Turkey and Mexico was converted into heroin during 1971.

Although the United States remains the main consuming market for these international supplies of heroin, addiction and use of the drug are on the increase in Western Europe. At the same time, efforts of the United States government and others to interdict and eliminate the international traffic in heroin are beginning to have an impact on international trafficking. Enforcement efforts by various governments have led to mounting seizures of morphine base and heroin both in the United States and Canada as well as in Western Europe. The tabulation below shows total recent seizures of morphine and heroin base in the United States, Canada, France, the Federal Republic of Germany, Italy, Turkey, and Southeast Asia in terms of their opium equivalents. In any case, despite the rising pace of seizures, the international market seems still to have adequate supplies to meet the demand in consuming countries.

Year	Tons of Opium
1969	6.6
1970	7.3
1971	21.6
1972 (January to mid-March)	9.0

Illicit Opium and Its Derivatives. The illicit processing of opium results in a decreased bulk and higher narcotic content of the commodity at each stage of refining. Opium and its derivatives move in illicit markets in one or more of the following forms:

The morphine content of *raw opium* varies from as high as the 14 percent level of Turkish opium to the 5 to 10 percent levels of South Asian and Southeast Asian opium. Raw opium has a strong odor; it does not keep as well as and weighs more than prepared opium. It is smoked, sniffed, or eaten chiefly by users and addicts in or near the areas where opium is cultivated.

Processed, prepared, or cooked opium is raw opium with moisture cooked out. Morphine content may range from 15 to 20 percent. It is ingested by users in the same fashion as raw opium.

Morphine base is opium from which most of the organic impurities have been chemically removed. The morphine content may range from the 50 percent level found in much Southeast Asian base to the 70 percent or higher levels preferred by European traffickers. Morphine base is not easily soluble in water and thus is not readily absorbed by the human body. Essentially an intermediate product, morphine base is converted into morphine salt compounds soluble in water or into heroin for consumption.

Morphine sulfate, morphine hydrochloride, and morphine acetate are forms of *morphine salt* used for legitimate medical purposes. There is little illicit production of these morphine compounds. For the most part, these compounds enter the illicit traffic as the result of pilferage from pharmaceutical houses and hospitals. Morphine injection addiction appears on a small scale in Singapore and in parts of Western Europe and the United States.

Crude heroin—specifically diacetylmorphine—is morphine base that has undergone acetylation. The narcotic properties of heroin are several times stronger than those of morphine products. Crude heroin may have a content of around 75 percent heroin. In Southeast Asia, crude heroin is converted into No. 3 smoking heroin or into No. 4 white heroin. The terms *No. 3* and *No. 4 heroin* are usages restricted to the illicit traffic in Southeast Asia and are not usually used elsewhere. The origins of the terms are unknown, but No. 1 and No. 2 may refer to morphine base and crude heroin, respectively.

Purple, or No. 3, heroin is a purplish or brownish smoking heroin favored by addicts in Southeast Asia. Strychnine and caffeine (to facilitate absorption of heroin by the body) and barbitone (to offset extreme intoxication) are added in large quantities which reduces the effective heroin content of No. 3 to around 15 percent. Consumption of heroin in this form appears to be restricted to Southeast Asia.

White, or No. 4, heroin usually has a heroin content of 95 percent or better. In Asia, No. 4 heroin tends to have a fluffy consistency much like soap flakes. In Europe and the United States,

white heroin resembles talc or flour in consistency. High-purity
heroin of an off-white or brownish color often appears in the American market and is customarily described as being of Mexican origin.
White heroin is adulterated as it moves down the several levels of
illicit distribution in the United States. Thus the heroin content of
an individual dose at the retail or street level may run as low as
3 percent.

Opium Processing. The conversion of opium into heroin in
so-called laboratories and refineries is no more complex than making
bootleg whiskey in the United States. Neither high temperatures
nor high pressures are involved in the process, the basic equipment
used is simple, and only small amounts of common industrial chemicals are required. Electric power needs (for heat sources and to
operate equipment) are modest; ample, but not unusually large
supplies of water are necessary. Processing does not require the
services of a graduate chemist. For the most part, processing operations are run by so-called heroin chemists who have learned the
trade through apprenticeship to other heroin chemists. Aside from
the chemist, only a few semiskilled helpers are involved in processing.

The operations at each stage are simple ones of soaking,
filtering, heating, precipitating, drying, and crushing. The basic
equipment required is inexpensive and can be quite primitive:
enamel pots or copper vats, strainers and filters, pans and trays, and
a simple heat source. The more sophisticated processors, particularly
in Europe, may use vacuum flasks, simple distillation apparatus,
and drying cabinets to shorten processing time at each stage. In
Europe, a laboratory capable of producing 100 kilograms of heroin
per week can be equipped for as little as $4000. Floor-space re-
quirements for heroin processing facilities are small. Refineries and
laboratories have been found in such diverse locales as hut complexes in Southeast Asia, several rooms in a villa in France, and a
bathroom in a Hong Kong apartment building.

The chemicals used at each stage of processing are common
industrial chemicals such as slaked lime, ammonium chloride,
acetic anhydride, chloroform, benzol, tartaric acid, alcohol, hydro-
chloric acid, activated charcoal, and ether. These chemicals are
produced in huge quantities in most industrialized countries and are
regularly exported to areas where they are not produced.

Acetylation is the key process in converting morphine base to heroin and can be accomplished using either acetyl chloride or acetic anhydride. Acetyl chloride is flammable, irritating to the eyes, reacts violently with water or alcohol, and requires careful handling in laboratory processes. For these reasons, acetylation using acetyl chloride is not favored by illicit processors of heroin. Although acetic anhydride is corrosive and requires care in handling, it is less hazardous to the user than acetyl chloride and hence is the key chemical used in illicit processing.

Enormous quantities of acetic anhydride are produced each year in the world's industrial countries. United States output alone was on the order of 700,000 tons in 1971, with comparable amounts produced in Western Europe and Japan. Acetic anhydride is a relatively inexpensive chemical. Prices have recently ranged from $0.21 per kilogram in the United States to $0.26 in France to $0.39 in Japan. Between 80 and 90 percent of world output is used to manufacture synthetic fibers, with the remainder going to pharmaceutical use (particularly the manufacture of aspirin) and other uses (plastics, perfumes, flavoring materials, and dyestuffs). As a general rule, the production of 1 kilogram of heroin requires 1 kilogram of acetic anhydride. Given the abundant availability and cheapness of this chemical, the quantity and value of acetic anhydride used in illicit narcotic production is minuscule. These factors make government monitoring and control of acetic anhydride production and distribution—as a means of identifying illicit heroin production facilities—difficult in an industrialized country such as France. On the other hand, such monitoring is simpler to accomplish in such countries as Laos and Thailand, where acetic anhydride is not domestically produced and must be imported.

Major Illicit Trading Networks. At present there are three major marketing complexes for the movement of illicit opium and its derivatives. The primary complex, which is the main concern of current enforcement efforts, begins in Turkey, encompasses many countries in Western Europe and the Western Hemisphere, and terminates in the United States. A second complex is the Southeast Asian market, which primarily serves addicts and users in that area and provides only small amounts to consumers in the United States and Europe. The third complex—composed of India, Pakistan,

Iran, and Afghanistan—is important chiefly in terms of the drug addiction problems in that area. All three markets are treated below —the first because it is now the center of the heroin problem and the second and third because of their potential for becoming crucial elements in the problem.

Mideast–United States Network*

The greatest amount of heroin smuggled into the United States originates from opium poppies cultivated in Turkey. The opium poppy is grown by poor peasant farmers, and they are required by law to sell their total production of opium to the government monopoly. The government pays the farmer $11 per kilogram for his opium. However, a great deal of the crop is diverted to illicit buyers, who pay the farmer approximately $25 per kilogram. Since the amount of opium produced per hectare is difficult to estimate, no one knows how much opium is diverted into the illicit market. Estimates run as high as 50 percent of the total.†

In order to have a clear understanding of the international heroin traffic, let us examine profiles of the principal figures, the organizations they control, and their method of operation.

The illicit drug traffic in Turkey is financed and controlled by a relatively small number of individuals. They are wealthy and usually establish their headquarters in either Istanbul or Izmir. While they amass most of their money from illicit narcotic transactions, they also engage in other illegal activities. One of their other principal sources of income is derived from smuggling arms from Europe to Turkey. While engaged in their illegal activities, they are successful in maintaining some degree of respectability in their com-

---

* This section of the chapter is the work of Andrew Tartaglino and the Staff of the Office of Criminal Investigations, Bureau of Narcotics and Dangerous Drugs.

† Turkey has outlawed opium growing beginning in 1973. This should considerably reduce the Turkish role as a source; however, illicit opium and morphine are reportedly warehoused in Turkey for future sales and there is a bill before the Turkish Parliament to reestablish production, so that the eventual role of Turkey cannot be finally ascertained. Experience to date has shown that when one country withdraws as a supplier, other countries take its place. Yet we may use the role of the Middle East heroin system as an historical base for anticipating how systems will operate elsewhere.—R.H.B.

munity. Funds from their illegal activities are invested in many diversified legitimate enterprises, from hotels to factories. They seek to divorce their illegal activities from their legitimate enterprises in order to present a good public and business image. Some are engaged in illegal money exchange and maintain large capital in foreign banks.

With the large money resources resulting from their illicit activities, they try to infiltrate police departments and political circles by doing favors for individuals and, in some instances, by bribery. By and large, police officers are undereducated and underpaid; consequently, they are easy targets for bribes.

The controlmen finance the production and distribution of opium and morphine base but rarely come in actual contact with the drugs. Like their organized-crime counterparts in the United States, they remain in the background and hire two or three trusted lieutenants as intermediaries so that controlmen are insulated from direct transactions. While the controlmen do not handle the drugs, they have the necessary contacts in France and other countries to assure the sale of their drugs, and they are responsible for guaranteeing that their organizations will meet their obligations.

To insure the organization an ample supply of opium, men travel to remote farming areas to purchase as much of the production as possible from the farmer. In some instances, it is contracted for before the harvest. Because the trafficker is willing to pay so much more than the government, the farmer agrees to sell to the organization.

Some of the opium is then transported to the various clandestine laboratories that are controlled and financed by the criminal organizations. The lieutenants of the controlmen finance the establishment of the laboratories and hire the chemists to convert the opium to morphine base. It takes 10 kilograms of opium to produce 1 kilogram of morphine base. The traffickers prefer to convert the opium to morphine base so that when the drugs are smuggled to other countries the shipment is more compact, which means a lesser risk without the profits being reduced. However, at times they smuggle opium directly to the other countries for conversion to heroin.

After the conversion, the morphine base and the remaining

opium are stored in Turkey awaiting orders from the customers. The principals in the organization maintain communications with their customers in France and other countries to arrange for shipments of the requested drugs.

The drugs leave Turkey by many routes and various means of transportation to reach the clandestine heroin laboratories. Some of the opium and morphine base are smuggled from Turkey into Syria, where they are converted into heroin. The heroin produced by these laboratories eventually is transported to Lebanon for traffickers in that country or for transshipment to the United States. These traffickers have associations with smugglers in the West Indies and the United States and route the heroin into this country by way of the Caribbean Islands.

Most of the opium and morphine base produced in Turkey is eventually destined for the clandestine laboratories in southern France. Over the years, the French heroin traffickers have depended on the Turkish producers for their source of raw materials.

The organization of the Turkish controlmen maintains elaborate smuggling systems to get the narcotics to their customers. One of the principal routes utilized by the group is by ship from Turkey to either Italy or France. Many small vessels run scheduled trips from Turkey to ports in Italy, France, and Spain. These vessels are used to transport large amounts of opium and morphine base to these countries. Such a venture is not the responsibility of one man; several or sometimes all members of the crew can be involved in such a smuggling operation. Although not everyone is aware of the hiding place of the drugs, the Turkish trafficker who ships the drugs pays bribes to the others to insure that they do not tell the police of the shipments.

Most of these shipments are unloaded in France and turned over to the customers. However, some of the drugs may be unloaded and sold to a middleman in Italy, who then resells them to the French laboratory operators. In Italy, some of the violators use the barter system and exchange the opium and morphine base for arms and ammunition. These then are smuggled back to Turkey where the trafficker can realize a large profit from their sale.

Another route used to smuggle the narcotics to France is overland in trucks and automobiles through the Balkan countries.

Some automobile garages in Turkey and France specialize in building false compartments into the trucks and automobiles, the location of the false compartment depending on the type and make of the vehicle. To get the narcotics to Europe, the shipper hires an individual to drive the vehicle, then registers the car in that person's name. This not only allows the driver to pose as a person on an innocent trip in his personal vehicle, but also protects the identity of the shipper in the event the car is seized by the police.

On many occasions, the trafficker in charge of the shipment does not travel with the shipment. He instead flies to France and makes the necessary arrangements to meet the vehicle when it arrives, then oversees the delivery to the customer. He then accepts payment for the narcotics and arranges to get the funds back to Turkey. The funds are on occasion transferred through secret Swiss bank accounts.

During recent years, Germany has become increasingly more important as a transshipment point for opium and morphine base going from Turkey to southern France. After World War II, there was a serious shortage of labor in Germany, and thousands of Turkish workers were recruited to work in German industry. These workers made several trips a year back to their homes to visit their families. As they were not subject to a strict customs search on their return to Germany they smuggled opium and morphine base to defray the cost of the trip. These relatively small quantities of drugs were sold to a middleman, who stored the opium and morphine base until he had a sufficient quantity to sell to the customers in France. As the traffic increased to Germany, the traffickers organized a regular smuggling operation to bring in large quantities of opium and morphine base. These same Turkish migratory workers, now over a million in Europe, provide a regular reservoir of smugglers through the Balkans for drugs going to Germany and to France. Traffickers have organized firms to give legitimate cover to their operations; and, in some instances, they have used systems already in operation to smuggle arms from Germany to Turkey. These operators, like those in Italy, use their smuggling channels for a two-way traffic flow—drugs from Turkey to Germany and weapons from Germany to Turkey.

In France, several organizations maintain control over the

production and distribution of illicit heroin. These organizations are headed by a relatively few controlmen, who have been in the narcotic traffic for many years. These controlmen are principals in the Corsican criminal organizations that govern most of the major crime in southern France. They have made a great deal of money over the years and now remain in the background to finance and control the distribution of the heroin. As in Turkey, they invested their money in property and legitimate enterprises so as to give the appearance of respectability. Most of their criminal activities are directed from Marseilles, France, where they meet associates and receive communications from other traffickers. They insulate themselves from the lower-echelon violator through lieutenants who handle most of their negotiations. They do, however, maintain communications with principal traffickers in Italy, the United States, and other countries with whom they have been doing business over the years. As these traffickers increased their stature among the criminal element, they also improved their image in the community and with the funds available to them have infiltrated police and political circles. Through their associations in these two latter fields they have been able to protect and expand their illegal activities.

The narcotic traffic in France is broken down into separate and distinct groups, each of which is responsible for its own phase of the operation.

When a shipment of opium and morphine base arrives in France, it is received by one of several organizations whose only part in the illicit traffic is to keep the laboratories supplied with the necessary raw materials. The top men in the organizations maintain close communications with the principals in Turkey, Germany, and Italy who supply them with the opium and morphine base. Through these associations, they negotiate price and method of delivery so as to insure that they or their men are not arrested.

Once the courier arrives with the illicit drugs, arrangements are made to transport them to a safe place. In most instances, they are not taken directly to their destination but are transferred in stages to insure that the police do not follow them to the cache. The recipient in France does not pay for the shipment until after he has received delivery in his area and is able to have control of the shipment. The opium and morphine base are then stored until ordered by the persons operating the clandestine laboratories for the conversion to heroin. The drugs are sometimes stored in several separate locations and brought in segments to the laboratory.

The second phase of the operation in France is the conversion of the opium or morphine base to heroin. Here again we have separate groups whose only function is the operation of the clandestine laboratories. The clandestine laboratory is usually set up in a rented villa in a rural area and is usually not a permanent operation. This group arranges for the purchase of the necessary equipment and chemicals, such as acetic anhydride, necessary to operate the laboratory and convert the raw materials to heroin. Once the heroin has been produced it is stored until arrangements have been made for delivery to a customer.

As in Turkey, the controlmen have middlemen who are buffers between them and the customers. These lieutenants deal with the lower echelon of the French criminal element, who arrange details for the delivery of the heroin. The controlmen and their principal lieutenants deal directly only with the controlmen in other countries. They have a close relationship with Italian traffickers in Italy as well as the Italian criminals in North America.

The heroin is smuggled out of France by many different ways en route to its ultimate market in the United States. The routes and methods of smuggling are too numerous to consider in detail, but let us look at the main routes and modus operandi utilized by the international traffickers.

Part of the French underworld is engaged in the smuggling of heroin from France directly into the United States, and although they purchase the heroin from the organizations in the Marseilles area, the Marseilles organizations do not come under their control.

An organization sends one of its members to the United States to establish residence here and to act as its representative. The trafficker in the United States is responsible for receiving the heroin, distributing it to the customers, and getting the funds back to Europe. The funds are sent back to Europe through the use of international banks and are deposited in numbered accounts in Switzerland.

The members of the group in France are responsible for purchasing the heroin and devising means to smuggle it into the United States. These groups establish themselves as businessmen and set up corporations to justify their travel and transfers of funds.

Their methods of smuggling vary from the use of couriers to use of vehicles with false compartments to commercial shipments in which the heroin is hidden in legitimate items imported into the United States for sale. Another method utilized by these groups is the recruitment of diplomats to use their diplomatic immunity to bring heroin into the United States. The diplomat who acts as a courier may be overextended financially and in need of money or he may have been compromised by the trafficker and forced into the drug business so as not to be exposed. The identities of diplomatic couriers are closely guarded. The service of a courier who has immunity from search is indeed a prize!

One of the principal routes in the past, but to a lesser degree now, was through Italy to the United States. The heroin traffic through Italy is controlled by Italian organized criminal elements in that country. The Italian criminal elements in the United States have strong ties with the Mafia in Italy and order their heroin from these violators. The Italian trafficker is usually an older member of the Mafia with some stature in that organization. He is also engaged in other illegal activities and maintains a strict control over his underlings. The Italian controlman requires that the customer pay part, if not all, of the cost in advance so that he does not suffer a large loss if the heroin is intercepted by the police.

Another route utilized to get the heroin to the American market is through Canada. In Canada there are Italian controlmen who have direct contacts with the principal controlmen in the Marseilles area. The principals in Canada are involved in many other illegal activities and control most of the organized crime in that country. The traffic in narcotics is only one of their illegal enterprises. Through their representatives, they order the heroin from one of the principals in Marseilles and usually pay in advance for the heroin. The heroin costs them from $4000 to $5000 per kilogram. They then utilize various smuggling operations to get the heroin into Canada. In some instances, they hire couriers who travel to Europe where they are given the heroin, which is then either hidden on their bodies or in false-bottom suitcases for smuggling into Canada. Another method involves shipment of cars in which secret compartments have been built for smuggling the heroin; the vehicles are carefully selected and must have excess space in the body cavity. This method is usually used when a large shipment of heroin is involved. Seizures of heroin concealed in vehicles have amounted to as much as 250 pounds in a single car.

During recent years, Spain has become an important link for the smuggling of heroin into the United States. The main traffickers in Spain are a combination of two distinct groups. Some of the principals are Cuban traffickers who came to Spain after Castro took over Cuba. They had a ready outlet for the heroin through members of the Cuban criminal element who came to the United States. Other principals in Spain settled there after Algiers became independent. This latter group was part of the criminal group in North Africa and had engaged in smuggling for many years. They had contacts with the French criminals and were able to gain access to unlimited quantities of heroin. These traffickers settled in the Madrid area where they purchased bars and restaurants in which they placed key associates. Here again, like their counterparts in other countries, they invest their funds in legal business enterprises and form partnerships with Spanish citizens to appear as respectable businessmen.

Since the traffickers in Spain had access to the sources of supply in France and the customers in the United States, they rapidly grew to be a major part of the international drug traffic. They recruit couriers from among the criminal element of Spain to smuggle the heroin into the United States. They also recruit couriers from among the poor peasants of Spain. These people, who have never had a great deal of money, are approached to carry packages to the United States. They are often ignorant of what they are actually involved in and merely see it as an opportunity to earn a great deal of money for their families.

Probably the most important route being used at this time to transport heroin from Europe to the United States is by way of South America. European settlement in South America has been continuing for centuries. Since World War II, some immigrants have been criminals who have continued illegal activities in these underdeveloped nations. The officials in these countries are poorly paid; and, with the funds available to them, the criminals infiltrated the police and other government agencies. One of the main sources of income for the criminals was the smuggling of whiskey, tobacco, electronic equipment, and other goods from North and Central America into the South American countries.

With stricter enforcement in North America inhibiting movement of contraband by way of known smuggling routes, the traffickers began looking for new routes and seized upon the opportunity to utilize the routes from South America that were already in existence. The heroin traffic in South America is controlled by a few key individuals who are responsible for most of the heroin that comes from France. They are of French extraction and have close ties with the heroin traffickers in the Marseilles area. They are established in the Buenos Aires area and own bars and restaurants. These traffickers have infiltrated the police departments in several countries, through bribery, and are kept aware of any police activities that may hinder their operation. The controlmen for the heroin traffic to South America do not engage in the smuggling operation, but sell the heroin to customers who are responsible for getting the narcotics into the United States. The principals who control the delivery to this country are very wealthy individuals who have been engaged in illegal activities for many years. They form corporations to legitimatize their operations, and they associate with the top members of government and society in South America. As in Spain, many Cuban exiles have settled in South American countries and have engaged in the smuggling of narcotics into the United States. They have a ready access to the cocaine sources of supply and are now receiving shipments of heroin directly from France. Most of their large shipments of heroin are smuggled into South America aboard vessels making scheduled trips.

From South America the heroin is smuggled into the United States by various routes and methods. Large shipments are usually flown into this country on nonscheduled airlines as commercial freight. The traffickers also have built into the airplanes false compartments that are capable of holding 100-kilogram lots of narcotics. Another method frequently utilized is to have a number of couriers who travel from South America to the United States with drugs either taped to their bodies or hidden in false-bottom suitcases. These couriers are usually petty criminals in their own countries, and they travel on false or altered passports. Usually the person responsible for these smuggling operations has a reliable associate meeting the couriers to accept the delivery of the narcotics or else he flies to the United States to be available for delivery.

For many years in the United States the heroin traffic was under the control of the Italian criminal element. The traffic of heroin was only one of the Italian offender's activities, which included loan-sharking, bookmaking, organizing prostitution, among others. As a controlman in several illegal areas, he financed the purchase of the heroin but did not come in contact with the merchandise. In view of the amount of money involved, at times several controlmen joined together to finance a shipment. The cost of 100 kilograms of heroin involved an outlay of $500,000.

With the money realized from his illegal activities, the controlman invested in various types of business to give himself the appearance of respectability. Initially, it was bars and restaurants, but subsequently he branched out into trucking companies, manufacturing, and various other enterprises. He moved his family to a rural area and gave the impression of being a legitimate businessman. He and his family were active in community and charity affairs and he tried to shield them from contact with or even knowledge about his criminal activities. He continued his association with the heads of other organizations throughout the country and his sources of supply for heroin in Europe.

In recent years, there has been a change in the heroin traffic, with the rise of the Latin-American elements in drug traffic. They have established their own contacts in Europe and South America and can obtain large amounts of heroin directly from the French suppliers. They have also established their own courier network to smuggle the drugs into the United States and the money back to the sources of supply. A great deal of the traffic resulted from the exodus of Cubans from Cuba to other parts of the world, where they have continued their drug activities.

The profit that can be realized from the sale of heroin and

the raw materials to make heroin is probably the main reason why so many people are involved in this traffic.

Southeast Asia Network*

The distribution of opium products, including heroin, is a big business in Southeast Asia. For the most part it is handled by large and well-organized trading networks. Supplies of opium for these networks come from hill people who grow it in the tri-border area of Burma, Laos, and Thailand. Annual production of opium in the area is about 700 tons. Of this, 400 tons is consumed by the hill people themselves and does not enter international trade. This 400 tons, however, serves as an important reserve supply to lowland dealers because growers can be induced to sell part of what they normally consume if offered an increase in price.

In normal years, about 300 tons of opium is brought to collection centers in northern Thailand, Burma, and Laos near the tri-border point, where it is processed and packaged for distribution to wholesale centers in Vientiane, Bangkok, and Hong Kong. The chief ultimate customers are the large opium and heroin smoking communities which exist in most big cities of Southeast Asia. Smoking is the main form of ingestion; injection is virtually unknown.

Before the development of the large United States serviceman market for heroin in South Vietnam, sales of Southeast Asian opium or heroin to non-Asians were very small. Before 1970, these sales probably amounted to less than 10 tons of opium equivalent annually and consisted mainly of high-quality, injection heroin (No. 4 heroin) produced in laboratories in Hong Kong and Bangkok for sale to international traffickers who came there to buy the contraband. In 1970 and 1971, Southeast Asian dealers produced large quantities of white, high-quality heroin for the United States serviceman market in Vietnam. This market declined sharply after June 1971 as a result of United States troop withdrawals together with stringent United States programs to inhibit the use of heroin by United States servicemen. Whether the big Asian heroin dealers will be content to revert to their pre-1970 situation, when trafficking in No. 4 heroin was a minor sideline for them, or will resume

* This section resumes the report of the Cabinet Committee.

production of No. 4 heroin with the intention of moving it to the United States and/or Europe on a large scale is not known. In any case, they are not likely willingly to give up their traditional opium trading activities, which have been profitable, relatively dependable, and safe sources of income.

Historically, there have been wide variations in the size and nature of opiate-consuming communities in Southeast Asia. Smoking of opiates is widespread in most overseas Chinese communities, for example, but not in the large Chinese community in Indonesia. The Thais are the only non-Chinese ethnic group in the lowlands of Southeast Asia to have taken up consumption of opiates in a large scale. Smoking of heroin, which is stronger and more addictive than opium, is the predominant form of consumption in Hong Kong and Thailand, but attempts to push heroin among the population in South Vietnam have been unsuccessful, and heroin use has not shown up in Singapore. Singapore and Malaysia have a small but growing population of morphine injecting addicts, one of the few pockets of morphine consumption in the world. This variation in consumption patterns means that wholesale suppliers in the Southeast Asian network must be flexible in their ability to provide a differing mix of products to different customers.

Markets. Hong Kong importers annually take about 10 tons of morphine base—for refining mostly into No. 3, or smoking, heroin in Hong Kong—and 50 tons of raw opium. The morphine base and opium both originate in the tri-border area and move overland through Thailand to Bangkok. From there, most is delivered to Hong Kong on Thai fishing trawlers that transfer the product to Hong Kong–based junks in the territorial waters of the People's Republic of China near Hong Kong. Some morphine base is smuggled from Bangkok to Hong Kong by civil air passengers and some is concealed in merchant ships. Hong Kong is both a consuming and an exporting country. It supplies the opium and heroin used in the small Chinese population in the Philippines (about 10 tons of opium equivalent a year), and small amounts of No. 4 heroin are sold to merchant seamen and other small-time international traffickers.

The number of addicts in urban Thailand is about the same as in Hong Kong—150,000—and the proportion of heroin smokers to opium smokers is three or four to one in each community. Whereas Hong Kong distributors refine their own heroin, opiate distributors in Thailand have their heroin produced upcountry near opium producing areas, where it is mixed with adulterants and shipped as a finished product overland to urban Thai markets. Before 1969, these refineries were in Bangkok, but during 1969 and 1970 most or all moved upcountry for security reasons. On the basis of dosage rates in Hong Kong, the quantity of smoking heroin consumed by Thailand's 120,000 heroin addicts totals about 100 tons gross weight of raw opium equivalent a year. Thailand's 30,000 opium smokers in urban areas use the product in either raw or processed form. About 50 tons of raw opium equivalent are shipped annually from the tri-border area south to meet urban Thai requirements for smoking opium.

The opium smoking community in South Vietnam, centered mainly in Cholon, the Chinese district of Saigon, imports annually about 15 tons of prepared opium. This is supplied from Laos, sometimes via Bangkok, by organizations that have ties with Saigon dating back to the days of French control of Indochina. In Vientiane and other cities in Laos, heroin as well as opium is smoked. Annual consumption here may be on the order of 10 tons of raw opium equivalent.

Finally, there is a significant market for opiates in Singapore and Malaysia. Together they account for about 30 tons of raw opium annually, plus small amounts of morphine base which distributors convert into an injectable form of morphine. Most opium for Singapore and Malaysia is delivered from Bangkok by fishing trawler to points off the Malaysian coast, where it is picked up for distribution to customers in Singapore, Penang, and other cities.

Trafficking Networks. The major trafficking networks in Southeast Asia are well-coordinated business activities. They tend to be dominated by ethnic Chinese merchants who have been in the business for years and who are often wealthy men well able to finance narcotics activities. They are used to dealing with high government officials to arrange protection and are also skilled at evading government controls when necessary. The key points in these networks are discussed below.

The distribution process begins in the Burma, Thailand,

Laos *tri-border area.* Until mid-1971, when governments in the area began increasing enforcement efforts, the collection and refining of opium was done more or less openly. Since mid-1971, however, the big narcotics dealers have had to conduct their operations more discreetly. The Laotian consortium, for example, relocated its refinery activities to Burma where it operates under the protection of the Burma Self-Defense Forces (Kha Kweyei, or KKY): numerous armed groups that occasionally support the Burmese army in battles with Communist insurgents but which remain beyond Burmese government control. To some extent, the large opium syndicates in northern Thailand have also moved their refining activities north across the Burmese border. They have similar protection arrangements with Chinese irregular, or KKY, groups in the neighboring Shan State of Burma, an area the Burmese government traditionally has been unable to control.

The movement of opium products south through northern Thailand has been handled for a number of years mainly by two Chinese irregular forces known as the Third and Fifth Kuo-mintang armies. They are remnants, still well-armed, of forces driven out of Southwest China in 1949. The Thai government has been putting pressure on them to get out of the opium business, however, and achieved some success in March 1972, when the government obtained and destroyed 26,245 kilograms of raw opium supplied by the two armies in exchange for land for resettlement.

In addition to the sizable flow of opium and its derivatives through northern Thailand south to Bangkok for consumption there or transshipment, there is a reverse flow, totaling many tons annually, of opium processing chemicals from Bangkok to upcountry morphine and heroin refineries. There is little information available, however, on the routes and methods used to move either opium products or opium processing chemicals through Thailand.

After moving undetected to *Bangkok,* products show up again in various smuggling systems out of the city. Most raw opium and morphine exported to Hong Kong, Malaysia, and Singapore is moved by various fishing trawlers under control for any given trip of the group of Bangkok traffickers financing the operation. There are three or four trawler trips a month, carrying 1 to 3 tons each trip. The same organizations that run the trawlers are believed to handle, at the wholesale level, the growing traffic in No. 4 heroin to international markets. This product is either sold in Bangkok to buyers, who have been mainly United States servicemen or United States veterans, or delivered directly to buyers in the United States by couriers run by Bangkok dealers themselves. One such smuggling system was broken up in January 1972, when United States customs inspectors in Honolulu arrested three couriers who were body-carrying No. 4 heroin from Bangkok for delivery to Chinese-American buyers in San Francisco and New York.

A consortium of Chinese merchants in *Vientiane* handles the processing and distribution of most smoking heroin and opium to urban markets in Laos and Vietnam. They also produced much of the No. 4 heroin supplied to United States servicemen in Vietnam in 1970 and 1971. Under pressure from the Laotian government, however, they relocated their refinery operations in mid-1971 to Burma near the tri-border area and are now believed to be producing only No. 3 heroin for the small market in Laos.

Police in *Malaysia and Singapore* believe there is one major organization, operating in Malaysia, that handles distribution of most opium products imported from Thailand. Members of this organization have been detected trying to smuggle No. 4 heroin that originated in the tri-border area to the United States and Australia, although the amounts they have succeeded in moving are believed to be small.

There are two or three major narcotics importing and distributing organizations in *Hong Kong*. They import opium in raw form and morphine base for conversion in their own refineries to No. 3 or No. 4 heroin. They supply the large markets of smokers in Hong Kong and Macao and a smaller one in the Philippines, and make available No. 4 heroin to international traffickers and to merchant seamen and other small-time smugglers. One organization in Hong Kong, which is probably typical, owns a gold and jewelry firm, gambling casinos, and other businesses, and has close ties with one of the Triad secret societies, which run protection rackets in Hong Kong. Perhaps because their diversified activities in Hong Kong are sufficiently profitable, the major dealers there have never shown much interest in actively developing markets abroad for No.

4 heroin. The product is readily available in Hong Kong, however, for pickup by international smugglers.

Middle East–South Asia Network

The main consuming markets served by the Middle East–South Asia network are Iran and, to a much lesser degree, Pakistan. The needs of Indian addicts and users are met from Indian opium. Afghanistan does not appear to have a major consumption problem. Turkey, once a major supplier in this network, now plays a minor role.

Iran. Until 1970, about half of the opium smuggled into Iran came from Turkey and the remainder largely from Afghanistan and Pakistan. In 1969, both Turkey and Iran tightened their border patrols, and Iran instituted the death penalty for opium smuggling. Seizures along the Turko-Iranian border dropped sharply, while those at the Afghan-Iranian border increased. Recent reports of the existence of opium processing facilities on both sides of the Turko-Iranian border suggest that opium derivatives, as well as opium itself, may be entering Iran from the west. During 1970, 90 percent of illicit opium seizures in Iran were made near the Afghan border, compared with an average of about 45 percent in previous years.

Opium seized by Iranian authorities near the Afghan border in 1970 amounted to 12.5 tons. In the six previous years, when Tehran's surveillance and enforcement procedures were far less stringent, opium seizures near that border averaged only 7.2 tons. Iranian consumption estimates suggest that as much as 300 tons of opium are smuggled into the country from all sources, and it is possible that the great part of Iran's needs is being met through the Afghani channel.

Most of the opium smuggled into Iran almost certainly originates in Afghanistan, and some probably also transits Afghanistan from northwest Pakistan. Almost all the traffic follows land routes through Afghanistan, but opium may also be smuggled by sea from Pakistan or even India. Some illicit opium probably also moves among India, Pakistan, and Afghanistan for local consumption.

Afghanistan. Most of the opium smuggled from Afghanistan

to Iran is handled by nomadic tribes. Local Afghan businessmen
and merchants sometimes act as middlemen between opium growers
and smugglers. There is no indication of substantial involvement by
high government officials. Some low-level enforcement officials
almost certainly cooperate with the smugglers.

The tribes most heavily involved in the traffic into Iran are
the Ghilzai (Pathan), Shinwari (Pathan), Baluchis, and Turkmen.
The Ghilzai carry opium from East Central Afghanistan. The
Shinwaris operate mainly near the Pakistani border but probably
carry opium into Iran as well. The western portions of the Baluchis-
tan desert are the usual areas of operation for Baluchi caravans. The
Turkmen route is across northern Afghanistan. The major border-
crossing area is in the vicinity of the road from Herat, Afghanistan,
to Meshed, Iran. Large camel caravans are the traditional carriers
of opium to Iran.

The tightening of border surveillance by Iran has reportedly
led to a shift in border-crossing patterns away from the major routes.
Also caravans are larger and more heavily armed, and the tribesmen, aware that they are likely to be executed if they are caught in
Iran, are prepared to offer resistance. Middlemen often hold smugglers' families as hostages to ensure they do not surrender to Iranian
border forces or fail to return with proceeds from the opium sale.

The sparsely settled mountain and desert areas in Afghanistan are well suited for smuggling operations. Indeed, smuggling is
a way of life in Afghanistan—and in parts of Pakistan as well. The
population along the Afghan-Iranian border is basically nomadic.
Families usually have relatives living on both sides of the border
and routinely cross back and forth without official sanction. Moreover, sheep-raising is the tribesmen's main occupation, and they
often cross the border with their flocks in search of grazing land.
Smugglers have built close relationships with the tribesmen over the
decades. In addition to paying for lodging, they also bring goods to
trade in local markets.

Pakistan. Most opium smuggled out of Pakistan probably
transits Afghanistan for Iran. Kabul, of course, claims that most
of the opium transiting Afghanistan comes from Pakistan, which
Islamabad vehemently denies. Pakistan and Afghanistan share a
900-kilometer border with only three custom posts, and the tribal

areas of Pakistan are a de facto free-trade zone. This situation undoubtedly accounts for the lack of seizures in the border area. About half of the seizures in Pakistan in recent years have been in the northwest, with the opium reportedly in transit for Karachi or India. But there have been virtually no seizures of opium in Karachi itself in recent years, although there have been many seizures of hashish destined for shipment abroad. Moreover, India in 1969 reported seizures of only 42 kilograms of opium that had been smuggled from West Pakistan.

Afridi (Pathan) tribesmen dominate the opium traffic in Pakistan. Trucks are probably the major carriers, but camel and mule trains, buses, and automobiles are also used. As in Afghanistan, tribal smugglers make payments to customs, revenue, and police officials to ease their path. Tribal relationships suggest that the Afridis pass their opium to the Shinwaris and Ghilzais in Afghanistan for movement to Iran if they do not carry it through Afghanistan themselves.

India. India in the past was an important source of illicit opium in the world market. In the period 1946–1951, for example, United Nations data show that Indian opium accounted for one-third of world opium seizures, almost exclusively in international traffic. Earlier, in the 1921–1931 period, when British India included most of the area from the Thai border to the Afghan-Iran border, India was a major source of captured illicit opium, with much of the traffic originating in the growing area north of Bombay.

In recent years, however, there have been few indications that Indian opium plays a major role in illicit international traffic. Indian government controls over opium are extensive, and New Delhi points to the small seizures in illicit export traffic as evidence of their effectiveness. Such seizures amounted to only 232 kilograms in 1969, with the average haul amounting to 26 kilograms. There are no details on the ultimate destination of this opium.

On the other hand, there have been three seizures of Indian opium in Ceylon in recent years, the largest being 291 kilograms. Ceylonese officials estimate that a minimum of 5 tons of opium are smuggled from India to Ceylon each year. There have also been unsubstantiated reports of opium being smuggled from Bombay to Singapore and Persian Gulf ports by sea.

Prospects. There are at present no indications that international opium trafficking organizations are operating in the area. Afghani and Pakistani opium is of poor quality with a low morphine content, making it a less desirable commodity in the illicit international market. There are also no firm indications that countries other than Iran illicitly receive any important amounts of opium from South Asia. Nevertheless, substantial volumes of hashish are regularly smuggled out of Afghanistan and Pakistan into international traffic through apparently well-organized channels. If illicit supplies of opium from other sources in the world are cut back, these channels have the potential for moving South Asian opium into the international market.

Illicit Market Prices

The clandestine nature of almost all transactions in illicit narcotics markets makes for a dearth of information on costs and prices of opium and its derivatives at each stage of processing and distribution. Enough information is available, however, to provide some insights into the characteristics, price levels, and capabilities for adjustment of some of the major illicit markets.

In general, the illicit markets for opium and its derivatives are sellers' markets from which the major supplying firms (individuals and organizations) receive extremely high rates of return on their investment. The profits that can be made in servicing the United States market for heroin are sizably greater than in any other market. Table 5 illustrates the comparative scope for profit in the United States market and in the Iranian heroin market.

Despite the large gap between wholesale and retail price, the largest profits apparently are realized by firms in the wholesale trade handling large volumes of the product. Typically, retail distribution is managed by dealers selling small quantities. Wholesale firms trafficking in opium and opiates operate as oligopolies. They are large and few enough for each to exercise considerable influence over the local or national market. Rather than acting independently, they tend to operate in explicit or implicit collusion to set prices, and they resemble cartels in their proclivities for dividing up national

Table 5

Market	US $ per Kilogram	US $ per Kilogram of Raw Opium Equivalent
United States		
Price to farmer for opium (in Turkey)	22	—
Wholesale price for heroin[a] (Marseilles)	5,000	500
Border price for heroin (New York)	10,000	1,000
Wholesale price for heroin (New York)	22,000	2,200
Retail price for heroin (New York)	220,000[b]	22,000
Iran		
Price to farmer for opium (in Afghanistan/Pakistan)	12 to 15	—
Border price for opium (Afghanistan/Iran)	80 to 110	—
Wholesale price for heroin[a] (Tehran)	2,600	260
Retail price for heroin (Tehran)	13,000	1,300

[a] When raw opium is converted to morphine and heroin the volume is reduced by a ratio of 10:1.
[b] If sold as pure heroin. In fact, heroin is greatly adulterated when it reaches the addict; the price for adulterated heroin—40 percent purity—would be about $88,000 per kilogram.

markets. As noted in the earlier discussion of the major illicit markets, this tendency is strongly manifested in the Southeast Asian market and only somewhat less so in the European market.

Another illustration of the profit opportunities available to traffickers serving the United States market, as well as an indication of some of the longer-term price changes in that market, is provided by the operations of French traffickers. Currently, morphine base is likely to cost French traffickers somewhere between $800 to $1500 per kilogram, depending upon the quantity purchased and whether purchased directly from Turkey or through middlemen in other countries. The traffickers must next pay about $400 per kilogram for the conversion of the morphine base into heroin. Each kilogram of heroin obtained in this manner therefore costs the trafficking group anywhere from $1200 to $1900 per kilogram. The lower figure is only about 10 percent higher than the levels prevailing in 1960. If the traffickers purchase heroin directly from an independent heroin laboratory or another trafficking group, the cost is about $3000 per kilogram. In 1960 the laboratory price was about $2000 per kilogram. The acquisition of 100 kilograms of heroin thus represents an initial investment of anywhere from a minimum of $120,000 to $300,000 for the French trafficking group.

The price of 1 kilogram of heroin delivered to a United States buyer by a French trafficking group stood at about $4000 in 1960. By early 1972, the delivery price had increased to about $10,000 per kilogram. This 150 percent increase is the result of both the increased demand for heroin in the United States over the last decade and the greater risks involved in smuggling heroin because of increased interdiction efforts. In any case, the initial $120,000 to $300,000 investment in 100 kilograms of heroin should have yielded the traffickers a gross of about $1 million. After subtracting courier fees, transportation and preparation costs, and other operational expenses, the net profits of a successful operation on this scale probably range from one-half to three-fourths of $1 million.

The demand for heroin in the United States market has burgeoned since 1960. However, Table 6, prices in 1960 and 1971 from the illicit European market, suggests that the effect of this increased demand on prices at the various stages of supply has been uneven.

Although the price data are admittedly tenuous, the decline in price paid for raw opium suggests that the sources of supply of raw opium have readily adjusted to the increased demand of the past decade. At the same time, the increased prices for heroin in both Europe and New York imply that the increased demand is being met, but only at higher costs than was the case in 1960. These increased costs, in turn, would seem to reflect the increased risks involved both in heroin processing in France and in moving heroin to the United States caused by strengthening of enforcement measures in recent years.

Table 6

	US $ per Kilogram		Percentage Change
	1960	1971	
Opium (from farmers)	28	22	-21
Heroin Converted by trafficking group facilities	1,100	1,200 to 1,900	9 to 73
Converted by an independent laboratory	2,000	3,000	50
Landed in New York	4,000	10,000	150

A demonstration of the adjustment of an established illicit market to sharp changes in demand was provided in the Southeast Asian opium market in 1970–1971. Up to 1970, Southeast Asian farmers apparently received around $17 per kilogram for their opium, most of which was used for production of smoking opium and No. 3 heroin. The Hong Kong wholesale price for white heroin —for which there was little demand at that time—averaged around $2000. The sharp increase in demand for heroin engendered by growing use of the drug by United States troops in Vietnam in 1970 led to an increase in prices paid to farmers for opium to $20 per kilogram and by mid-1971 to a doubling of the Hong Kong wholesale price to $4000. Furthermore, new operators entered the heroin production business at this time. By early 1972, the collapse of the United States serviceman market had led to a drop in prices paid to farmers and a decline in the Hong Kong wholesale heroin price to around $3500. Moreover, most of the new producers who had entered the market earlier apparently went out of business. Some of the established traffickers in the market may have suffered losses when the sudden decline in demand caught them with unusually large stocks of heroin. Aside from this aspect, the Southeast Asian market appears to have adjusted flexibly to rapidly changing conditions.

Another point of interest suggested by the price changes in this market in 1970–1971 is that the difference between the selling price of heroin and the price paid to the farmer for opium is so huge that the trafficker clearly is capable of absorbing increased costs for opium. For example, prior to the price increases of 1970, 1 kilogram of heroin valued at $2000 in the Hong Kong market represented only $255 worth of opium procured from farmers; after the price increases, 1 kilogram of heroin valued at $4000 represented only $300 worth of opium.* If the trafficker decided to pass on the increased costs incurred by payment of higher prices to farmers for opium, the effects on wholesale and retail heroin prices would likely be small. For example, a 100 percent increase in the price paid to farmers for 15 kilograms of opium (from $255 to $510) would have the effect of raising the Hong Kong wholesale price of heroin by about 13 percent (from $2000 to $2255)` and would be likely to raise the retail price of heroin in the United States by only 0.1 percent (from $250,000 to $250,255). These observations suggest that traffickers are well able to pay higher prices for opium procured from farmers than is the case at present. This factor is likely to act as a strong counterbalance to attempts at eliminating poppy cultivation.

Multilateral Drug Control Efforts

The development of multilateral drug control efforts has been slow, largely because of widely varying national attitudes toward the drug problem. Differences in national laws and policies regarding drug trafficking and drug abuse, in attitudes toward extradition procedures, and in customs control and enforcement systems have hampered the development of an agreed international position toward drug control. Similarly, there have been great disparities as regards the resources each state has been willing to allocate to the problem. These differences have complicated the problem of inter-

* The calculation assumes that because of the lower morphine content of Southeast Asian opium, 15 kilograms of opium (rather than the general rule of thumb of 10 kilograms) are required to produce 1 kilogram of heroin.

national regulation of trade in licit opium and its derivatives for many years. More importantly, these differences are regularly and skillfully exploited by the illicit international trafficker.

In the years subsequent to the International Opium Convention of 1912, the effort to develop a common international approach to the problem made only slow progress and then chiefly under the auspices of the League of Nations. Much of the work of the League served as a point of departure for similar efforts conducted by the United Nations. In the past few years, international approaches to the opium problem and other narcotics problems have gained momentum. As indicated below, a large number of multilateral bodies both within and outside of the United Nations are now engaged in the effort.

United Nations' Efforts. The *Single Convention on Narcotic Drugs* was adopted in 1961 and entered into force in 1964. The convention provides the mechanism for continuous international cooperation on narcotic drug control through essentially voluntary restraints on the cultivation, production, manufacture, and import and export of opium and opium products. Supplanting eight previous narcotics control treaties, the Single Convention consolidated the United Nations' narcotics control machinery and increased the then existing methods of control. Overall supervision of the Single Convention rests with the United Nations Economic and Social Council (ECOSOC), while the specific provisions of the Single Convention are implemented by the Commission on Narcotics Drugs (CND) and the International Narcotics Control Board (INCB). At present there are 90 parties to the Convention.

After a three-week plenipotentiary conference, a protocol to amend and strengthen the 1961 Single Convention on Narcotic Drugs was adopted in Geneva on March 24, 1972, without a negative vote. The United States and 29 other countries cosponsored the amendments, which will make the Single Convention more responsive to the current world narcotics situation. The amending protocol, adopted by a vote of 71 to 0, with 12 abstentions (Algeria, Bulgaria, Burma, Byelorussian SSR, Cuba, Czechoslovakia, Hungary, Mongolia, Panama, Poland, Ukrainian SSR, USSR), is open to signature by countries which have either signed or become parties to the Single Convention. The protocol will enter into force when 40 parties to the convention have adhered to it. By June 23, 1972, 47 countries, including the United States, had signed the protocol.

The most noteworthy improvements in the amending protocol are: (1) For the first time the INCB will be assigned specific responsibility for attacking the illicit traffic in narcotics. (Heretofore, it concentrated primarily on regulating the licit cultivation, production, manufacture, trade, and use of narcotic drugs.) The INCB's powers will be substantially increased to carry out this new responsibility. (2) For the first time, the INCB will have authority to require the reduction of legal opium poppy cultivation and opium production in countries where there is evidence of diversion into illicit traffic. (3) The INCB will have access to more and better information from a wider range of sources, including the United Nations, the specialized agencies, and certain intergovernmental and nongovernmental organizations with narcotics expertise. (4) For the first time under a narcotics control treaty, the INCB will be authorized to recommend to United Nations bodies that technical and financial assistance be provided governments to help them carry out their obligations under the Single Convention. (5) If the INCB has reason to believe that a country is becoming a center for illicit narcotics activity, it is authorized to take the initiative in proposing on-the-spot studies to develop necessary remedial measures. (6) If a country fails to cooperate when requested, the INCB may publicize the situation among the parties to the Single Convention and at all appropriate levels of the United Nations. This could also include consideration of the matter by the United Nations General Assembly. (7) The protocol will extend to narcotics offenses the same kind of improvements in extradition that have recently been accepted in multilateral conventions on hijacking and other offenses against civil aviation. The new provisions will have the effect of including the full range of modern narcotics offenses in existing extradition treaties between the United States and other countries ratifying the amendments. This will significantly improve the capacity for prosecuting narcotics traffickers. (8) For the first time in international narcotics control, parties to the Single Convention will undertake an obligation to give special attention to drug abuse prevention, and to the education, treatment, rehabilitation, and social reintegration of drug abusers, as well as to more effective law enforcements. (9) The INCB, a body of technical experts serving in their individual capacities and not as representatives of government, will be increased from 11 to 13. Also, the term of office of its members will be increased, and the independence of its Secretariat will be strengthened.

The *United Nations Commission on Narcotic Drugs* (CND), a functional commission of ECOSOC, is the policy-making body in international narcotics control and presently consists of representatives from 24 nations elected by ECOSOC. ECOSOC recently has voted to expand the CND to 30 members. The CND meets biennially to review developments, suggest new measures, and recommend the adoption of resolutions to ECOSOC. The CND in September 1971 created the Ad Hoc Committee on Illicit Traffic in the Near and Middle East to promote more effective cooperation and increase mutual assistance in efforts to eliminate the illicit production and traffic of drugs in the region.

The *United Nations Division for Narcotic Drugs* (DND), which is part of the United Nations Secretariat, is the administrative office for drug matters within the United Nations. The Division is a central point for much of the United Nations documentation on narcotics; among other things it receives, analyzes, and disseminates reports from governments on drug seizures, production controls, and antismuggling efforts. The DND operates a laboratory in Geneva, which is developing methods for identifying the origin of seized narcotics.

The *United Nations Fund for Drug Abuse Control* was established in April 1971 by the secretary general following action by the Economic and Social Council and the General Assembly. Ambassador Carl W. A. Schurmann of the Netherlands was appointed as the secretary general's personal representative in charge of the Fund.

In establishing the Fund it was generally recognized that, in carrying out a worldwide program, financial resources far in excess of those available in the regular budgets of the United Nations and its specialized agencies would be required. Consequently, the United Nations secretary general called upon governments and private sources to make voluntary contributions. The Fund was launched with an initial pledge of $2 million from the United States. As shown below, contributions and pledges to the Fund totaled over $3 million by mid-1972. In addition to money, assistance in the form of personnel and facilities will be accepted.

CONTRIBUTIONS

United States	$2,000,000
Canada	150,000
France	100,000
Federal Republic of Germany	310,482
Vatican	1,000
Morocco	2,000
Saudi Arabia	2,000
Sweden	20,790
Turkey	5,000
Vietnam	1,000
Nongovernmental	6,830
	$2,599,102

PLEDGES

Canada	$250,000
Cyprus	2,550
Iran	5,000
Italy	101,350
Norway	74,626
Sweden	41,580*
Greece	2,000
United Kingdom	125,000
	$602,106

* (FY 1973)

The Fund will finance a Plan for Concerted Action Against Drug Abuse executed by the competent United Nations organs and as such has the following among its objectives: (1) to expand the research and information facilities of the United Nations drug control bodies; (2) to enlarge the capabilities and extend the operations of existing United Nations drug control bodies; (3) to limit the supply of drugs to legitimate requirements by ending illegal production and substituting other agricultural crops; (4) to promote facilities for treatment, rehabilitation, and social reintegration of drug addicts; and (5) to develop educational material and programs against drug abuse in high-risk populations.

It is anticipated the United Nations specialized agencies will play a major role in implementing the Plan.

The World Health Organization (who), for example, has a significant role in the control of narcotics and dangerous drugs. In accordance with Article 3 of the Single Convention on Narcotic Drugs, who may recommend the addition or deletion of substances from the schedules of the convention. The who Expert Committee on Drug Dependence has provided guidelines for governments engaged in revising their laws on drugs and in bringing additional drugs under control. The latest meeting of the World Health Assembly voted to expand who's program on drug dependence. Under that decision, who Expert Advisory Panels would provide regular reports on drug dependence in various geographical areas, and monitoring systems also would be developed.

unesco will undertake projects of an educational nature and related social research, the International Labor Organization (ilo) will deal with rehabilitation of addicts among workers, and the Food and Agricultural Organization (fao), with the substitution of crops to limit or eliminate the growing of narcotics.

Other Multilateral Efforts. The members of the European Community (ec) have devoted only limited attention thus far to cooperation against drug abuse and trafficking. The initiative of French President Pompidou in August 1971—detailed in a letter to the heads of government of the five other ec nations and the United Kingdom—proposed specific areas of cooperation within the ec on the drug problem. The Pompidou initiative contained proposals for coordination of police efforts, legal prohibitions, and medical and social research. Several follow-on meetings have discussed the package proposal, but there has not yet been any concrete action.

The *Committee on the Challenges of Modern Society* (ccms) of the North Atlantic Treaty Organization was set up in 1969 at United States initiative to explore the social problems of urban life. The Committee currently has under way a study of the prospects for international cooperation in drug rehabilitation.

The *International Criminal Police Organization (Interpol)* assists national police forces by collecting, collating, and disseminating information on international crime operations; it is not an enforcement or investigative agency. Interpol, which has its headquarters in St. Cloud, France, maintains its own radio network, library, and criminal records. The 111 nations that belong to Interpol underwrite its activities through annual membership dues based on population, living standards, and use made of the organization. The 1971 budget was a little less than $1 million.

Interpol generally suffers from a shortage of manpower, a lack of funding, and the use of outmoded equipment. Manpower deficiencies have a particular bearing on the organization's effectiveness in the narcotics field: in 1971 Interpol's staff of 107 included only 12 personnel working full time on narcotics matters. Although Interpol dues were increased in 1969, a number of countries have been delinquent in payment, and the small operating budget prevents needed improvement of communications and information processing facilities. Interpol's effectiveness is also restricted by erratic reporting from member countries, which are obligated to report the arrests of foreign nationals, and the prevalence of strictly national police problems such as poor communications, weak administration, and corruption.

The organization is devoting increasing attention to drug control efforts. The fortieth session of Interpol's General Assembly —held in Ottawa in September 1971—discussed illicit drug traffic at length and, among other things, reached agreement on measures to streamline the exchange of information in Europe. The general secretariat of Interpol subsequently selected three police officials— from Italy, Sweden, and West Germany—who have assumed responsibility for improving the flow of narcotics information within their respective regions. Interpol maintains permanent contacts with WHO and the United Nations Commission on Narcotic Drugs.

The *Customs Cooperation Council* (ccc), with a membership of 67 countries and a budget of $1.2 million for the 1972 fiscal year, is active in all aspects of customs operations. Headquartered in Brussels, the ccc makes its major technical and policy decisions at annual Council sessions. Frequent gatherings of subordinate technical committees are held throughout the year. Its principal role is to coordinate and resolve customs technical problems and to facilitate the development of international trade. It also provides a mechanism for the exchange of information between customs administrations on customs law violations and offenses but has only recently focused on the customs role in the specific area of narcotics. The Council adopted a recommendation in 1971 for the spontaneous exchange of information between customs administrations throughout the world on the illicit traffic in narcotics and psychotropic substances. Bilateral and multilateral agreements for such exchanges are encouraged in the recommendation. Turkey, most East European countries, and all principal West European nations are members. The United States joined the ccc in 1970.

The Council of Europe presently has a membership of 17 countries and has several standing committees which discuss greater cooperation on social and criminal problems. The European Committee on Crime Problems (ECCP) was established by the Council of Europe in 1957 to develop a program for the prevention of crime and the treatment of offenders. In March 1972, the Council sponsored a Multidisciplinary Drug Conference to work out a European strategy for attacking drug addiction and trafficking. Many of the proposals resulting from this conference are to be implemented within the framework of existing working agreements between the Council and Interpol and United Nations' organs.

5

Considerations on
Law Enforcement

Richard H. Blum

Our interest in this and the following two chapters is in constraints
on and strategy of law enforcement at the local level vis-à-vis
dealers. Our studies of two California departments—one in a major
city, the other in a university town—were limited in scope, resting
as they did on voluntary labor and on existing—and often inadequate—police records. The shortcomings of our inquiry are, fortu-
nately, counterbalanced by the availability of several previous
studies that focus on the narcotics law enforcement apparatus in
California, one of which has intensively examined the activities of
the vice squad in the city that is also the object of our study. In
addition, that city's police force has been the object of a careful
study that provides an overall perspective on its style and philosophy of operation. California data also figure strongly in the reports
of Kaplan (1970), Morton and others (1968), Skolnick (1966),
Wilson (1968), and Blum and Wahl (1964). We restrict our view

to a limited aspect of local narcotics enforcement and do not here consider the issues of the functions and the appropriateness of the criminal law as applied to drug use. These major—and troublesome —issues have been dealt with by, for example, Kaplan (1970), Schur (1965), Duster (1970), and Packer (1969).

Morton and his colleagues (1968), reinforced by a foreword by Kaplan, report on their interviews with police officers in Los Angeles County and their observations of the disposition of drug arrest cases there. With regard to the operation of the law, they agree with the statement by Packer (1969):

Enforcement of the marijuana laws suffers from the same difficulties encountered in the enforcement of laws concerning other consensual crimes. There is no victim to complain and there is little social pressure to conform to the law within the various subcultures involved. The police compensate for these difficulties by developing aggressive techniques designed to ferret out the illicit activity, including the use of informants, undercover operators, and field surveillance.

Given the incidence of use, compared with incidence of arrest, the result of such an enforcement problem is inefficient enforcement (Kaplan calls it erratic); that is, there is greater chance that a criminal act will be undetected and its perpetrator unpunished than that the act will be detected and the criminal punished. Note that efficiency, as we use the term here, relates only to detection and arrest; we are not referring to effectiveness of enforcement as deterrent or corrective relative to drug use or dealing. Kaplan (1970) calculates that in California in 1968, on any given occasion, the chance for arrest for marijuana use was 1 in 200; but he notes that this risk is unequally distributed, the risks falling more heavily on persons who more readily come to police attention, usually lower-class or visibly deviant youth.

Kaplan's point is readily supported by California arrest statistics (Morton and others, 1968), which show disproportionate numbers of Mexican-American youth arrested for narcotics violations. Observations on arrests among college youth (Blum and Associates, 1969b) permitted the conclusion that less than 1 percent among students who use drugs had experienced a narcotics arrest. These data on the infrequency of arrest in at least one relatively immune population should not lead us to disregard what we have already learned from our sample of variegated Bay Area dealers, namely, that approximately 41 percent have suffered at least one narcotics arrest, whether for possession or for sales. On the other hand, in terms of arrest, there were two clear subgroups among the experienced dealers: the lower-class opiate-using criminal dealer, with multiple nonnarcotics arrests, and the cool-man-hip dealer, the active middle-class psychedelic pusher, with relatively infrequent arrests for narcotics or other violations. From this analysis emerges the proposition that as a person becomes more actively involved in dealing (as opposed to casual use, for example)', he runs a greater risk of arrest. However, this risk varies considerably depending upon other conditions, type of drug sold and used, type of clientele, background in terms of class and propensity to violence, personality, and the like. Thus, the risk of arrest can be predicted on the basis of dealer characteristics, one of which, the degree of involvement in the drug life, is most important. Data reported in *The Dream Sellers* (Blum and Associates, 1972a) reveal that dealers who make the most money have a greater chance of arrest than little-money dealers, that the more violent dealers are more often arrested than less violent ones, and that psychedelic dealers avoid arrest more easily than heroin peddlers. In any event, arrest risk is never certain, for even among the "losers," or heavily involved dealers, there were some who had never been arrested on any charge.

The police are certainly aware of the inefficiency of enforcement of laws against the users. The former chief of the Los Angeles Police, Thomas Redin, has been quoted as saying that all the police can do is try to keep marijuana under control. At best such a strategy implies prevention of spread of use. However, given California statistics showing prevalence of use increasing over time (San Mateo County School Study, 1968 through 1972) and those showing arrests doubling each year (Morton and others, 1968)', the realities of enforcement in California dictate a strategic goal that can hope only to slow the expansion of use (or reduce regularity of use by interdicting supply)'. An alternative or concurrent goal might be procedures that raise the cost of being a dealer (and of what is sold) through the hazard of arrest.

Enforcement, in the face of widespread prevalence of sales and use, may also serve simply as a drill: the police "do their duty" without much hope of impact or with the hope of delayed impact, that is, that at some future time their efforts will pay off. Given the results of studies of the motives and morality of police recruits and working officers (R. Blum, 1964; Blum and Osterloh, 1966), it is possible—even likely—that individual officers make drug arrests because they are convinced that drug use and dealing are immoral as well as unlawful and that their function as moral men maintaining the proper order of things is to punish such wrongdoers. Given these individual motives, it does not matter so much that the overall enforcement system is erratic or ineffective, for a moral and presumably personally satisfying purpose is served whenever a convinced officer makes such an arrest.[1] Such arrests also serve a symbolic function; they are an expression of the disapproval of one group of people for the life style of another. Morton and coworkers (1968), for instance, observed that the risk of drug arrest to hippies is greater than for straights because officers are more likely to stop a hippie-looking youth for stop-and-frisk. Officers whom they interviewed not only were aware that "long hairs" were more likely to be drug users and sellers and thus better targets but also disliked them as a group: "There was a particular contempt for the older hippies . . . who the police believe introduce many high school age juveniles to drug use." Just as drug use becomes symbolic of a life style—a point made by Goode (1970) and Colon (1971)—so also can the detestation of that life style, as expressed by arrest for drug use, become a police response. In such a context, the efficiency of enforcement is secondary; the police as opposition do what they can to impose the morality of the class that they represent. In the

---

[1] An analogy is the clinician in medicine or psychiatry, for example, in a medically underserviced region, who feels he has done his job well when he successfully treats a patient with a disorder, even though, from the public health standpoint, there is evidence that most people with the same disorder go untreated and that even treated patients relapse. We must distinguish, then, between officer as "clinician" doing what he feels is right and the appraisal of the public impact of his work.

same vein, the drug-using youth do what they can to propagate their morality—and its symbols—and to resist the alarms and incursions of traditional (especially working-class and lower-middle-class) views about "vice."

Further evidence (Blum and Wahl, 1964) about the personal views of California narcotics officers supports the notion of their involvement, not just with dutiful enforcement, but also with the conviction that their own personal actions are moral in the finest sense, protecting the community from imminent danger originating in bad people. Heroin users, for example, were described as self-indulgent, greedy, and exploitative; marijuana smokers were —back in 1964—considered disrespectful of and rebellious toward authority and exploitative; hallucinogen users were seen as disrespectful of and rebellious toward authority and as self-indulgent, professing "superior" moral ideas.[2] When police were asked to rank various groups in terms of the degree of menace they presented to the community, these views of individuals combined to place heroin users second below the first-ranking Communist Party and worse than the Syndicate, burglary rings, and confidence men. Marijuana users ranked sixth as a menace, ahead of the Mafia, black nationalists, white supremicists, dishonest real estate promoters, and others on the list, all of whom were more menacing than LSD users who were, in turn, thought more of a menace than civil disobedience demonstrators, homosexuals, and the like. Indeed, in discussing ideal penalties for various offenders, these experienced narcotics officers would punish only homicide more severely than drug-dealing—with most wanting death for the murderer and six to ten years in prison for the drug peddler. Companions to the peddler in this preferred long-sentence group were, next, the rapist, then the armed robber. In these views, the officers saw themselves as generally supported by the public, which, they believed, was fearful of the spread of drug use and was responding to that use with disgust and revulsion. In this perception, if we may take the 1970 and 1972 Gallup opinion polls as evidence, the officers' views of 1963 and 1964 remain correct.

[2] Implicit here is a class variable, for early hallucinogen users were drawn from professional and other upper-middle-class strata (see Blum and Associates, 1964), whereas most officers come from lower-middle-class or working-class backgrounds (see R. Blum, 1964).

In terms of the stated strategies of the police, Morton and colleagues (1968) differentiate (1) the federal officers (Bureau of Narcotics and Dangerous Drugs [BNDD], Customs, and Border Patrol on the California-Mexico border) along with the California State Bureau of Narcotics Enforcement, whose mandate is to detect and apprehend major traffickers; (2) departments of larger cities and counties, whose narcotics units or juvenile narcotics squads are aimed at local dealers; (3) smaller departments with part-time narcotics officers only, whose mandates appear less clear; and (4) the patrol division, whose officers are "the last link in the enforcement chain" and who account for most narcotic arrests, usually of individuals in possession of drugs, that is, users. Unlike the investigations of the higher-echelon specialists, which rest upon informants (professional, local contacts, or "turned out" arrestees) and field operations (field investigation units or undercover agents) and which require penetration of dealer groups and, over time, the setting-up of informants and then agents (in sequence) for buys, the arrests by patrol officers are essentially "accidental"; that is, they are not based on planned, long-term investigation. Morton and others (1968) found that patrol arrests for possession occurred in consequence of "(1) the stopping of a vehicle for a traffic violation, (2) confrontation of allegedly under-age juveniles for curfew violations, (3) the investigation of a loud party, and (4) the frisk of an individual stopped under the stop-and-frisk doctrine." The authors give no data on the relative prevalence of any of the arrests, but they do observe that the procedures, as set forth, are discriminatory. Discrimination can occur "accidentally," that is, in consequence of unrelated policies (for instance, greater patrol for high-crime areas where some groups are then automatically at higher risk, for example, black youth); because of personal or departmentally sanctioned intent, for example, the aforementioned police disapproval of hippie-looking youth or of disrespectful delinquents (Werthman and Piliavin, 1967); or in consequence of departmental policy from which discriminatory strategies ensue. Since all enforcement must be selective, given the magnitude of the problem, certain policy decisions determine priorities; for example, Morton and coworkers (1968) note that the Los Angeles Juvenile Narcotics Division desires to concentrate on adult pushers believed to be supplying to juveniles. Since most of the data from the study by Morton and others

(1968) relied upon interviews with (a few) police administrators and officers, we have no way to know what informal policies—as opposed to public postures—may also dictate enforcement. Skolnick's (1966) participant observer study in one of the California police departments, which we have also examined, provides insights into the day-to-day operations of their narcotics squad. Skolnick sketches the narcotics officer's "working personality," which is responsive to potential danger; his role as authority; and the need for efficiency. Since danger is real,[3] the officer discriminates in his environment between those who are likely assailants and those who are not. Because drug users are presumed to be unpredictable (Blum and Wahl, 1964) as well as criminal and are in fact drawn from the potentially more violent population sector (being predominately male, young, and, increasingly, armed [Blum and Associates, 1972a]), users are among the feared groups whom Skolnick calls symbolic assailants.

In examining narcotics work, Skolnick (1966) emphasizes the importance of the informant and the working relationships developed between officer and "snitch." He also describes the (constitutional) unlawfulness of some of the investigative steps that take place and the officers' justifications of the moral and expeditious grounds for these. As an analyst of a working system created by the pressure for arrest in the difficult vice arena (see Schur, 1965), Skolnick suggests that the need to use informants to make buys can —by employing public money and creating "buyers," some of whom will later testify in court—actually serve to create "dope rings." The "smashing" of such "dope rings," as reported in the press, is at best exaggerated, not only in the implied sizes of the "dope rings," but also in the values set for "dope" seized. Skolnick also discusses the impossibility of "full enforcement" and indicates the discretionary role of the officer and the prosecutor, who, in making judgments as to whether to investigate, arrest, charge, and prosecute, implicitly or explicitly set priorities for enforcement. We shall shortly see what some of these priorities are in the narcotics area.

The operational realities for the individual policemen—and

[3] In the first six months of 1970 in the United States, 48 police personnel were killed and 1,031 injured.

the values and assumptions that operate to form these—are well presented by Skolnick. Wilson (1968), on the other hand, provides a view of police administration in that same department, which Wilson describes as emphasizing formal hierarchical authority (over informal clique authority), legalistic, stressing technical efficiency (against inefficiency measured by the production of arrests or in records keeping), sensitive to citizen complaint and willing to discipline officer misbehavior, emphasizing selection of middle-class men (or standards). Wilson stresses the importance in enforcement of abstract justice and "punishment," rather than—as occurs in other departments—reliance on handling of cases where the officer's "magistral" powers are enhanced in that he is granted more discretion in dispositions (see Barrett, 1962,[4] for a consideration of the officer as "curbstone magistrate"). The arrest rates are much higher in a legalistic department than in an informal one. Wilson observes that there are 50 times as many vice arrests of blacks for gambling in this city as there are for the same offense in a comparable informally policed city. Whether we shall be able to discern the impact of these features, so ably observed in the mid-1960s, from a look at the operation of that city's narcotics enforcement in 1970 and 1971, we shall see in the next two chapters. In any event, the picture given by Skolnick (1966) of informal procedures is not fully compatible with that of Wilson (1968), although both stress efficiency and managerial skill. Wilson emphasizes pressures for "justice" as well as production, whereas Skolnick perceives narcotics endeavors as proceeding by unconstitutional means; indeed, he pleads: "What must occur is a significant alteration in the ideology of the police, so that police 'professionalization' rests on the values of democratic legal order, rather than on technological proficiency" (p. 239).

With this background, we turn to our work and findings. We think the data speak for themselves as we examine priorities, arrests, and outcomes for drug law violations—use and dealing—in the two communities.

---

[4] Barrett's observations of 1962 were also conducted in this city.

6

The Narcotics Law in Action: A College Town

Richard H. Blum, Andrew Gordon

Call it Comfort. A pleasant place, with tree-lined streets and a median household income of about $11,000. A fine town and next to it a fine university. Most of its (95 percent white) citizens are law-abiding and they think well of their town and its police. Next to Comfort are two areas about which its citizens may have two minds; one is a large unincorporated area that has approximately 65 percent black citizens whose crime rate is higher and from which comes a spill-over of lower-class crime. In that black area, drug use is common, as is alcoholism. In the other direction is the university; some of the students are dissident and among them many are regular users of illicit drugs. In Comfort itself is a Free University, which attracts some unusual students. Some of these students live in

114

town and, with wandering other visitors, comprise a small population of street people, some of whom live in in-town communes, give rock concerts, and, of a warm spring night, may not see eye-to-eye with the city fathers on when to go home. In this group, too, illicit drug use is high.

Based on our data (Blum and Associates, 1969a,b), and those of Manheimer, Mellinger, and Balter (1969) and Robins and Murphy (1967), we estimate, on the basis of the identifiable population strata in and next to Comfort, that there should be about 13,000 persons who occasionally or regularly use marijuana and/or other illicit drugs. In the course of a day or month, most of these 13,000 will come to Comfort.

Comfort has a police department of more than a hundred men, which, by most standards, is a fine one. It has what many other small towns do not have—a narcotics enforcement program under its Investigation Division. This program is the work of one full-time detective; we shall call him Burden. In this chapter, we shall try to understand the limits on and the priorities for narcotics enforcement in Comfort, and how Burden handles his task.

Budget

One kind of reality begins with money. By understanding money one learns about a major set of constraints on narcotics enforcement. Comfort has an operating budget of nearly $13 million. Since its citizens, middle-class people, already pay high federal, state, county, and city taxes, one guesses that they might resist tax increases. We conducted a survey of these citizens, taking a random area sample of 100 householders. It confirmed our expectations. Citizens think their taxes are already high enough or too high. They think their police department is a good one, and they do not wish to spend further moneys to make it better. These citizens think drug abuse is an important matter, but not the town's most pressing police problem. Even though the city is now operating below its tax ceiling, we may take it as a given fact that the upper limit on police expenditures—short of a major criminal threat to the city— has been set. Indeed, a tradition has already been established, for over the past ten years the police have been awarded the same piece of the budget pie, each year gaining a little more in absolute funds since the city budget has increased (by 14 percent each year) but given inflation, expanding personnel costs through retirement, and the like, and the increased cost for more complex equipment, real capabilities have not expanded grandly.

A program budget for the police department shows that its greatest costs are incurred in the Uniform (patrol) Division. The Investigation Division, which gets 13 percent of the total budget (about $225,000), is manned by a captain, a lieutenant, two sergeants, and eight detectives. Burden is one of the detectives. Occasionally he works on other cases, but he also calls on other men to help him on narcotics cases. We assume that these trade-offs balance out so that the budget of the Narcotics and Dangerous Drug Branch *is* Burden. With his salary, a rented car, and miscellaneous funds ("buy" money,[1] per diem, informants' fees, and the like, totaling $2000), his direct costs are $16,000 or 7 percent of the Investigation Division budget. Overhead costs add more—the budget estimates allow about $2000 per man for management expenses. We assume that, as of 1970 and 1971, the worth of narcotics enforcement *via investigation* to the citizens, city council, and police administrators of Comfort—all of whom determine enforcement priorities—is 0.7 percent of the police budget and 0.001 percent of the city budget.

Cost of Making a Case

What does that budget mean for enforcement via investigation in terms of cases? There are two ways for calculating case costs: one uses the basis of man-hours, which are calculated to include all police costs, resulting in a figure of $8.10 per police man-hour to the city of Comfort; the other is a case-cost calculation by expense items and salaried man-hours. We find upon review of narcotics branch cases that there are two kinds: little ones and middle-sized ones.[2] Burden's mandate is to make cases against dealers. Big cases

[1] If more buy money is needed, the department has a special fund of $600 to use. Any situation that requires more is considered a heavy case and is transferred to other authorities.

[2] A small case involves a lid of grass, a gram of hash, 5 tabs of hallucinogens, 5 to 10 pills (a deck), up to a $20 paper of speed, up to 12 reds (barbiturates), or up to "15-cent" to "25-cent" bags ($15 to $25) of heroin. Medium cases involve up to a key (kilogram) of grass, an ounce of hash, 100 tabs of acid, 200 amphetamine pills, an ounce of speed, or an ounce

are referred to state or federal agents and are not handled locally except for liaison. Using one of the middle-sized (big for the branch) cases, we established a total cost of $713 by the man-hour method and $725 by the expense-item-and-salaried-time method—nice agreement for the two cost methods. Splitting them down the middle, we can say it costs Comfort $720 to investigate, make an arrest, follow up, and present evidence in court (court costs are for the police and their agents only) for a "big" case; the one cost analysis was based on one of the biggest, a sale of two kilograms (4½ pounds) of marijuana. It involved six officers from three jurisdictions and a federal officer.[3] Cost analysis of a little case revealed costs of $81 by the man-hour method and $139 by the itemizing method. The discrepancy was caused by the need in that case for required "extras"—such as a rented electronic bug and a $25 informant. Let us assume that through investigation, bust, follow-up, and court, it costs Comfort $110 for a little case; the one analyzed involved the sale of $100 worth of LSD.

If Burden spent all his time making cases—and could draw on all the extra help he might need just to do that—he could, conceivably, make 22 "big" cases (middling ones, that is) or 145 small ones a year. Burden cannot spend all his time on cases. He must go to staff meetings, have coffee, talk to worried parents, give lectures in schools, check the scene, train other officers, be kind to research assistants working on projects like this one, and the like. He works a 9- to 10-hour day but much of it, as any organization man knows, is taking care of business, not doing business.

If we estimate that 40 percent of his time is spent doing business[4] that is, directly related to making and prosecuting particu-

---

of heroin. Larger transactions, if known in advance, are referred to state or federal agents.

[3] It did not turn out so well. The officers, attempting to follow their informant's car, managed to follow the wrong car. The undercover agent, who thought he was making a buy, had been set up by his "customers" for a rip-off. In robbing him, they found his police radio in his car, panicked, beat him up, stole most of his buy money, and stole and wrecked his car. These "exceptional" costs—the agent, the car, and the buy money—were not calculated in figuring what a "big" case costs since it was not supposed to have cost that much. Two of the four thieving, car-wrecking, assaulting dealers were later caught.

[4] This out-of-the-hat guess comes from a study (Blum and Downing,

lar cases, and that one-half of his cases are big ones, we would expect Burden to make about 32 cases a year. Case does not mean persons, for there may be several persons arrested. Yet, the record shows that Burden made 15 cases and arrested 32 persons. Burden either made more big cases and/or could not put in 40 percent of his time making cases.[5]

However, more than 32 persons were arrested on narcotics charges in Comfort in 1969 and more than 15 cases were made; 152 people were arrested on 109 cases. For, as has been seen in the two other studies (Morton and colleagues, 1968, in Los Angeles; Blum and Associates, 1972a), most narcotics arrests are made by the patrol force as a result of "on view" activities, furtive movement, stop-and-frisk procedures, and the like. Such arrests are almost always for possession for use, although the records do not tell us that clearly.

What does it cost for a patrol arrest? If we assume about five hours (using the man-hour rather than itemized-expense base) for arrest, report writing, and court appearances in those exceptional cases where plea bargaining does not wrap the case up without a trial, we obtain a total cost of $3700 for all patrol cases or about $40 per case. Obviously, if the objective were to make cases cheaply, the patrol division should be spurred on to "have at it" busting users.

We would expect the patrol division to get the careless offenders. If discretion is learned with age and with becoming a serious dealer, the weight of arrest would be expected to fall on the younger users who, as we have seen elsewhere (Blum and Associates, 1972a), are not the serious dealers. Indeed, a review of Comfort's 1969 statistics suggests that these are the people they get anyway, even if there is a Narcotics and Dangerous Drugs Branch with its investigatory effort. The 1969 arrestees had an average age of 20. There were 123 men, 29 women; whites outnumbered blacks 8 to

---

1964) we did on the distribution of professional time in a mental health agency, where we found that professionals spend about 40 percent of their time in activities directly related to their stated tasks.

[5] Another thing Burden did was to give credit to younger patrolmen who helped him on the bust. When that happened, arrests appear as patrol arrests even though they were, in fact, arrests subsequent to investigation and setting-up for buys.

1; and nonresidents were arrested more often than residents by a ratio of 1.2:1.[6] Most were unemployed and had completed high school.

Results

Presumably the number of cases made depends on how many officers are working on drugs. The record for Comfort shows 18 adult drug arrests in 1966, 34 in 1967, 72 in 1968, 97 in 1969, and 75 in 1970. During this same period, juvenile drug arrests jumped from 5 in 1966 to 27 in 1967, to 83 in 1968, back down to 55 in 1969, and to 36 in 1970. Three factors—manpower, support, and priorities—help to account for these figures. Until 1966, there was no detective assigned to specialized narcotics duty; Burden was a juvenile officer and his drug arrests appeared in the juvenile column. In 1967, the first narcotics detective (Burden's predecessor) was appointed; and, in 1968, Burden took over with the added advantage of the liaison and support system that had been developing, that is, informants and a working relationship with other departments. In 1970, a new element was created in response to citizen protests over unsafe streets. An undercover "mod squad" of from three to ten men covered "the action" in Comfort and made 50 to 60 arrests per month. Their cases contribute to the 1868 (all offenses) 1970 arrest statistics.

The third factor to account for the statistics on the different patterns of adult and juvenile arrests is a shift in police policy and resultant priorities. In Comfort, juveniles who are arrested must necessarily sometimes be the offspring of citizens who count. Where increasing drug use and dealing make the arrest of these young indiscreet dealers otherwise inevitable, only a policy shift can reverse the trend. The change in policy was politic as well as humane, for it reduces potential conflict between "good families" and the

---

[6] If we calculate color not on the basis of the 95 percent of Comfort residents who are white but as a proportion of the approximately 100,000 people who do business in Comfort, there are about 14 percent black, which is very close to the arrest ratio. Similarly, our estimate of 100,000 doing business in Comfort gives an about 50:50 ratio of regular visitors over townspeople. Given the slightly higher nonresident arrest rate one assumes, quite safely, that the visitors are younger and thus more likely users. The university and street people account for such a risk group.

police and can be justified by beliefs shared by many to the effect
that the older user-dealer is a greater menace. Other departments
have the same policy; for example, in Los Angeles the juvenile
bureau prefers to concentrate not on juveniles in the drug area but
on adults who supply children, even though our data (Blum and
Associates, 1972a) make it clear that such adults are *rara avis* indeed. In showing declining juvenile arrests from 1968 to 1969 and
from 1969 to 1970, Comfort differs from the rest of California
where juvenile drug arrests, after a tremendous increase from 1967
to 1968 of 117 percent, increased an additional 12 percent from
1968 to 1969. The state figures for 1969 and 1970 show a decrease
of 0.3 percent with a changing pattern of arrests—a 19 percent increase in marijuana arrests coupled with a 20 percent decrease in
arrests involving dangerous drugs.

Manpower does increase arrest capabilities, but we had contended that Comfort had reached its taxation limit for narcotics and
that no further increase in funds for narcotics enforcement costs
could be expected. We reckoned without the rest of the world for,
although Comfort's police costs are born by taxes from the town, we
had a surprise in 1970. The county, in the face of public agitation
over rising taxes, applied for and received $1 million of Law En-
forcement Assistance Administration (LEAA) money to support
increased county-wide narcotics enforcement. Comfort received a
portion of this windfall, which they chose to use by assigning two
new men, in January of 1971, to drug cases. With their presence
can we expect dealer arrests to at least double or—given some
bureaucratic inefficiency as staff is expanded—at least to increase
considerably again? We doubt it for several reasons.

One reason is that the focus on adults rather than juveniles
will make drug arrests more difficult if, as we assume, adults are
more careful than young offenders and if their education in caution
is augmented, as we have seen in the history of dealers it is (Blum
and Associates, 1972a), by learning about the perils of pushing
from one another as well as from their own bad luck. More serious
dealers tend to speak of the need not to be visible; insofar as their
lessons are learned elsewhere, the wise dealers—and it is on the
dealers that both men in the enlarged branch are supposed to focus

—will be harder to spot. We scanned the mug shots of those arrested in 1969 and 1970 and found the majority wearing the hippie costume. These were easy targets.

A second reason is that officers are becoming more cautious. As the dealing scene becomes more violent and the "symbolic assailants" are viewed as more dangerous, officers take more time to plan a bust, and they take along reinforcements when they make it. Burden said: "I used to bust alone, but not anymore. I used to be able to walk up to a dealer, make a buy and bust him on the spot. Now I won't go out without at least one or two other guys. Safety first. . . . With certain types of people like Afros, Panthers, and Hell's Angels I have to take several cars."

On a recent raid of suspected drug-using Panthers, Burden took five cars and ten men. They burst in both front and back doors to find their prey in an opium stupor. Even so, he said, "If one of them would have moved, I'd have reacted. You can never tell when someone's going to put a program on you."

And he reflects, "After a while you begin to wonder if it's worth it. . . . I've been thinking about getting out of this. . . . I'm getting too old for this type of work; and a nice, easy desk job wouldn't be bad."

In addition to the slowdown required for logistics—imagine the time it took Burden to arrange those five cars and ten men from outside his own bailiwick—and the more insidious restraint associated with fear, the "is it worth it?" question also arises because so many of the cases made with such effort do not end in convictions. Skolnick (1966), Blum and Osterloh (1966), and others have commented on the irritation—if not discouragement—that the officer feels when the courts deliver a different sort of justice than that which the arresting officer feels is appropriate. Not that a trial is the usual outcome, for in 18 out of 20 drug cases, the offenders pleaded guilty to, in many cases, a lesser charge. Only 14 percent of all Comfort's drug arrestees were found guilty as charged, 25 percent were dismissed or acquitted, and 20 percent were "carried over" or otherwise delayed for a year or more. No wonder that Burden complains about court inefficiency and leniency and admits to often being unhappy about how his hard work turns out.

Another powerful constraint on Burden is also related to the courts. The plea bargaining[7] and delays are only symptoms, for the problem is that the prosecutors and courts are so overwhelmed that they are ill-prepared to handle an increased rate of arrests. The district attorney, in our presence, asked Burden to "stop giving me anything but good drug cases for a while" and Burden later said, "I have to slow down and make more complete cases."

All these factors mean that, whatever the external pressures and even with the infusion of outside money for enforcement, a markedly increased arrest rate is uncertain. That being so, the number of busts is not the "name of the game." Burden cannot judge his competence on his "production" only, nor will his superiors, who also know conditions, rate him on production. Priorities that are and will be set should permit cases to be made at approximately the rate allowed by the system—Burden's time and doubts, his support capabilities, and the prosecutor's receptiveness. Priorities, of course, may not be set explicitly, (although sometimes, as in the case of the cutback of juvenile arrests, they are) but will emerge at each of the points of discretion at which Burden may elect to act.

Judging Competence

Competence in narcotics enforcement in Comfort is a matter of playing the game according to the local rules. Part of the "dirty game," as Burden calls it, is to maintain and expand the informer system, showing consideration when necessary in return for information (see Skolnick, 1966) and "pretending to like drug users I don't like" in order to keep relationships going. The game also includes bluff, threat, harassment, and old-fashioned hard work.

But it is not a numbers game; rather, payoff depends on how well Burden gets along in the department and with liaison personnel. Effective work is informal work—getting the five cars and ten men was not achieved through filling out forms in triplicate and sending them through channels. As with most other coordinated actions, it was done informally through phone calls and acquaint-

[7] For a dramatic account of the plea bargaining system in New York City see *Life* (March 12, 1971).

ance networks. A man who can get the system to work for him and who can work within it gets "brownie points." He must be willing to give and take, working with other detectives when they ask him to make a bust with them.

Since "work" is valued, he must show how busy he is; the overtime he puts in proves his dedication and initiative. He must conform to the general stance of the department, which we suspect is to the right of center; and he must, when necessary, know when *not* to enforce the law in order to avoid embarrassment. For example, interviews with others in the Comfort police department have led us to believe that marijuana use by officers is not unknown; nevertheless, whatever knowledge Burden had on that score was kept to himself and, when pressed, he parried the query. He is—as we believe most policemen are—a "good guy," genuinely so, and his superiors will measure him by his competency and not by his production of arrests, which are controlled by factors beyond his reach.

What satisfies colleagues and superiors might not satisfy the public or indeed the officer himself, as they, and he, think of what "is" compared with what "ought to be" in the control of narcotics. Perhaps in reaction to this deficiency, Burden and others may make more of what they accomplish than the facts warrant. Skolnick and others described how drugs seized from wholesalers are priced, when the newsmen ask, at high retail values. The narcotics agent does what the embezzler may do, he "kites" the value to get more out of it than was originally there. In doing so, he has a responsive, if not encouraging, partner in the newsman who knows that $10,000 worth of marijuana makes a better headline than a haul valued at $500—and also in the reader, who prefers his fables writ large.

Priorities in Enforcement

Since the law, duty, the public, and Burden's own moral as well as professional obligations require that there be enforcement, arrest actions involve problems about whom not to go after as much as those of getting evidence that will stand up in court if a bust is made. These choices may be viewed as ways of controlling work flow or as matters of practical politics, expenditure, or individual morals and emotions. They are probably all of these. The priorities, as they may be inferred from outcomes or statements, may be examined as a matter of an order of menace in drugs and their users or as a matter of the social rank of persons who are potential arrestees.

By drug. As best we can interpret Burden's remarks, priorities based on drugs used are set by a mix of beliefs about given drugs. These beliefs are related to the presumed seriousness of drug effects (dependency potential as measured by addiction and/or regularity of use, bizarre or unpredictable behavior, associated criminality, personality change, and the like), the amount of the drug available (the more there is, the greater the need to exert control), the number of users (if there is spread, then there must be counteraction to control spread), and the setting in which the drug is taken (use on a high school campus or on the streets requires action, use in the home does not). In 1970 and 1971, this mix of beliefs had led to a shift in stated priorities from marijuana to heroin and opium as these later had become more available, their use more obvious, the spread of use to adolescents noticeable by virtue of indiscretion—or informant penetration—and subsequent police observation. Heroin use is regarded as producing the most harm to the community because, says Burden, "Many addicts have to steal to support their habit. We don't care about "weekenders" who shoot up maybe $30, $40 worth occasionally but we do care about a guy with a $100 a week habit. He has to steal."

Burden believes that barbiturate addiction is worse for the individual, since dosages are purer and more powerful, with associated toxicity, and since someone coming down off reds can be in real trouble, that is, experiencing pain, convulsions, and even death. These drug effects are not believed to be associated with menace to the community; the barbiturate user is not so likely to engage in other criminality to support his habit, and therefore he is considered less of a menace. This addiction involves less nondrug criminality because barbiturates are cheap and their users are young. However, because reds are addictive, are increasingly available, are used indiscreetly, and are used by the young, they do rank second on the control priority list that Burden enunciates. He ranks amphetamines third on the target list and the hallucinogens—among which he includes marijuana—fourth. Marijuana can be ranked last now, according to Burden, because it does not compel regular use, does not create dependency and so need not interfere with conventional conduct.

By group. Priorities are also set according to the nature of the user, that is, his social characteristics. Adults are now given a higher priority in enforcement attention than are juveniles. Users who are likely to use publicly (that is, in indiscreet ways) are likely targets, as are those who engage in other criminality. The classification of people who steal to support their heroin habit has finer distinctions, based on Burden's estimation of the seriousness of the crimes they ordinarily engage in. In his book, the greatest threat to community comes from the armed robber who robs citizens (non-addicts); the next greatest menace is the robber who robs other addicts, followed in order by burglars, check and papermen (or "paper-hangers," those who write fraudulent checks), shoplifters, and petty larceny thieves. Since Burden is convinced that confrontation with risk of violence is greatest with robbers and burglars, he accords differing priorities for investigation and arrest of heroin users within the criminal group.

At the other end of the scale from those who harm the community are those who do, or may shortly be expected to, belong to it or "help" it. We asked Burden to translate his conception into what we call a scale of social worth. There emerge five categories—ranked mostly by occupation—from people who are very important to the community to those who are of no importance to it. Burden says of the former that they deserve "a little leeway." He conceives of the latter as "threats." In his Rank I, most important, Burden puts policemen, professional people (doctors, lawyers, college professors), and students in high school, college, and graduate school. His Rank II is comprised of businessmen, skilled workers, artists, and second-level professionals (veterinarians, pharmacists, nurses, store owners, craftsmen, journeymen, and the like). In Rank III he puts the great mass of clerical and less skilled folk, the petty bourgeoisie (officeworkers, salesmen, clerks, tailors, small farmers, and the like). Rank III includes a man out of a job who would like to work. Burden's Rank IV is limited to hippies who are "sponges" (not willing to work), a variety of drug users, and marijuana dealers. His Rank V contains all mainlining (intravenous-injection) users; all users of methamphetamine, heroin, and hallucinogens; and all drug dealers, excepting those who sell marijuana.

We see that Burden's order of social merit depends on education and occupational prestige for the first three classes and upon presumed drug effects and associated life styles for the bottom two ranks.

Other bases for classifying people bear on their priority for narcotics investigation and arrest. One is political, for political radicals are given high priority for investigation. Another is practical in terms of police work; informants who are delivering the goods are not to be arrested (see Skolnick, 1966, on this point). Indeed, an issue of contention exists between local enforcement departments and state and federal organizations because agents of the latter two tend to pick up users indiscriminately, including those who are working for local departments and deserve (require) protection as sources. Practicality also allows distinction among those in the Rank V group, for Burden says of hallucinogen users that they are unpredictable and undependable in contrast to the heroin addict who, because of his habit, can be counted on to show up when everything is set up for a buy that will be the basis for arrest. Consequently, Burden, who does not want to waste time and energy, prefers to concentrate on the dependable addict.

Within the Rank I group of worthy citizens who deserve "leeway," Burden is not indifferent to or unaware of distinctions among users, nor need he be inactive even if he may not arrest. He is likely, for example, to turn over information about suspects to such institutional authorities as school administrators, parents, and professional societies.

Practicality, in terms of responding to citizen pressure, may lead to temporary shifts in priorities or, if no shift is possible, to a quandary for Burden. He spoke of a spate of letters from angry parents of high school students, who were demanding that he do something about the Free University where, said the parents, their children had purchased drugs from "flagrantly open" dealers. Burden, who had been fully aware of the dealing, realized what the parents had failed to take into consideration, that is, arrests of the dealers on that campus would also require that high school and college student buyers (users) be arrested. He also felt that the Free

University, because it was educational, had social worth. In consequence, the protesting parents challenged his priority system by demanding that Rank I students be arrested and their institution "hassled"; it also challenged the family interests of those same parents—and of many others whose children would also be caught in the sweep. That the Free University allowed "outsiders" (hippies and others in his Ranks IV and V) to come freely to deal, further complicated affairs for Burden since the presence of nonstudents did in fact mix the priorities for investigation at the Free University. Implicit here is a "rule" we shall shortly examine, that of sanctuary.

Within Rank I there are physicians who do use drugs illicitly. When such information comes to Burden, he turns their names in to the State Bureau of Professional Vocational Standards, for handling and treatment within the in-group. Similarly, when he learns of a lawyer user he advises the bar association and takes no further action. His assumption in such actions goes beyond that of social worth to presume the capability of self-policing and self-help within professional groups concerned with their reputations, who, sharing Burden's standards of propriety (see Blum and Associates, 1972a, chapter 26 on pharmacists for a related discussion), are valuable as allies working in concert—and dangerous as enemies when crossed, as might occur if their valued members were arrested. ("I don't trust some of these lawyers; they can fix anything," remarked another officer who was working a case with Burden.) Burden distinguishes a class of "croaker doctors," who sell opiate and amphetamine prescriptions to users; he argues that they are older men "ready to die," otherwise they would not deviate so from the standards he and their colleagues have set for them. Such challenging violations (that is, drug-dealing) put the offenders in Burden's Rank V threat category. They are no longer simply users deserving "leeway"; they are no longer among the worthies of Rank I. Burden would like to arrest the croaker doctor but, he says, it is too difficult to make a case. He refers suspects to state agencies. Again we see that practicalities of time and money rearrange priorities.

Policemen are also Rank I; and their use of drugs, which Burden must suspect, also creates quandaries. According to others in the department, persistent users, who do not respond to admonition (self-policing), are dismissed quietly, for no scandals are desired. Detectives are particularly suspect since, in their work, they may well seize drugs in the course of other investigations. Some of them also have taken to keeping drugs in their offices to show to interested parents and others. We cannot say whether Burden resents this intrusion into his speciality; we are aware that there were signs of suspiciousness that such access and interest might be associated with experimentation. Burden would only reluctantly, we believe, "put the arm" on a fellow detective; and it would be most awkward if their position of privilege were to be abused by such indiscretion that their drug use came to Burden's attention.

Sanctuaries

The term *sanctuaries* implies that there are places of safety where law does not intrude, even though the police know what offense has been committed and where the offender can be found (see Lindesmith, 1965, for a related discussion). Considering the scale of social worth, we can say that persons who restrict themselves to using—as opposed to dealing—who use the low-risk drugs, and who maintain themselves in the worthy roles of Ranks I, II, and possibly III, will have a sanctuary. The term *sanctuary* also implies that both offenders and police agree on the rules of sanctuary. Consequently, if social worthies know and play by the rules, they and the police have agreed on a quiet contract for acceptable illegality, or tolerated "deviance."

Sanctuaries are not just occupational; they are institutional and geographical as well. Insofar as the occupation also has an institution and occupies a special place, its sanctuary is duplicated. We can suggest that drug users are the more immune from arrest the more duplication there is in their sanctuaries, that is, the more they can claim sanctuary based simultaneously on social worth, on institutional affiliation, and on separate locale. The on-campus college student enjoys all three and is, for all intents and purposes, immune from drug arrest either as user or dealer as long as he does not violate the rules, that is, as long as he does not fail to play "fair" or is not otherwise indiscreet. The high school student enjoys only social worth sanctuary; he has lesser degrees of institutional membership and protection (compared, say, to the medical society or the police department) and lesser geographical distinction (his campus is not so removed from daily life of the town as is the ordinary college campus). The physician who uses drugs at home also enjoys three sanctuaries; the police officer who uses at work enjoys only two but flagrantly violates the rules of the game by choosing the wrong locale—the police station instead of his home. Similarly, the college professor who violates his social-worth sanctuary by becoming simultaneously a "political radical" and visible as a drug proselytizer (as did Timothy Leary in his Harvard days) not only violates the condition of sanctuary but flaunts the violation in order to demand counteraction.

We can posit then that the sanctuary rule will work only as long as the user is aware that there is a set of rules and abides by them—which means that he is discreet and that neither neurosis, stupidity, nor drug effects interfere with his judgment and self-control. Indiscretion by definition becomes any act that breaks the sanctuary rules in such a way as to embarrass the police, that is, by making it clear that they are not doing their duty unless they investigate. Similarly, anyone who calls attention to the quiet contract breaks the rules by doing so, for the public or formal stance is that there is no such agreement. Witness the trouble that the angry parents visited upon Burden by demanding he arrest the dealers at the Free University. He could not tell them the terms of the quiet contract between the police and the Free University, for those parents, in their naïveté, expected a different set of rules—impossible rules that would require public police action against dealers who were dealing openly and that would at the same time protect their children who were openly buying from those dealers. His quandary was intensified because the Free University was also violating the rules, by letting outside dealers exploit the university's institutional sanctuary in a way that also violated the geographical sanctuary—children as outside buyers were allowed "on campus," were allowed to come to the building, thus making a "private" institution public.

Most of the constraints of the sanctuary are on the user; after all, he is the illicit chap, and communities require discretion of those who would be both respectable and illicit—be that in sex, gambling, income tax evasion, or drug use. However, the rules also apply to the police. That famous Sergeant Sunshine in San Francisco who insisted on inviting the press to watch him light a joint of grass on the Hall of Justice steps was an example of a two-headed man—being both police officer and drug user—who violated the rules for both sides. A clearer example comes from the university next to Comfort where, a few years ago, two unwitting and overly enterprising campus officers, passing by the open windows of an eating club, observed two undergraduates who were smoking marijuana. The policemen entered and made arrests. There was a campus outcry, with various law professors rushing to the defense and, we assume, quieter administrative directives to the police to refrain from future indiscretions. Till the time of this writing, at least, there had been no campus arrest, even though regular use of one or another illicit drug could be estimated with some assurance at about 40 percent. Students were observing the quiet rules; enjoying sanctuary. The police, it appeared, misconstrued the requirements of discretion about geography, not understanding that the students' lounge was the private territory of the university. We suspect that a host of examples of police indiscretion—and of their "punishment" for such indiscretion—might be found upon analyzing cases that were not prosecuted by district attorneys or were dismissed by judges.

Here let us call attention to the fact that many constitutional safeguards (that is, the safeguards arising from the Fourth Amendment) are designed to protect the sanctuary of a man's home, vehicle, and person from the literally "unwarranted" and procedurally unjust intrusion of the police. In these matters, the contract regarding sanctuaries is not a quiet one but public, writ strong in the Constitution, and based on a conception of the rules of the game derived from basic beliefs about the humanistic doctrine of the inviolable rights of man and the political danger that can be inherent in police activity. Many of the cases of "bad" police procedures that led to a spate of decisions protective of citizen rights during and since the Warren Court[8] developed from narcotics investigations. This situation demonstrates not only the oft-cited difficulties faced by the police in enforcing the criminal law in

[8] See, for example, *Miranda v. Arizona*, 384 U.S. 436, 1966.

areas of consensual crime, but also the fact that the police are bound by community rule that they shall not violate the various rules of sanctuary that govern the constitutional concept of citizen-police interaction; that is, they must not be indiscreet in reference to those rules. We would further note that, for all their notoriety, the police cases that come to court attention because of the use of unconstitutional procedures are few in number compared with all the cases investigated. Therefore, we can make two inferences: (1) Narcotics officers do in fact for the most part observe the public (that is, constitutional) rules in their investigations. (2) When they do not observe those rules, most such violations are not indiscreet; that is, either they do not come to attention, or, if they do, they occur in circumstances in which the cost to the accused may be greater if he complains than if he makes a deal.[9] In situations in which making a deal seems preferable, the quiet rule is still maintained; earlier indiscretions on the part of both parties are elements in the plea-bargaining negotiations.

Priorities in Action

Granting the existence of priorities and varying mixes of elements contributing to these priorities, we focus now on how they affect enforcement practices. There are three levels of enforcement practice: One is public policy as announced by the police department, another is informal policy as practiced by officers, and the third is spontaneous action as an officer approaches or is faced with a decision point in a case. For Burden's branch, official policy, for example, states that his mandate, in law enforcement, is to arrest dealers but, in peace-keeping, is to maintain surveillance and to control the addict community so that drug-related crimes and the spread of drugs are kept within bounds. Illustrations of informal policy include all those geared to priorities and sanctuaries: adults, but not juveniles; hippies, but not students; dealers, but not informants; and so on. These formal and informal policies influence the basic strategies employed; that is, what kinds of informants are sought; what kinds of information are bought; how informants are deployed; and what leads from citizens, seized dealers' records,

[9] *Life*, March 12, 1971.

neighborhood surveillance, and the like, are to be followed. Deployment of probes is essentially a matter of selecting a suspect population for investigation and may be considered as the selection of the unknown case. For the patrolman, the equivalent is his response to a complaint about a loud party when he has no reason to believe that the loud ones are also going to be found (or not found) to be using drugs. Obviously, the discretionary power of the investigator is considerably greater than that of the patrolmen in this stage; the officer must answer the call, whereas Burden decides in advance whether to work informants on the campus, in a street people's hangout, or wherever.

The second decision point is faced when there is a possible suspect. Burden gets information that X may be dealing or that Y's number is included on a telephone list found in a dealer's pad. Does he pursue the lead or not? At this stage, formal and informal policy must be linked to what he suspects, or knows, about X and Y or about the population of which X and Y are members. The patrolman faces a similar choice point when he sees a "furtive movement" by an occupant of a vehicle stopped for speeding or when he suspects he smells marijuana in the car.

Probably suspicion is the third choice point. There are suspicions about illicit sales by a 13-year-old youngster. What does Burden do? In this case, he did not go further than suspicion, since juvenile grass dealers have low priority. In another case, that of the demand of the irate parents to crack down on the dealers at the Free University, he acted, but as he would with the medical society. He told the Free University of his information, gave warning, and demanded that they clean house. The patrolman who observes a felony (for example, that there is marijuana in a car) has a similar choice. It is easier for the patrolman, since he may arrest for possession. Burden, however, is aiming at dealers; and, if he decides to pursue a case, he must at this point of "probable suspicion" begin the hard work of setting up the dealer so that the buy transaction engineered by Burden becomes evidence to be used in court.

A fourth decision point for Burden may occur when satisfactory evidence is in hand or can be had in hand. Ordinarily, this moment will not be one of choice since it results from a planned investigation that included setting up the offender for a buy. It may also occur by happenstance if Burden, in the course of an investigation, comes upon satisfactory evidence of dealing before he expected to do so or evidence that nails another nontarget offender. At this moment of arrest, a new set of priorities may well operate. Recall Burden's fear of violence? In a recent case, he had set up to buy from a Hell's Angel and was himself doing so but, contrary to plans, in the company of other Angels. He decided the risk to himself was too great to make the arrest at that time (the arrest was made later). In another case, an "on view" offense, he and another detective observed two young men, street people, smoking marijuana publicly; they would have made an arrest but for the fact that the offenders were in a group of their own. Caution dictated retreat. Burden noted the men and arrested them later when they were alone. In doing so, he revealed that his own formal priorities, set by the departmental mandate to arrest dealers before users, do not operate when there is an "on view" offense and when no sanctuaries exist to protect the offender. Also, Burden may not have been sure that his fellow officer shared his priorities; in such a situation, concern over criticism for nonenforcement from a man who might be a Crusader Rabbit (a gung-ho enforcement type) could have been a factor pushing Burden to followup. Perhaps pride, smarting from the frustration resulting from refusal to arrest because of fear, led to a compensatory insistence upon following up.

We shall not dwell on complications that arise, not from priorities, but from constitutional questions. We shall note, however, that the officer, Burden or a patrolman, may have evidence of drugs or drug-dealing that is practical but not admissible because of some "due process" violation. To illustrate, a Comfort patrolman arrested a Hell's Angel on a traffic charge. In the course of a frisk—which was undertaken on grounds that all Hell's Angels deserve to be frisked—a syringe kit and drugs were found. These could not be the basis for a drug charge unless some excuse for the search could be conceived. In conference with the district attorney, the patrolman and the DA decided that the syringe kit was about the size of a switchblade and would have appeared like one to the patrolman, and so in retrospect it became the reason for the frisk.

Such considerations are associated with the fifth decision point, at which Burden must decide whether the case can be made in court. "If there's the slightest doubt, we'll drop it." Here priorities may express themselves in the sentence recommended by Burden in his report or in conference with the district attorney. For instance, Burden recommended severe sentence for a dealer who had been known to be dealing heavily over a long period of time. In another case, the accused was the brother of a boy who had been disabled as the result of a bomb explosion and who was friendly with many officers; Burden asked for a light sentence out of consideration for the disabled boy and in hopes of rehabilitating his brother.

We have considered the priorities set by the department and by Burden and have noted that these apply primarily to investigational cases; patrolmen arrest when they witness the crime or when they investigate subsequent to such suspicious happenings as furtive movements, the odor of marijuana, the sight of drugs within—or being tossed from—a car, or intoxication.

Outcomes

If these priorities were in fact operational at all times, all Burden's investigative arrests should be of high-priority offenders, that is, those who are without sanctuaries; who are adult dealers in opiates, barbiturates, or amphetamines; who are not informants; about whom evidence that is admissible in court is gathered fairly easily; who may be political radicals; who are likely to be criminals and especially aggressive criminals; and who will be arrested in situations posing least danger to the lives of the arresting officers. In 1969, Burden initiated 32 arrests of record. Of the arrestees, 26 were 23 years old or younger, 5 were juveniles arrested in company of adults or on premises raided. Among adults, 23 were white, 21 were male, most had previous offenses that included nondrug crimes (burglary and theft foremost), most were not students, and all were in Rank III occupations; indeed, 19 of the 23 adults (only on adults do the records show background data) were unemployed and only one was a college graduate. Five were high school dropouts. Marijuana and hallucinogens were the primary drugs involved (19 of 23 cases) and 16 persons were arrested for sale or sale and possession as opposed to possession only.[10]

[10] We have not undertaken to go beyond the police blotters to learn

Given these statistics on arrests resulting from investigation (for the most recent year for which records were available), it is apparent that Burden's social-worth categories, by occupational prestige and employment, dovetail with actions taken, that is, except for students (four adult and five juveniles), no one from the more prestigeful Ranks I and II was arrested. No campus arrests were made, but homes were the arrest scene in 16 instances. Warrants have been issued in two cases in which the suspects "eloped." The priorities expressed both by policy and the menace of Ranks IV and V are not reflected in the data. Although marijuana and hallucinogens are said to be lower-priority drugs, they account for most of the cases; and, although dealers are supposed to be Burden's only targets, 8 cases of the 27 were for possession not for sale.

Among the variables affecting who gets arrested as opposed to who ought to get arrested if Burden's priorities were affecting action is an important one we have yet to mention except by implication. Serious dealers learn something about concealment and develop means for avoiding identification, informants, set-ups, and the rest. In our dealer data in *Dream Sellers* (Blum and Associates, 1972a), we characterized as "losers" those who were early in crime and early arrested; they had not learned the requisite skills. Presumably evasive skills of dealers as well as police priorities determine who gets caught. For example, successful psychedelic dealers among students were middle-class folk with good cover jobs or stories, and many avoided the hippie look that dominates among the mug shots of Burden's arrestees. We assume that these skillful dealers are harder for Burden to catch; and, given the time and costs involved, Burden is less likely to try. Indeed, the skilled dealers will be dealing in quantities and prices considerably higher than Burden's level of

---

about the arrested sample. We suspect that the younger ones would prove much like the drug-using delinquent type identified and validated by Stein, Sarbin, and Kulik (1971). These are described as coming from broken homes, running with delinquent gang companions, involved in school and other difficulties with the law, uninterested in the approval of the straight world, and enjoying delinquent rather than conventional morality. In the sample surveyed by Stein and colleagues, as for California juvenile arrestees in general, Mexican-Americans are overrepresented. This is not the case in Comfort where almost no Mexican-American population exists.

aspiration—or available buy money—so that Burden would, in any event, refer them to state or federal agents for investigation.

The other side of the skills coin has to do with Burden himself. He tells us he had only eight hours of formal training in narcotics investigation, plus some additional time spent working in coordinated cases with his superior. He has, he says, "picked things up by reading books"; and he has tried to learn by watching narcotics detectives from other jurisdictions. Burden would be the last to claim that he is well-trained for his job, although he is doing his best. He feels that his most valuable training derived from his involvement with juveniles and his experiences on the street. In consequence, the lack of formal training of Burden pitted against the greater cunning of his dealer prey might mean that whatever the priorities, it would be the naïve, the stupid, or the otherwise disadvantaged dealer who falls.

Who does fall? We have already given the statistics on overall arrests; the young and the unemployed predominate. And now we quote Burden himself: "The ones who get arrested are the stupid ones, the careless ones, the real abusers; the easy and the obvious are the ones we bust."

Comment

We have reviewed Comfort's enforcement campaign against drugs as conducted by its Uniform Division and by Burden, a skilled and insightful officer who is its one-man Narcotics and Dangerous Drug Branch. We have seen that the priorities set at explicit and implicit levels are complicated by practical considerations of what can be done and who comes into range. Given the characteristics of those who have been arrested in the Comfort campaign, there is little question that few or none among those with sanctuary are at risk. On the other hand, the evidence also shows that only a few of the high-priority targets are, in fact, caught at all, although some high-priority cases are referred to state and federal agencies. Most arrests are made among those who are not protected either by sanctuary or by practical considerations that deter arrest, such as the risk of violence or the inutility of evidence—nor are the arrests made among the highest priority targets. Thus the group at highest risk for local narcotics enforcement arrest are those who are the losers: visible deviants who act indiscreetly; who do stupid things publicly; who are not skilled enough to avoid detection; and who possibly possess personality, intellectual, and social deficits that contribute to their unfavored position in the straight or the psychedelic-dealing or the criminal opiate-dealing worlds.

We have not examined the operations of state or federal enforcement and so cannot say whether or not the big-time or clever dealers who do not fall to Burden do fall to these higher-echelon agencies. Our own dealer data suggest, on the basis of narcotics arrests, that many but not all of them do. At the local enforcement level, however, it is clear that the risk is to the indiscreet user; and, even then, it is only a minimal risk. Given our estimates of the prevalence of regular illicit use in and near Comfort compared with the annual incidence of narcotics arrests (and assuming that there are no rearrests), in 1969 about 13,000 persons were using illicitly and regularly and only 154 were arrested. That is a rate of about 12 per 1000 of user-dealers at risk of arrest for narcotics offenses by local enforcement.[11]

Summary

Constraints, priorities, and practical considerations that limit and set investigation and arrest targets among drug user-dealers in one middle-class town were examined. Taxpayer priorities, and available funds, limit police capabilities; and social status, institutional affiliation, and geographical or other physical insulation protect illicit user-dealers. We suggest that the concept of sanctuary will be useful, not only in predicting who is immune to arrest, but also in helping to define discretion, for both the police and the illicit user-dealer. Other factors that apparently affect the risk of arrest on narcotics charges include political stance, friendship patterns vis-à-vis the police, community flap potential, and informant status. In addition, the user-dealer who has a potential for violence or is in a group with that potential, as perceived by the police, is initially protected. Similarly, the skill of the illicit user-dealer in con-

---

[11] We can see why serious dealers rated local drug enforcement as ineffectual compared with state and federal endeavors.

çealment operates to protect, whereas user dependability in terms of an addiction that enables the police to predict buying habits may—according to the police—increase risk of arrest. Another set of variables that affect priorities for arrest have to do with police estimates of the danger of the drug used and of associated criminality and their obligation to act to interdict drugs believed to be "spreading" to younger population segments. The skill of the officer may also affect the practical outcome of cases as does the element of "accident" or at least an associated misfortune or delinquency that results in an arrest because patrol officers become aware—"on view"—of a narcotics violation without previous knowledge or investigation of that offense.

For all the priority considerations, the actual outcome of investigations shows that priorities are rarely operative in the sense that the most sought-after targets are in fact arrested. Priorities do operate, in that protected or immune populations are not arrested. On the basis of these findings, we suggest that the nonimmune non-high-priority user-dealer is at greatest risk of arrest from local enforcement. That person appears to be visibly hippie, a marijuana or hallucinogen user, indiscreet, unemployed, young, male. Possibly he suffers intellectual and/or personality deficits that could account for his occupying neither a protected position in the straight world nor a protected or successful middle-class one among psychedelic dealers or the criminal opiate-using lower-class dealers. In any event, the risks of arrest by local law enforcement are low; we estimate that, in the area studied, for regular users of any illicit drug the prevalence of arrest relative to use, annually, was on the order of 12 per 1000. We cannot say what added risks are incurred for the successful dealers by the practice of referring bigger cases to state or federal agencies for investigation. On the basis of our earlier dealer data (Blum and Associates, 1972a), given the reported rate of narcotics arrest and dealers' own evaluations of enforcement competence even for successful dealers, apparently higher-echelon agencies with their larger resources will be more effective than local ones in arresting dealers.

7

The Narcotics Law in Action: A Major City

Richard H. Blum, Terence Egan

Gertrude Stein, speaking of it, complained, "There is no there there." Its Convention Bureau would take a more laudatory view. For our purposes, the city—let us call it Steinville after that famous daughter—was an excellent one, for it offered an opportunity to work with its cooperative and modern police department to observe the action of local law enforcement vis-à-vis the drug scene.

The city has a population of more than 360,000, 34 percent of whom are black. It is an industrial center and busy port, and it has its share of fine residential districts and of poverty areas. It also has its share of illicit drug users and dealers for, as any San Fran-

139

cisco Bay Area urban center must be, it is part of the California drug scene.

Our interests in drug law enforcement in Steinville were not, as with Skolnick (1966), an intensive study of process or, as with Wilson (1968), management. We simply wanted to know who was arrested on drug charges, what the circumstances of their arrests were, how they were dealt with, and how those arrested compared with the estimated "real" population of regular drug users who constituted the reservoir from which dealers are drawn. Our methods were also considerably simpler than those of the other scholarly observers who worked more intensively with Steinville's police. We chose a month in 1969 (November) and examined available statistics for that month. We spent a year talking to officers about those statistics. With the help of the chief and the narcotics bureau we gathered additional data. Then we made some estimates and some leaps of inference, and we finally arrived at certain conclusions about what local law enforcement accomplishes in the drug scene and what issues arise in consequence.

Among the persons who were arrested in Steinville in November of 1969 were 210 whose major offense was some violation of laws against narcotics and dangerous drugs.[1] The arrest record and identification file of each of these 210 arrestees was subsequently followed through July of 1971. To be sure that November was not unusual, we compared it with its eleven calendarian fellows; it was not different from other months in that year with regard to the number and types of crimes committed.

Who was arrested? Mostly minority group members (61 percent). Fifty-three percent were black. Men were also predominant, constituting 88 percent of all those arrested. Young people rather than old were arrested, for 86 percent were 29 years or under, with 52 percent between 21 and 29. These drug-arrest statistics, compared with those for Steinville's November arrests for all other offenses, indicate that the only major difference is that drug arrestees are more often male. The city's drug arrestees, compared with California state arrest statistics for the year, are found

---

[1] There were 71 additional arrests for which narcotics charges were filed, making a total of 281. However, in each of these cases the drug charge was deemed subordinate to another, probably more serious, crime and was not filed or coded as a drug arrest.

to include more juveniles (34 percent to 28 percent), more males (88 percent to 82 percent), and more minorities (61 percent to 27 percent) and particularly more blacks (53 percent to 16 percent). However, Steinville has considerably higher concentrations of blacks (34 percent) than the state as a whole (7 percent), and when we compared ratio of blacks arrested to the black population we found that for the state the narcotics arrest rate is 0.013 percent and for Steinville 0.012 percent—an inconsequential difference. About 40 percent of the city's drug arrestees indicated that they were employed, 20 percent were unemployed, 14 percent were students, the remainder did not say. Almost all listed working-class occupations, with "laborer" first, "factory worker" second, and specific trades following. Only a very few could be considered white-collar or professional workers, for example, one social worker and one modest chap who listed himself as President.

Arrests for drug offenses were made by three police divisions: the patrol squad, the vice squad (vice includes narcotics offenses), and the Community Relations and Youth Unit.[2] Among these, 80 percent of all arrests were "on view" patrol arrests, 13 percent were vice arrests, and 7 percent were juvenile arrests. We do note that patrol arrests include those made by other police agents ranging from guards in the jail to highway patrolmen booking arrestees in the city. What is immediately apparent is that planned arrests, following investigation of the sort necessary to interdict dealing, occur rarely. Most violators are apprehended accidentally by patrolmen.

Arrests by Patrol Squad

When we examine the particular circumstances of the 168 patrol (or other police agent) arrests, we find that these fall into six major categories, as shown in Table 7-1.

[2] NOTE: Among the 210 cases that were followed, nearly two years after arrest 38 had no disposition on file with the Police Department. Of these, 22 were juvenile cases in which the official disposition would be "referred to juvenile court." It is not likely that the conviction rate would be significantly higher or lower for these cases. Another dozen apparently are record-keeping failures, that is the identification file number that was written on the arrest record did not correspond with the file of the suspect who had committed the crime. The remaining four cases may not yet have been disposed.

Table 7-1

CATEGORIES OF DRUG ARRESTS BY PATROL SQUAD,
STEINVILLE, NOVEMBER 1969

	Number	Percent of total sample (N = 210)
Arrests related to traffic or motor vehicles	70	33
Arrests subsequent to investigation of suspicious conduct	46	22
Arrests subsequent to investigation of suspicious person	9	4
Arrests made in the course of investigating nondrug crimes	19	10
Arrests made subsequent to a citizen's complaint	13	6
Miscellaneous	11	5

Of the 70 arrests that were related to traffic or motor vehicles, 31 were made subsequent to a moving violation; 22, subsequent to a patrolman's observation of a mechanical or legal deficiency in a vehicle; 9, subsequent to investigation of a suspicious vehicle (that is, a vehicle that may have been stolen or used in a recent crime); 3, subsequent to investigation of a vehicle with outstanding warrants; 2, subsequent to a patrolman's observation of furtive behavior of the vehicle's occupants; and 3, subsequent to a patrolman's observation of drug use in a vehicle.

Mechanical or legal deficiencies in a vehicle included one instance of no red cover on a rear light, two of mutilated registration tabs, and three of nonfunctioning license-plate lights. Moving violations included, as one might expect, ignored stop signs and reckless lane-changing maneuvers.

An officer's observation of a "furtive move" can range from watching the suspects stuffing some substance into their mouths as he approaches to noticing nervousness or apprehensive glances from another vehicle. Of course, something odd or suspicious about the vehicle or its occupants must first attract his attention, since any movement or gesture, in a suspicious context, might be interpreted as "furtive." If the circumstances and the observations of the police indicate that some criminal activity may be in process, the officer then has the right to search the occupants of the vehicle. The exact nature of the furtive move has caused much controversy in the courts.

Of the 46 arrests made subsequent to investigation of suspicious conduct, 10 involved violent or unruly behavior in a public place; 18 involved suspected intoxication (staggering or unconsciousness) in a public place; 3 involved furtive moves; 2 involved officers' observation of use of drugs in public; 6 involved officers' observation of handling or selling of drugs; 1 involved association with a suspected intoxicated person; and 6 involved drinking in public.

Those observed drinking in public were usually charged with a drug offense when the arresting officer found drugs on their persons as he searched them incidentally to arrest for public drunkenness. Occurrences of violent or unruly behavior ranged from arguments or fights with family or friends under the influence of drugs to, in one case, a boy who had been inhaling spray paint, screaming, and yelling for hours in a church yard. The two who were observed using drugs in public were two school boys who were seen walking down the street smoking marijuana. The suspect who came to the attention of the police by being associated with an intoxicated person was a man seen in an alleyway, bending over the body of an unconscious friend. He was searched and arrested for possession of restricted drugs. Many suspects were observed staggering or obviously intoxicated in public, and four were found unconscious. One of these had passed out in his seat in a theater, and another was in the gallery of the superior court.

It is evident that violations of the vehicle code give the patrol-car and motorcycle officers considerable opportunities for contact with citizens from which drug arrests can arise. In this mechanized era, police contact with pedestrians may be less common, at least at the same level of scrutiny as after a vehicle stop.[3]

[3] Virtually the entire patrol force is deployed in vehicles. A few walking policemen are regularly assigned to patrol one area in which there

If, when passing a pedestrian on foot or by car, an officer does observe something amiss that leads him to suspect drugs, he may ask the citizen to take a street sobriety test,[4] which is a series of "clinical observations" including standing on one foot and walking a straight line. If these confirm the suspicion by showing coordination failures, the suspect is brought in and given blood tests. If intoxication is determined, arrest may follow. Such arrests are, probably by virtue of this "testing," more solid, as measured in terms of convictions, for among subjects so arrested 41 percent were convicted as compared with a conviction rate of 30 percent overall in the sample.

Nine arrests were made subsequent to the investigation of suspicious persons. A suspicious person, in this context, is someone who, by his nature or situation, or by information previously known about him, attracts the attention of the police. Such a person need not be seen doing something that appears to be illegal. The circumstances of initial contact in the 9 cases that fall under this category included street search for "youthful appearance" (3); questioning and search for making a "field contact report" (2); offender answering the description of a suspect in a recent crime (2); offender (a known drug user) observed loitering (1); and offender among a group of loitering blacks (1).

Three suspects searched because of their "youthful appearance" were young black males, who were seen walking out of a used-car lot late one evening. They were found in possession of three matchboxes of marijuana, 44 reds, and $34 in cash. Charged with

---

are many bars and in which there are often many people late at night. Some officers patrol the downtown shopping districts during the daytime, when there are large numbers of people on the street, according to the one supervisor, who could not cite foot-patrol deployment figures except to say "there weren't very many; these men are just there to keep people happy and feeling safe." Intersection traffic duty is undertaken only during holidays and other emergencies. There are no personnel regularly assigned to this. We see almost total mechanization.

    [4] The arresting officer cannot by law compel a suspect to take a street sobriety test. It requires the agreement of the suspect. If the suspect seems intoxicated, but refuses to take the test, the officer can arrest him anyway. If he refuses the test and the officer is uncertain about his inebriation, the officer may let him go. A vehicle driver can lose his license by refusing to submit to a blood test, urine test, or breathalyzer, but the pedestrian has nothing to lose by refusing any of these. An arrested pedestrian may request such a test to prove that he *is* sober, but he must pay for it himself.

possession of marijuana and dangerous drugs for sale, they were later convicted.

A "field contact report" is a routine form made out on persons who are observed loitering, or otherwise "up to no good," so that, in the event that a crime is later committed in that vicinity, the police will know that such persons were nearby. It is seen as a good method of contacting people who fall just short of the basis for being arrested. The two persons listed under this heading were approached by the arresting officers with this in mind, but they either refused to cooperate or made secretive gestures on the officer's approach. One suspect was released because of insufficient evidence, and the other was later convicted.

The known drug user who was observed loitering was arrested at a drive-in restaurant, where in fact he had been arrested the night before. He claimed that he was an undercover agent in the employ of another branch of the department, but he was convicted of burglary.

These arrests on suspicion can be delicate from the constitutional standpoint and do require careful exercise of discretion on the part of the officer. That this is exercised may be deduced from the conviction rate of 44 percent in this category. From the standpoint of narcotics law enforcement, we can see that these are all situations in which the suspect placed himself in jeopardy by unusual behavior or visibility that, when noticed by the police, led to an arrest in the course of which a drug violation was determined.

Thirteen arrests were made subsequent to citizen's complaints. In seven of these, the complainant was a relative or close acquaintance. These include wives, mothers, sisters, girl friends, or a girl friend's mother, and, in only one case, a male relative, a father. Complainants, apparently not knowing the suspect, refused to identify themselves in five cases; in the sixth a pharmacist called the police. These arrests are an exception to the "rule" that drug arrests are crimes without complainants (or victims, as the case may be). Even so, following arrest, prosecution is more difficult since family members appear less likely to press charges or appear in court. Among our seven cases, convictions were obtained in four. The other aspect of these complaints is implied in the sex of the relatives; women, not men, complain about the drug use or drug conduct of their relatives who were, without exception, all males. One wonders if this occurs because women are unable to handle the drug-using relative and thus rely on the police to intervene, whether they are more likely to sit in moral judgment to deliver a punitive sentence—to be exercised by the police they call, or whether the drug use of a male relative or acquaintance is a hook upon which a woman may hang a male at whom she is annoyed for other reasons. It is an intriguing question.

The city's police claim that they follow any lead that promises to uncover illicit drug user-dealers. Anonymous phone calls are followed up on the principle that these are not low-yield or crank reports. Vice-squad personnel comment that such anonymous calls can come from drug dealers intent on eliminating competition legally. The squad counts on rivalry of dealers or exasperated buyers who have been burned (cheated) to yield leads as much as their own paid informants do. The squad also recognize that anonymous calls may come from citizens with legitimate complaints who fear involvement or retaliation. Informants are, of course, often used in Steinville. Skolnick (1966) described the complexity of their employment. Discussions with officers indicated that they had some concern about the use of informants as part of the parcel of "dirty tricks" but that "there is no need to call on higher moral standards in handling narcotics dealers than those dealers use with each other." Officers noted that certain "sophisticated" elements of society looked down on "turning out" informants from among those just arrested or just paroled and in jeopardy of revocation. It was apparent that this "sophisticated" morality contradicted the pragmatic moral position of vice-squad officers who would hold that it does not "break the rules" to set one criminal against another. One captain said emotionally, "There is *no other way* to uncover information about drug use and drug dealing than working with undercover agents and turned-out informants. I object to accusations of police immorality about this. Those who do the accusing from their ivory towers don't themselves have to deal with the criminal's moral code."

In Steinville in November 1969, 19 arrests were made for narcotics violations of which the police became aware while investigating other crimes, which included suspected of receiving of stolen property (4); suspected burglary (7); suspected trespassing in a condemned building (3); suspected shoplifting (3); and suspected desertion from the armed forces (2).

Much more often than not, in making the 210 drug arrests during our sample month, the investigating officers had no reason to believe that drug crimes were involved as they initiated arrest proceedings. This includes the warranted arrests and all arrests made by the Vice Control Section. That some other suspicious activity, or past offense, does lead to a drug charge suggests linkages among criminality, suspicious conduct, and drug use. Put another way, one may say that persons who are delinquent, indiscreet, careless in driving, or otherwise incongruous enough to attract public complaint and police attention are also inclined to be drug offenders. If we examine the 210 who do constitute our drug arrest cases, we find that less than one-fifth did not have a record of prior non-drug offenses in their city police records. Conversely, one could argue that the use of drugs leads to such conduct, the investigation of which by the police uncovers drug violations. Other data on the criminality of drug users—or the drug use of criminals—supports such an association, as for example Ball and Chambers (1970) and our own findings in Blum and Associates (1972a). At this point we do, however, note two things: one is that only 8 percent of all the November arrests made in Steinville led to any finding of a drug violation (this includes our 210 base cases plus the 71 additional ones for which narcotic charges were filed but dropped as subordinate to more serious crimes). Second, that no drug charge was filed in the remaining 92 percent of all arrests does not allow the conclusion that any given suspect was not a drug user or dealer, for the test of a charge upon arrest is direct evidence, whereas the test of being a user or dealer is, for us, a self-report. Consequently, we do not know what percent of all offenders had, in fact, engaged in illicit drug conduct.

Vice Control Section Operations

In Steinville, the six officers who are chiefly responsible for narcotics investigations are part of the Vice Control Section. Constituting less than 1 percent of the department's active officers, these six are the only members of the force whose job it is to *seek out* suspects involved in drug crimes. Their stated policy is to concentrate their attention only on "the most dangerous narcotics criminals"; this means drug dealers. To be effective, the officers institute priorities. High on their present list of priorities are (1) bulk dealers of what the officers hold to be the most dangerous drugs (heroin, methamphetamine, and the like.) Lower in priority, but not unimportant are (2) the dealers in less dangerous substances, like marijuana and LSD. Of lesser interest are (3) smaller dealers in any of these drugs; that is, the lower echelons of the marketing pyramid where very little profit is made. The officers recognize that most of the dealers at lower levels are likely to be users as well. They hold that upper-echelon dealers are not so likely to be users. Although not high in priority, a user found committing a drug violation will be arrested unless to do that would "blow the cover" of officers working under cover or unless the user is himself working under cover as an informant.

The Vice Control Section was responsible for 27 (13 percent) of the 210 November arrests. Of the 27 arrested persons, 18 were dealers and 14 were charged with dealing (and possibly other offenses). Among the 14 prosecuted for dealing, 6 were convicted. Of those convicted, 4 served time and 2 paid fines. We may look at these outcomes several ways. We may say that only one-third of all dealers known as such to the police were actually convicted. Conversely we may say that 100 percent of the persons proven to be dealers in the courts "paid for their crime" by fines or imprisonment. This is in contrast to 59 percent in the total sample of disposed drug arrests who were, upon conviction ($N = 40$), "let off" with probation, agency referral, or some other nonpunitive action. The overall rate of conviction for prosecutions on arrest by the vice squad is slightly less than that for drug arrests by the patrol or juvenile divisions—22 percent (or 33 percent if we include only cases of records disposed after nearly two years) compared with 40 percent conviction of the patrol/juvenile drug arrests. Since most vice squad arrests were by warrant (19 of 27) as compared with few if any by warrant in the case of patrol/juvenile drug arrests, one must conclude that warranted arrests—that is, planned arrests following investigation and allowing an officer legally to search the house of a suspect—do not provide better evidence, as measured by convictions, than do the "on view" arrests by noninvestigation officers. One may, on the other hand, assume that the work of the vice squad with its dealer priorities is the more difficult, for two-thirds of their arrests were of dealers (although only half resulted in charges of illegal supplying) as contrasted with 20 percent of all other arrests that led to a dealing charge.

If we measure effectiveness of the vice squad by pitting priorities against outcomes, we could conclude 50 percent effectiveness on the basis of dealing charges over total arrests. Measured in terms of types of drugs or amounts involved, three-fourths of the cases involved hard drugs or large quantities[5] of hallucinogens or cannabis. Using convictions, 6 of the 27 arrested were convicted.

Types of Evidence

Material evidence was listed in 174 (83 percent) of the 210 cases. "Nonmaterial evidence" that might have led to some arrests included needle marks on the arrested offender's body or perhaps failure to pass the street sobriety test.

47 cases (22 percent) involved evidence of approximately 1 ounce of marijuana or less.

26 cases (12 percent) involved evidence of fewer than ten pills or capsules.

21 cases (10 percent) involved more than 1 ounce of marijuana.

36 cases (17 percent) involved more than ten pills or capsules.

35 cases (17 percent) involved quantities of some hard drug (any drug of the opiate or methamphetamine class or, for our purposes, any substance found in powder, crystal, or liquid form, which the police might believe to be a hard drug).

12 cases (6 percent) involved paraphernalia only.

61 cases (29 percent) implied some use of hard drugs on the part of the suspect (evidence here includes quantities of suspected hard drugs in powder, crystal, or liquid form, needle marks, or paraphernalia for the preparation or injection of such drugs).

1 case (0.4 percent) involved two forged prescription slips.

[5] Defined as ten or more pills or capsules, more than 1 ounce of marijuana, or several doses of some other narcotic substances.

1 case (0.4 percent) involved a bottle of pills with a prescription label.

2 cases (0.9 percent) involved smoking pipes, in which it was suspected that marijuana or hashish had been smoked.

Among the 36 cases for which there was no material evidence, the following nonmaterial evidence was offered:

5 offenders (2 percent) were arrested for needle marks only.

8 offenders (4 percent) failed to pass the street sobriety test.

2 offenders (0.9 percent) were arrested for needle marks and for failure to pass the street sobriety test.

2 offenders (0.9 percent) were arrested on their own admission of having taken drugs. (They were both escapees from the Nevada State Mental Hospital.)

5 offenders (2 percent) were arrested subsequent to the arresting officer's observation of their strange behavior.

The greatest amount of illicit drugs found in possession of— or in a sale transaction with—any suspect was 21 balloons of heroin. For the most part, drugs are found but not in large quantities. From this we conclude that, from the standpoint of evidence, Steinville's police do not appear to be interdicting major traffickers.

Dispositions for Dealers

If the amount of evidence cited in the arrest reports, as well as the arresting officer's account of the circumstances of each arrest are assumed to be accurate, we can make a rough estimate of the number of dealers arrested by combining the number of suspects who were actually observed selling drugs with the number of suspects caught holding more drugs than they were likely to be using immediately for themselves,[6] or who had quantities of drugs packaged in such a way that the inference of intent to sell is reasonable (for example, wrapped in small tinfoil or cellophane packets). There were 11 suspects observed dealing by the arresting officer or

---

[6] This amount was set arbitrarily at ten or more pills or capsules, more than 1 ounce of marijuana, or several doses of some other narcotic substances.

another police agent; 54 suspects were apprehended holding large quantities of drugs, or drugs especially packaged, making a total of 65.

Fifty-seven suspects, or 27 percent of the total sample, were actually charged with possession of drugs for sale or another dealing-related charge. Perhaps leniency on the part of the arresting officer accounts for the discrepancy in charging people for dealing (a crime that is always a felony). On the other hand, most officers stated that they ordinarily charge a drug suspect with as many offenses as can be applied, in hopes of convicting him or, alternatively, of being able to use the weight of these multiple charges to elicit a confession or to bargain for information leading to the arrest of others who may be involved. Turning out informants can be one goal of the "bargaining" process by the arresting officers prior to arraignment.

The penalties handed down to those suspected of dealing, even when compared with those for the rest of the sample, were not heavy. The following breakdown does not include 38 members (18 percent) of the total sample whose dispositions were not available. Most of these 38 were juveniles, whose cases had been referred to the county's juvenile court, with the results not recorded with Steinville's identification section. Some other cases had not yet been disposed. We assumed that 65 suspects of the total sample were dealers (on evidence only—not self-report); and, for 50 of these, records of dispositions were available.

38 (76 percent) were charged with sale of drugs or possession for sale as one of the charges.

22 (44 percent) of these probable dealers were convicted.

13 (26 percent) were fined or sent to prison.

9 (18 percent) were convicted, but were given suspended sentence or probation.

28 (56 percent) were dismissed, released, or otherwise not convicted as of July 1971.

Of the 122 suspects assumed to be nondealers (again, on evidence only, not self-report):

15 (12 percent) were fined or sent to prison.

46 (38 percent) were convicted.

*31 (25 percent) were convicted but given probation or suspended
   sentence.*
*76 (62 percent) were dismissed, released, or otherwise not con-
   victed as of July 1971.*

We find that those charged with drug-dealing are more than
twice as likely to be fined or imprisoned than are other drug-law
violators. Most of the prison sentences ranged from 30 to 90 days.
The longest, one year, was given to an unemployed heroin addict,
who was arrested on a warrant by members of the Vice Control
Section.

Risk of Arrest

The question arises: Is the risk of a drug arrest in Steinville
the same for each sector of the population? The answer is No. Recall
that blacks constitute 34 percent of the city's population but account for 53 percent of the arrests. Males are 48 percent of the
population but contribute 88 percent of the arrests. Adolescents 16
to 20 are 4 percent of Steinville's citizenry but provide 27 percent
of all drug arrests; the United States census age categories 21 to 34
are 11 percent but the police-arrest age category 21 to 29 contributes 46 percent of the cases. The young black male is obviously the
high-risk citizen in Steinville as far as drug arrests are concerned.

Is the young black male also the drug delinquent? That is,
do arrest rates fairly reflect the actual rate of drug offenses in the
real population? If so, then law enforcement is efficient, justice is
equitable, and the canons of democracy are served. Otherwise—

There are no survey data from Steinville that tell us who
among its citizens most often violates drug laws, whether as users or
dealers or both. There are, however, several studies of drug use and
dealing in the San Francisco Bay Area and, in addition, some data
are available on drug use by urban blacks. We shall extrapolate
from these sets of data to estimate the likely prevalence of regular
drug-law violations among Steinville's various population sectors,
a procedure that will allow us at least to guess whether or not narcotics law enforcement as conducted by a modern and fair-minded
force in an ordinary American city does in fact operate equitably.

One pilot study of normal population drug use in the Bay Area (Blum and Associates, 1969a) was conducted in 1966 and 1967, a period characterized by notably less drug use than later years (at least among younger users). At that time, 17 percent of the quota sample interviewed admitted to one-time or more illicit-exotic[7] drug use. The majority of illicit-exotic users were young, had some college education, and earned incomes of less than $10,000 per year. Ninety-seven percent were white. The illicit-exotic sample was heavily weighted with students. We recognize the several mismatches in the two groups—neighboring cities rather than the same cities, different years, the exotic-drug classification including some not yet illicit, sampling inadequacies in the pilot study, and so on. Nevertheless, we may note that, within groups identified as drug-law violators, the differences are so considerable on the two variables of race (3 percent in the study, 53 percent in Steinville arrests) and student status (36 percent and 14 percent) as to suggest that Steinville's narcotic enforcement may be hitting blacks more than whites and the working class and unemployed more than students or middle- or upper-class people.

A larger and more recent survey concentrated on marijuana and LSD use in neighboring San Francisco. Manheimer, Mellinger, and Balter (1969) found that 13 percent of the adults admitted one-time or more marijuana use and 3 percent admitted LSD use and that marijuana use was greater among men and younger people (under 30)—indeed, half of the 18- to 24-year-old men had used marijuana as had one-third of the women. Young black and white males did not differ in their marijuana use rates, but white women more than black women were users; older black males did have greater use rates than older whites. Were we to extrapolate, we would expect in Steinville that marijuana offenders would be concentrated in young males. Racial differences would be slight.

A third survey was done in a nearby county. Included in the sample were commuters working in Steinville. This household survey of persons over 18, conducted in 1969, found that 12 percent of the population had taken marijuana and 2 percent LSD. As in San Francisco, young people were the greatest users of these illicit

[7] Exotic drugs embraced LSD, glue-sniffing, and the like, which prior to that time had not been illicit to use in California.

drugs. Data on regularity of use show that experimental use occurs most often among women but that half of the women and two-thirds of the men were moderate or heavy users.

Additional data come from high school and college surveys in the Bay Area (San Mateo County School Study, 1968 to 1971; Blum and Associates, 1969b; Garfield and others, 1971; Garfield and Garfield, 1972), all of which show that the majority of students in high school and college have used drugs illicitly and that an estimated two-thirds use one illicit drug, marijuana, regularly. These are, because of the predominance of whites in the Bay Area, mostly white students. Observational data are offered by Carey (1968) on the street people who live adjacent to or in Steinville. Carey estimates that between 15,000 to 25,000 such folk are heavily involved in use. Yet another study (Blumer and others, 1967), conducted in Steinville itself, demonstrates the heavy utilization of illicit drugs among some youth, differentiating kinds of use and attitudes in relationship to social variables.

If we add to these Bay Area data the Robins and Murphy (1967) study in St. Louis, which focused on urban black males (about whom drug-use observations are to be found in Chein and others, 1964; Finestone, 1960; Ball and Chambers, 1970), we learn that the youthful urban male black does engage in considerable illicit drug use. Consequently, any city with a black population is likely to have a large pool of user-dealers that can be a police target. In Robin's sample, for example, half of the male blacks admitted to illicit use, although only 13 percent had ever been arrested for any drug-law violation.

This concentration of illicit use among young blacks does not, however, exceed the prevalence of illicit drug use as found among young whites in the various Bay Area studies; half of the San Francisco young white males also admit to illicit use; white women more than black women appear to be users; and, though the unemployed may be greater users than their student age peers, both groups report considerable illicit experience. If we add our own data on drug dealers sampled within the Bay Area (Blum and Associates, 1972a, 1972b), we learn that these more serious drug violations occur almost without any significant racial differences, although the styles of drug traffic and the substances sold and used may be linked to race in particular locales. Using dealer data from our various school studies, we achieve a remarkably constant estimate of 7 percent of junior and senior high school and college students engaged in illicit traffic. These are almost entirely males. Within schools for which we have racial data, there is no evidence that blacks deal more than whites.

What does this hodge-podge of findings—all of them remarkably consistent for one Bay Area city compared with another—suggest as we compare it with Steinville narcotics arrests? It suggests that young people do use drugs more than older ones and that they are arrested in due proportion for that. However, we suspect the arrests are concentrated more heavily among older youth, that is, 21 and over, compared with our estimate for actual use among especially early and mid-teen-agers. It is evident, we believe, that the risk of arrest for narcotics offenses does not reflect the prevalence of illicit use experience nor does it reflect, as best we can estimate and extrapolate, the frequency of illicit use. If that be so, certain discrepancies between drug arrests in Steinville and actual drug-law violations in that community call for explanations.

At this point, we can only speculate. One might invoke the notion of priorities, remembering that the vice squad aims to get dealers and wants to concentrate on hard drugs and on those trafficking in large quantities of any drug. Yet most arrests are made by the patrol division, not by the vice squad; and, overall, dealers are a minority of those arrested. It is likely that, before 1969 (see Ball and Chambers, 1970), as contrasted to 1970 (see Bentel and Smith, 1971), black users were much more likely to have been involved in hard drugs, which were a priority target for the vice squad and—perhaps by a ripple effect—for other divisions as well. Were that the case, then a portion of the discrepancy between being a drug-law violator and being at risk of arrest would be a function of the kind of drugs one used, that is, hard drugs as compared with others. Indeed, review of the cases shows that 46 percent were suspected of "hard" drug use (our term); Steinville's police are not in agreement among themselves on drug dangers. We surmise that heroin and amphetamines are ranked as most dangerous. However, the vice squad captain does not approve either of the priority system or of a hard/soft, dangerous/less dangerous classification. Presumably that would do violence to the requirements under the law that all illicit drug users-dealers be police targets. The priorities in fact are functional, representing beliefs, policies, capabilities, and trade-offs. This 46 percent is far greater than the expected prevalence for opiate and amphetamine use among all illicit users; for instance, overall levels of 2 percent for lifetime illicit heroin use were obtained in our normal population and student studies in the Bay Area. Illicit amphetamine use rates in these same populations were 17 percent.

It has already been observed that most of those arrested for drug offenses were not suspected primarily of drug offenses at the time of investigation or arrest. They were suspected of vehicle violations and/or criminality. After apprehension, they were found to be drug violators, and examination of their police records reveals that 80 percent were previous offenders (narcotics and/or other offenses).

This very high rate of previous offenses among a sample most of whom were arrested accidentally for drugs suggests that a very special population—chronically delinquent—in Steinville act in such a way as repeatedly to draw police attention and, subsequent to that, booking. The record of "priors" also shows a correlation between drug offenses and nondrug crimes of the same sort seen in our other dealer data, especially the group we referred to as "criminal" dealers (Blum and Associates, 1972a). Those "criminal" dealers tended to have lower-class backgrounds, parents with criminal histories, little schooling, and the like. Yet even among well-to-do youth there is the same trend for drug use to be associated with other delinquency; that is, nonusers are less delinquent (Garfield and Garfield, 1972).

If these arrests represent an accurate reflection of "real" crime committed, we can conclude that in Steinville much of the vulnerability of the young—especially the young minority male—to drug arrest is accidental, for it is a consequence of his engaging in criminality, not drug dealing or use per se, that brings him to the attention of the police.

The accidental nature of drug arrests is underlined by the actual rate of arrests. For the year 1969, 2813 drug arrests were made in Steinville (including those for which the drug offense charge was dropped). Compare this with the estimated prevalence in the city of regular illicit users (extrapolated from an average survey use estimate of 40 percent for all youths 16 to 30), which we estimate to number about 35,000 males and females, plus additional regular users especially among the older black males, the many additional thousands in the experimental user categories, and users in the age-15-and-under bracket. Let us use the total figure of 40,000 drug-law violators. Put conservatively, in any one year—and assuming no rearrests which is in fact not the case—no more than 0.07 percent of all estimated regular users of illicit drugs are arrested.

Focusing on dealers, it is the same story. Goode (1970) has shown that most regular users have been illicit marijuana suppliers at one time or another; Ball and Chambers (1970) data show about half of opiate offenders also admit to dealing. If we assume that half of our estimated regular users have violated dealing laws and that, as extrapolated from our institutional studies, 7 percent have been consistent dealers for profit, we arrive at the estimate of at least 20,000 dealing law violators in Steinville, of whom 1400 are or have been serious—not necessarily economically successful—dealers. Against this estimate, we place the 65 arrests of persons believed by the police to be dealers. Assuming the police view corresponds to role realities, this yields an annual rate of about 2.2 percent of dealers arrested.

We have no wish to argue for the accuracy of our estimates, but we believe that these "ballpark" figures, even if off by factors of two or three, help place in perspective the risk of arrest by local police for users and for dealers in Steinville.[8] What is clear is that the risk is low, that it is associated with delinquent life styles in general rather than drug use in particular, and that it is associated with enforcement policies that do not, in fact, appear to be aimed at planned apprehension of drug users at all nor indeed with any intense effort aimed at dealers either. Consider that most dealers were also arrested accidentally and that in the course of one month a six-detective vice squad arrested only 18 people it considered dealers.

[8] Is the risk of arrest for Steinville's users and dealers substantially increased by the work of state and federal narcotics officers? Neither agency has figures available for arrests by city, but after reviewing area activities, we estimate about 36 arrests per year in Steinville by these enforcement echelons.

Expanded, this would give us a rate of 36 dealers per year per vice detective. That figure may be compared with the annual rate of arrests for gamblers (129) and for prostitutes (103) for each detective in that same vice squad as we saw in Blum and Associates (1972a, chapter 28) and an arrest rate in a nearby city for each detective of up to 600 user-dealer per year.

In discussing factors that are linked by inference to the risks of arrests for males and blacks over and above the likely incidence among them of drug law violations, there lurks one as yet untouched but hardly unnoticed possibility, the fact of being black per se, for the visibility of the young male black delinquent comes in two ways: one by virtue of his indiscreet criminality, dangerous driving, or otherwise suspicious conduct; the other is his color. We have no data that bear on this matter. We do know that in the past the Steinville police have been charged with such discriminatory practices; we are aware that the department has a policy set by its leadership that stresses nondiscrimination and constitutional practices in enforcement. The department has been described by outside experts as highly legalistic (Wilson, 1968), that is, not allowing prejudice or favoritism to affect its efforts. The lieutenant in charge of the Vice Control Section states that officers are allowed no discretion in making arrests. "If the law is observed to be broken, the offender must be arrested." "Observed" is a key word, for most arrests were made on the street or in public places—only 51 (24 percent) took place in a residence or other private premise (29 of these 51 were on warrants, 12 made during investigation of some other crime, and 10 made after a call for assistance by a resident or neighbor). The captain in the patrol division agrees that it is *not* the policy to seek out narcotics offenders, but to arrest them when observed. This is fortunate for hippies and other costumed folk who advertise their way of life; if they wore dark clothes and a mask, and carried flashlights, they would be of interest to the patrol division whose obvious mandate is to seek out offenders whose offenses are crimes *with* rather than without victims.

On the other hand, there are shades of grey. When Mrs. Jones, plump, white, and middle-aged, who is driving her 1970 station wagon filled with dogs, kids, and groceries, sees a squad car and drops her cigarette in her lap, the patrolman is not likely to take notice. If Jose Morales, who is cruising in his '57 Ford with seven friends, does the same thing, it may resemble a "furtive move," which brings the cop over to take a closer look. If Mrs. Jones was smoking a joint and Jose a Camel, okay; if it goes the other way, one may view it as discrimination or, if one is a cop, as attentiveness to those incongruous characteristics that, on a statistical and experiential basis, officers know to be associated with increased risk of wrongdoing. Being criminal, being incongruous—or being disrespectful (see Barrett, 1962)—are things that draw attention and/ or incite response by the police. As far as Steinville's police are concerned, the drug offender who gets busted has placed himself in jeopardy and, in consequence, has only himself to blame.

Public Policy and Costs

Reality not rhetoric is the best measure of local policies. In Steinville, the reality is that dealers are not at greater risk of arrest than users but the risk to both groups is minimal. Drug-law violators in general are not major targets of the police endeavor. This is stated by the police themselves and is, moreover, evident in funding priorities. The city budget of some $62,000,000 (1969) allocated 26 percent to the police department. The Vice Control Section of 23 men has 6 assigned to narcotics; the latter's total cost (salaries and their portion of maintenance and overhead) is about $89,000 a year, which is 0.0054 percent of the police budget and 0.0014 percent of the city budget. At the level of reality, the taxpayer cares to enforce narcotics laws to the tune of 0.0014 percent of his total tax bill. For this, he gets his average 200 arrests a month, which, in the vice squad, cost exactly $273.62 each when all costs are divided by the number of arrests. The patrol arrests are more difficult to calculate on a cost per case basis, but appear to be $214.30 per drug case.

Another way of measuring real policy is in outcomes. Given the incompleteness, halfway through 1971, of disposition records for 1969 cases, we cannot be exact. As of the date of our last look, only 36 percent of Steinville's suspects had been convicted. This compared with a conviction rate (all cases adjudicated) for the state of 78.4 percent. If, further, we limit ourselves to those receiving only fines or prison sentences, "paying for their crime" as it is called, only 12 percent of all suspects are "punished." None, it will be recalled, in our sample month, paid with more than one year even though California law provides, for dealing, penalties of one to ten years for a first offense and up to life in prison—with a five-year minimum—for a third offense.

We assume that the courts, like the tax collector, the city manager, and the police department's administrators, reflect what Steinville *really* thinks about drug-dealing and about drug use in terms of community priorities.

Summary

Police operations in one medium-sized Bay Area city were examined using as a base statistics for one month in 1969. A comparison of those arrested with city population characteristics showed that young people, minority members, males, and the unemployed or working classes were more at risk of drug arrest than were other citizens. Projections for the city based on Bay Area drug-use data suggested that, although illicit drug use and dealing were more likely concentrated among young people and more frequent use among males, the overrepresentation in arrests of minority members and unemployed or working class folk could not be attributed to real prevalence of drug-law violations among them. It appears that males, blacks, and those with lower-class attributes are more at risk of drug arrest than other drug-law violators who do not share those features.

Inspection of arrest circumstances shows that most drug arrests are accidental, that is, incidental to apprehension on suspicion of other offenses—dangerous driving, theft, family complaints, and the like. Informal policy statements, budget allocations, and conviction rates all point in the direction of enforcement priorities directed at offenders other than drug violations. The predominance of lower-class black males among arrest subjects may be attributable largely to their involvement in these other offenses or, in the minds of investigating officers, to the probability of those acting "suspiciously" being involved in such offenses. What is clear is that drug offenders per se, including dealers, are at little risk of arrest providing they do not engage in such other criminal, provocative, incongruous, indiscreet conduct as to attract—indeed demand—the attention of the police.

It is our impression that the city has other things to do than to spend its money—or law enforcement capability—on narcotics law enforcement. The police department itself is refreshingly free from rhetoric and states it does not seek out drug-law violators. There is some effort to interdict dealers but this effort is minor compared with levels of investigation for other crimes. What does appear to be the case is that the police attend not to "the drug problem"—whatever that may be—but to problem people who, in the course of driving dangerously, committing crimes, bothering others, or acting in indiscreet or incongruous ways, are apprehended and found to be drug users or dealers as well. Whether or not the city's enforcement policy is "fair," not in the sense of the exercise of their duties by the police, but from a sense of proportion, becomes a major question. Those suspects actually found to be engaged in major violations other than drugs are not charged with drug crimes; the remainder are. The outcome is that a very few, on the order of 13 percent of all charged offenders, end up going to prison or jail because of drug-law violations, none for more than a year, even though minimum sentences of two years for dealing are called for and life sentences are possible under state law. Over the course of a year these most severely punished offenders constitute no more than an estimated 0.006 percent of the city's residents who have violated narcotics and dangerous laws.

8

Juvenile Detention Centers

Richard H. Blum

One of the measures taken by communities to deter and correct young offenders is to commit them—or hold them before sentencing—in juvenile detention centers. The nature of these institutions varies widely across the land and within states, ranging from despicable jails to quite comfortable cottage settings, from heavy security to open doors, and from custodial to maximum treatment endeavors. One assumes that children and youth sent to the more comfortable, more therapeutic, and more open of these facilities are at least exposed to opportunities to reconsider or otherwise correct or outgrow their delinquent conduct. It is also probably assumed by many citizens that, at least during the period of detention, children are protected from exposure to delinquency, including the illicit use of drugs.

Are they? It is to this latter that we address ourselves. We ask if there is, in fact, insulation from illicit drug use during the detention period for a population of children and teen-agers very likely (because of their delinquency) at higher than ordinary risk of illicit use? If there is not, we ask how drugs are distributed within such centers and what the pattern of dealing inside may be? Our limited funds and capabilities did not allow us to sample broadly from among juvenile facilities. We were fortunate enough to secure the cooperation of the juvenile probation department of a San Francisco Bay Area county that operates two facilities: one a secure detention center used primarily for processing juveniles for short-term holding or for juveniles who cannot be placed in open-door facilities and the other a rural facility, less secure and honor-run, for longer-term male offenders. The average monthly population at the secure facility for 1970 was 345 and at the rural center was 60.

Our interviewer was a special staff professional in a counseling position who became acquainted with many of the juveniles in detention while they were there. His position—as special chaplain—meant that he did not report any violations of institutional rules or confessions of delinquency that came to his attention. He held a special position of trust and respect within the system, although, because of this, we must note the possibility of underreporting of delinquency from those juveniles who wished to maintain the better half of their image in his eyes. The procedure employed was to interview detainees as part of the release process from the facility. Because time did not allow all to be seen, every Nth name upon a roster of those to be released was selected for interview. We present results of these interviews that describe illicit drug use and distribution for the two facilities separately.

Rural Minimum Security Center

Fifty boys, aged from 14 to 18, who had been in the rural center for from two months to one year were seen. Forty-three were white, seven were black. Only three were repeaters; for the rest it was their first stay there. A brief drug-experience inquiry indicated that most said that, before detention, they did drink, did smoke, and did use illicit drugs. Indeed, only one denied any illicit drug experience in his life. All but one (98 percent) had used marijuana, the majority doing so regularly (four times or more per week). Over half had used LSD—36 percent of those experiencing it having used it one or more times a week. The majority had not used speed, heroin, barbiturates, or special substances, although up to one-third had used one or more of these drugs.

Turning to drugs inside, most of the boys (72 percent) said they knew that drugs were used inside the rural center. We did not ask them about their own inside use, but about that of the boys they knew (that is, estimates not by name identification). Almost all said that cigarettes were smoked, even though contrary to rules, but most denied that liquor was used inside. Marijuana was the most available drug; sometimes LSD and barbiturates were also on hand. Marijuana, barbiturates, and LSD were secured by barter or were shared. They were not reported sold for cash, since money is not permitted at the facility. A few boys reported that these drugs were available at least once a week; most boys were not aware of such accessibility and described availability as a once-a-month or so phenomenon. Speed, the least available for most boys, was nevertheless the one drug more often available for those few who knew how to get it. One boy reported cocaine use. Nearly all the boys reported that only small amounts of any illicit drug were on hand (for example, five joints, five tabs); on the other hand, a few knew of moderate and even large amounts. All were in agreement that there were no cash transactions in the center for any drugs. In lieu of cash, candy or cigarettes were sometimes bartered for drugs.

Describing those who were likely to use these substances, there was agreement that neither the very youngest (14) nor the oldest (18) employed them; the 15- through 17-year-olds, who are the most frequent inmates, are also the users. Length of stay appears linked to drug use; there was agreement that use—and necessarily access to sources—did not occur until a boy had been in the center for approximately one month, and the population of users was skewed, boys estimated, toward greater use by those who had been in at least four months. (The average length of stay for our sample is six months.) It was also a matter of general agreement that those most likely to use were in for violation of narcotics laws; auto thefts ranked second. (Our sample consisted primarily of boys charged with robbery/theft/burglary [30 percent] and violation of the narcotics laws [28 percent]; runaways, the next most reported offense, comprised 10 percent.) For comparison, the juvenile hall monthly admissions, from which our rural minimum security population is derived, usually consist primarily of incorrigibles and runaways followed by theft/burglary/robbery, then narcotics/dangerous drugs/liquor laws violations. No group was seen as immune to use except those who were "straight" or who were intent on getting out.

Were there any problems associated with illicit drug use? Most boys felt not, but some noted that there was nervousness about being caught. Occasionally noted was aggressiveness, expressed either in fights or in threats to get possession of drugs. What about benefits? The majority saw none, but a goodly minority held that drugs made life in detention more pleasant.

How do drugs come into this minimum security rural center? As earlier noted, distribution is through sharing as boys get together out of sight and sound of supervisors. What are some of the tricks of the juvenile trade when it comes to getting illicit drugs into the rural center? One is to go on sick call and to keep rather than take medication given, sharing it later with one's friends. Another is to bring in drugs held in the mouth rather than in clothing or other searchable objects. Concealment in clothing, including transfer from street clothing to facility attire in shower rooms before search, in candy or gum wrappers, and the like, is also practiced. Some boys, when returning from leave, hide the drugs along the road or trails coming in, then pick them up at their leisure.

Secure Facility

The age range for our sample drawn from the security detention facility is broader, ranging from 12 to 18 although, as with the rural center, most are in the 15- to 17-year-old range. Eighty-five boys and 15 girls were interviewed—a distribution that approximates the normal male population there but was an undersample from among the population of girls.* Compared with the rural center there were more blacks, 24 percent, and the length of stay was much more varied: from one-third who had been there one week or less to three who had been there nearly a year. The majority had been detained for less than one month. There were

* This was an accident of the "run" of releases during the interviewing period.

many more repeat visitors, more than 70 percent returning two or more times, with one-quarter of the recidivists having been in six times or more.

Responding to inquiries about their "outside" drug use, 72 percent affirmed alcohol use, 82 percent tobacco use, and 78 percent the use of illicit drugs. Most had used marijuana; and, for those who used it, the most prevalent practice was of frequent use (four or more times per week). About 50 percent had used LSD, about 25 percent speed, 15 percent barbiturate, 9 percent heroin, 12 percent glue-sniffing and glue-ingestion. In discussing what went on within the juvenile hall, 63 percent said they knew of illicit drug use, and 83 percent knew of tobacco smoking (against regulations); but only one juvenile said he had known alcohol to be consumed inside. There was agreement that marijuana was the most easily available drug, barbiturates and LSD ranked second and third, speed fourth. Heroin was very rare. For all these drugs, acquisition was through sharing or barter; no cash exchanged hands. Although amounts in use units of less than five (five caps, joints, or whatever) were most frequently reported, a substantial minority held that larger amounts occasionally got in, that is, ten joints, caps, or whatever, which represented an estimate of the total amount available at any one time. It was generally agreed that, for all drugs, access was occasional, not more than once every two weeks; on the other hand a minority did estimate much more frequent accessibility: for 20 percent weekly and for 10 percent almost daily. These reports were consistent across the spectrum of drugs; that is, each of the major substances available was reportedly available to (the same) minority on a weekly or daily basis.

Those who used drugs within the facility were said to span a wide range of age and length of stay. Nevertheless, the majority of users were in the 15- to 17-year age range that characterizes the total institutional population and our sample. On the other hand, females nearly as often as males were said to be users, although there was a greater proportion of males in the facility and in our sample. Length of stay appears associated, in these estimates, with access to drugs. While 80 percent stay in the facility less than one month, there is a tendency for those who are in for more than one month more often to be characterized as users than are the short-timers.

The consensus among the juveniles is that those who are in for narcotics offenses more often use drugs in the facility than do others; runaways are ranked second, and auto thieves third. For comparison, 30 percent of our sample were admitted for robbery/burglary/theft offenses, 21 percent for violation of the narcotic-drug laws, and 19 percent for runaway.

The majority of our sample (55 percent) estimate that 16 percent of the detainees have used drugs while in the institution. There is a bimodal distribution, for 45 percent contend that they are not aware of the inmates who have done so. The same bimodality holds for tobacco use; 22 percent contend there is smoking inside, 78 percent say there is none. There are few "immunizing" features noted; a few contend that the younger inmates are least likely to use or that the "straighter" ones do not.

What about problems? The majority of those who are familiar with drug use inside do describe problems in connection with illicit use. These are mostly seen as fights ensuing over or in consequence of use and of threats associated with failures to share or supply, and the like. Almost none think that there is apprehensiveness associated with use; a couple do report that inmates become ill from drugs they take. The majority of our sample reported no benefits from such use, a minority contend that use in the facility served to calm and relax the juveniles; others said that it made their time easier to serve.

What about the manner of smuggling? We find concealment in clothing (transfer from street to hall clothes) on the way in to be most often reported. Accomplices are also said to climb the security fence to bring drugs in or, as visitors, to throw drugs inside the fence, so that the detainee can later retrieve them (from a bush, in a special wrapper, and the like). A few report that drugs given on prescription are hoarded and later used or shared.

Comment

Our method of estimating what others do rather than sampling adequately within each facility has its liabilities, but circumstances did not allow us to do better. We shall accept the estimates as reasonable ones on two grounds. One is that other evidence on estimates of drug use (Blum and Associates, 1969b) shows that for less-well-defined populations—college campuses—estimates of prevalence of use were most accurate when offered by those who themselves used. We have also seen (Blum and Associates, 1972a, chapter 23) that our high school dealers estimate dealer prevalence quite accurately. In our sample here, most of the informants were themselves users of illicit drugs. The second ground for accepting these as reasonable estimates is the fact that both units are small facilities in which inmates become acquainted and do have opportunity to observe one another. This is especially true for the long-term juveniles in the rural facility, and we note that in this facility there is the greatest agreement on the actual number of individuals using drugs. Disparity must also be acknowledged, especially that between the minority in both institutions who deny any illicit use and the majority who specify who uses what and how it is done. Perhaps the minority can be accounted for in terms of their actual ignorance—since the estimation technique required no self-revelations and indeed nearly all had already described a wide range of illicit use for themselves. If this be so, we suggest that there are within the detention center populations at least two subgroups: one the con-wise who know what is happening and are probably a part of it, the other the naïve ("straight Johns" they used to be called in adult prisons) who are not part of the action. Probably because of their youth and shorter stays as well as their own lesser illicit use, there are more naïve juveniles in the security facility.

In looking at the drug estimates, one identifies a third subgroup: the juveniles who have nearly daily access to all of the drugs that float through the (secure) institution. We must presume with our informants that these are the drug-wise crowd—youth who are experienced not only in drugs and their use but also in obtaining drugs as well. It is likely, therefore, that those who have engaged in dealing on the outside—becoming visible enough thereby to be arrested on narcotics charges—will be the importers and traffic routes for drugs on the inside as well. We cannot test this surmise further with our present data.

It is not surprising that within both institution estimates of drug use conform fairly well to estimates for the total population, for today's delinquent (as our data show) is also a user and, as we have seen elsewhere, regular users tend to be suppliers if not dealers.

It is also not unexpected that use—and by definition illicit traffic within the institution—is a function of length of stay. The short-timer takes a little while to learn his way around and to be accepted. Also, the longer he stays, probably the stronger his urge to relieve boredom or otherwise act out some of the same delinquent tendencies that may have brought him through the gate in the first place. It is also likely that longer stays are associated with greater gravity of juvenile offense, in which case an association with delinquent involvement (that is, gravity) and being drug-wise con-wise would be proposed.

It appears that the more densely populated, higher-turnover, more heterogeneous, shorter-term, detention center, with its higher recidivist population, has the greater availability of and traffic in drugs. Paradoxically, this is also the more "secure" facility; our observations suggest certainly that staff oppose such traffic and seek as much control over drugs as possible. We must conclude that, given the dispositions of the juveniles, drugs will come through, at least for the minority whom we have presumed to be cleverest in such matters. Perhaps a hopeful sign is in the relative lack of illicit traffic, defined by amounts and frequency of availability, in the open-door rural center (security is limited to body counts—approximately every two hours), with its policy of weekend leaves and its population of experienced drug users all on long-term commitments and so presumably seriously delinquent. These detainees could manage an increase in traffic if they wanted to do so; consequently, one must ascribe to their environment—and that means supervision as well as physical features—elements that mitigate against pursuing the easy illicit conduct that drug traffic seems to be.

Our final comment is tangential. To round off the interview, we asked each juvenile how he would like to see drug laws changed. Most wanted relaxation in marijuana laws, with permissive clauses for teen-age use. They also wanted alcohol and tobacco to be made legal for users in their age '(average 15 to 17) bracket. Most accepted present laws controlling other drugs as proper. Since most of our informants were already '(regular)' users, it was obvious that present laws had not deterred—even if they might have inhibited —use. The pressure for legalization from this constituency goes beyond that of college youth and their supporters, demanding that age limitations be dropped to some level below where they now are. It is apparent that any of the currently proposed revisions in marijuana statutes will not affect these young delinquent users, and, consequently, we shall continue to face in juvenile detention centers the problem of illicit traffic. One might propose that if we could learn why that traffic does not extend to alcohol, as clearly it does not in our two centers, we might be on the road to preventing illegality. We guess that problems of sheer bulk plus unfashionableness may account in part for the absence of alcohol.

Summary

Samples were drawn from among juveniles as they were released from a minimum security center and from a maximum security facility, both serving a San Francisco Bay Area county. Most reported themselves to be regular drug users and most reported illicit drug use within the juvenile detention facility where they had been. Traffic depended on barter and sharing, not cash exchange, and amounts of drugs available are small. The major drugs in both facilities are marijuana, LSD, barbiturates, and methamphetamines in that order. Most inmates appear to use infrequently, some not at all; but we suspect the presence of a small drug-wise and con-wise group in the maximum security facility for whom drugs were readily available. We propose—without direct evidence—that these are likely to be older, longer-term (or recidivist) juveniles with previous experience in drug traffic.

The secure facility has greater drug availability than the minimum security one. We propose that environments—including supervisory practices and institutional atmosphere—as well as population differences can account for differences in illicit traffic within juvenile detention centers.

9

Prisons

Nicholas Munson, Ingemar Rexed, Robert Packard, Richard H. Blum

Lest it be thought that society "solves" the problem of drug dealing when the dealer is sent to prison, we thought it well to attend to drug use and traffic behind the walls. As with much first-stage inquiry, the prison study yielded what was, for us, fascinating information of the sort to delimit the nature and type of activity, but it did not consist of quantitative data that provide incidence statistics or allow accuracy as to what kinds of places, people, or conditions were associated with levels of traffic in particular drugs.

Method

Each of us brought to the study a certain bias. One of us is an ex-convict, recently graduated from the California prison system. One of us is a San Francisco police officer, acquainted by virtue of work with some inmates and, by affinity, with personnel in the administration of justice. One of us is a Swedish judge who is active in Sweden in the convicts' union and other prison enterprises which, viewed with American eyes, seem, if not eminently Swedish, then "far out." One of us took an internship in one of the prisons under study, living inside at the time, and has, over the years, maintained some ties with the system—both inmates and administrators.

As we approached the problem of assessing traffic in the prison, we accepted as ideal our Swedish member's proposition that inmates themselves should conduct the study; but the ideal is sometimes not practicable. In consequence, we plan, one day, to assist in a study of prisons that the inmates themselves conduct. In the interim we relied on less satisfactory devices. These included (1) interviews with inmates just after they were released, (2) discussion groups held in half-way houses in the San Francisco Bay Area where ex-convicts lived during the period following release, (3) individual interviews and discussion groups within prisons, (4) memos written within prisons by inmates and sent to us by one route or another, (5) interviews with prison personnel ranging from guards to administrators, and (6) interviews with parole officers. From among these groups about 140 persons contributed actively.

Guiding our inquiry to each person or group was a set of questions, which, in essence, asked what illegal traffic within the institution was like, who participated in it, what factors affect that traffic, what kinds and proportion of users are involved, and how did it all work. Since prisons are closed and intense communities (Goffman, 1961) one factor will stand out; we shall see that, in a "dynamic" system in which a change in one part affects all parts, the major factors or issues in prison life express themselves in drug traffic. Conversely, drug traffic is likely to be more important in a prison community in terms of its immediate ripple effects than is such traffic outside where most citizens are relatively unaffected by it.

Initial Observations

Each prison has its own character. What that is depends on many things. These include the average age of the inmates, the distance of the prison from big cities, the reputation of the institution, the selectivity of assignment of inmates (type of offense, number of previous convictions, probable length of confinement), the attitudes of the staff toward the inmates and of the inmates toward the staff, and the customs that have become part of life there.

Because drugs are part of prison life, these too contribute to institutional character. At the very outset let us discriminate prisons on the basis of (1) the availability of hard drugs, principally heroin, and (2) the value assigned to other psychoactive contraband.

As to the prediction of this prison character, we believe that, of the two, heroin is easiest to anticipate. If the prison contains young inmates (under 40) who are lower-class habitual offenders and have themselves been heroin users or addicts, if it is close to a big city, if it permits physical contact between inmates and visitors, and if it allows prisoner release on work-furlough, conjugal visits, or 72-hour passes, then that prison will have a heroin character.

Anticipating the value placed on other contraband is easier after the fact, which means that we do not know how to predict it except as there are expressions of interest (just as the best predictor for alcohol problems is the expressed interest in and belief in the varied utility of alcohol among drinkers according to Cahalan's 1970 findings). Glue-sniffing, for example, is common in one institution and glue is therefore salable contraband there; in another prison, glue is only what one uses to cement broken pieces together. In one prison "pruno," the fruit wine locally made, is of interest only to the hobbyists—that is, vintners who consume their own product—but it is, so to speak, not "a drug on the market" for no one else cares. Elsewhere pruno is in keen demand; salesmen have pruno routes and, to bring customers to their supplier, offer free samples. In the same way, other contraband depends on the atmosphere. In one place, a good knife ("shank") will cost the buyer a $50 balloon of heroin; in another institution, the weapon will change hands freely, as long as it is believed destined for use in a good cause, that is, racial war.

At the outset and with regard to contraband, let us offer one proposition. It is that anything that a prisoner wants he can get, providing that it is concealable and that he is patient and ingenious, and further providing that he can afford to pay through goods or services and is willing to take risks. Although contraband moves through many channels—family and other visitors, staff, and the like—the major artery is through those prisoners within the institution who, as trustees or men with "honor" status, have, thereby, relative freedom of movement and contact. Insofar as trusties may move freely within the prison, they deliver goods and receive orders. Insofar as they work on the grounds, in fields, or in buildings outside maximum security zones, they are enabled to deliver orders to and receive goods from outside contacts. They are, in essence, each institution's free trade zone. A further consideration is that contraband traffic is not always remunerative. It can be done as part of a game or conspiracy of prisoners against the system. Contraband traffic can be run as one act in a chain of mutual favors that engage, pay off, and re-engage obligations among men whose needs are great and whose resources are few—and in such a setting, mutual obligations serve the collective. Contraband can also be run not because of favors received and given but out of emotion as well, be it terror or love. And finally, it can be done for money or in-kind payment. Almost no prisoner is so isolated that he cannot participate in the contraband chain. One in isolation (solitary) or on death row may get his heroin balloon on a piece of string lowered from his window or inside his mashed potatoes—but get it he shall if the will is there.

Insofar as any inmate who feels himself to be a member of the prison social system (that is, pitted against authority) is in a position to manipulate any aspect of prison life in favor of contraband traffic or other inmate interests, he will do so. For example, in one prison an inmate clerk was responsible for assigning guards to their daily posts (that is, making up the duty roster). This power allowed him to respond to an inmate requesting that a guard who was "messing" with his illicit enterprise be moved elsewhere. Guards requested duty assignments that they preferred. And on one occasion, before an escape attempt, the inmate clerk conspired to position and schedule guards to assist the escape endeavor. The point here is that inmates, who have little power individually, compensate by organizing a social system that patiently gains as much control over its own environment as it can. There was, for example, a twice-weekly chess club meeting in the dining hall. Contraband items were delivered to them by the kitchen crew which, as it went off duty, was searched and found clean. The chess club members, not a suspect crew, left search-free, and in that prison, were an integral part of the contraband chain.

Staff members, also, are part of the contraband chain, although usually in benevolent ways. Friendships do exist between inmates and counselors, teachers, or guards. Genuine on both sides, such friendships may lead to the math instructor's bringing special books to the inmate, to the counselor taking a letter out, to a social worker shielding a methamphetamine party from discovery, to a young intern taking a shiv (knife) from his inmate aide to protect him from discovery during a surprise search. For the most part, inmates manage drug traffic so satisfactorily that they do not require employees as "mules" to bring in the goods. However, it does appear that two groups of employees are more likely than others to be involved in such traffic if it does occur: hospital workers and freemen kitchen crews. Hospital workers have easy access to drugs within the prison; they may also assist in their legitimate delivery from outside to the pharmacy. Perhaps, too, they are in their work because of a desire to help people and do then more readily respond to the appeals of inmates for drugs couched in "help me" language. Culinary workers are a different lot. For one thing, they control items of great interest, for inmates desire food goodies for pleasure and barter such as, for example, yeast with which to begin a pruno batch. Civilian kitchen crews appear to be paid less than most staff and their status is not enhanced as is the guards' by power; furthermore, turnover is higher and qualification checks are not so keen. The kitchen workers seem more willing than others to smuggle for money or otherwise to enjoy the limited benefits arising from their posts which, to the outside world, are lowly but to prisoners are more important.

Life of the City

A penal institution is like a small city, except that the resident wakes up in a six-by-ten cement tomb with a barred door that looks out on another barred door. He has a roommate. They use the toilet, wash, shave, then wait for someone else to open their front door so they can go to breakfast, and then on to work. These roommates may spend that morning period in hostile silence or with a few mumbled words of rough civility or in the normal exchange of long acquaintanceship or even in the affection of lovers. In some cells there may be a carefully timed heroin injection by one or both inmates while the other stands near the cell door and listens for the tread of a guard.

The day's work may be janitorial, secretarial or clerical, welding or plumbing, carpentry, electrical, cabinetmaking, trade school, accounting, in the laundry or jute mill, stamping out auto license plates, herding cows, raising vegetables, culinary, landscaping, or tending a gate under the supposedly watchful eye of a guard. Work includes all the activities necessary for the functioning of a small city. In addition, there may be other production work agreed on by the body politic as not being too competitive with "free" labor and industry.

Each of the movements of prisoners in the work and social life of that city means a mass of inmate contacts and interactions. Notes, drugs, money, salutations, scowls, threats, hidden recognitions, weapons, and promises are exchanged. Only a little is observed by the custodial officers; it is likely less of it is understood by them. Contraband passes.

What is contraband? Anything forbidden that has value in the life of a convict. Dirty pictures, pornographic books, paint thinners, glues with volatile fractions, currency, heroin, methedrine, marijuana, knives, nutmeg, barbiturates, yeast or bread dough, cleaning fluid, letters to be sent out, letters clandestinely received, female undergarments, escape tools, specially tailored items of clothing, pieces of twine, allspice, tranquilizers, stimulants, cigarettes in large quantity, a filet mignon, a quart of pruno, two plastic bags and a length of plastic hose, a package of condoms, a pint of vodka —the list is limited only by the fancies of men in confinement.

During each day, scores of tourists, visitors, vendors, employees, and either incoming or outgoing prisoners come and go. All have some sort of contact with inmates. Some are exposed to a modicum of security, some to none. Some visitors feel the oppression of confinement as they enter; others, aware that they are free to leave, never notice it. But the inmates are constantly aware of it, suffer it, and rebel against it in a way that gives them a cohesive body. After an inmate has a visitor and he is searched to the skin, his ears, mouth, hair, and his inner anal orifice, he is enraged by the indignity of it and moves more deeply into the pool of hatred that stands the convicts against the prison. Contraband traffic then becomes symbolic as well as useful; each item in or out is a small triumph over the hated place.

When "open" visiting is permitted in an institution, the flow of narcotics into the place is freer. Visiting rules vary, but they are becoming more relaxed over time. Typically, an inmate may see one individual as a visitor no more than four times each month, with weekends reserved for families, but there is no restriction on how many different visitors he may see in a month. "Open" visiting normally means that visitors and inmates sit around tables for four or more, as in a cafeteria. There is frequently a row of soft drink, cigarette, candy, sandwich, and other vending machines in the room. Inmates are normally not permitted to have money, but these visiting rooms become so loose that visitors can give change to the inmates so they can go to the machines and get what they want, for the novelty of it. The guards pay little attention. There is so much motion and sound that almost anything can be passed from the visitor to the inmate. Eating and drinking mask the inmate's swallowing of drugs or currency in a balloon or condom. Swallowed contraband is one thing a "skin search," including a rectal examination, will not reveal.

In one institution, before a grinder was placed at the right point in the sewage system, a constant flow of drugs went in through the toilets in the waiting and visiting rooms. The method required only that the visitor go to the toilet and drop a balloon or condom containing the drug and the prisoner's name on a piece of lightweight paper into the toilet and flush it. The little packet would emerge at the other end of the pipe to float to the surface of the settling tank, which was the first stop in the sewage disposal system. The trusties working there would skim the packets off the top, wash them, open them to see whom they were addressed to, and see that proper delivery was made—for a price.

Even though cigarettes are the principal medium of exchange in a prison, they cannot be amassed in large quantities and concealed, since an inmate is normally permitted only three or four cartons of cigarettes in his cell at any one time. If he wants to have available value greater than a few cartons of cigarettes, he has to convert the cigarettes into money, because money is much easier to transport or conceal. Whenever money is found in an institution there is a good probability it figures in the narcotics trade. One can buy heroin with cigarettes, but it might take three or four cartons to get a weak $10 paper.

Trusties move with relative freedom. That is why they are one of the principal routes for drugs through the main wall. Trusties' jobs take them to the outer prison grounds, an area separated from the free world usually by no more than a high cyclone fence. Contraband is poked through the fence, tossed over it, or left under it at some prearranged place. To illustrate, recently in one prison a map drawn to scale and accurate in detail was intercepted on its way out. It showed an unguarded area of cyclone fence with an unused gate, and there was an arrow pointing to one place with instructions, "Throw it over here." In addition, there was a small note indicating that the guard post near the gate was unmanned at night. The fence shown is along a county road with totally unrestricted public access. Convicts returning from outside passes use this route, too. It is a busy receiving zone.

Guards are generally busy. Inmates have time to sit around and scheme. Out of these creativity sessions come new ways for getting narcotics into the "joint." As one proud con said, "That's why we outsmart the guards regularly." If the cons can get a guard involved in an illicit conspiracy, they will play him as long as they can. Inmates refer to the guard as being "in the trick." At the beginning, when a guard is set up for a delivery, the recipient of the contraband may have other inmates watch what happens, taking notes. These constitute testimony—evidence if ever they need to put pressure on the guard.

Shortly before our inquiries a guard who had gotten himself "in the trick" carried illegal mail, narcotics, and, we think, some weapons. But he fell in love and planned to get married. He wanted to stop packing in order to make his job more secure. The cons would not let him off the hook, but he backed out anyhow. They threatened to expose him until he made a deal with them: he would bring in one last load of stuff. One of the inmates sent a note to the warden. In it were included his name, the date, time, and what he would be bringing in. When he came on duty, he was searched by other guards. He had his "one last time" load on him. This "mule" had been sacrificed when he was no longer useful, and the prisoners who turned him in made some points.

One guard noticed that the incoming mail included numerous individually rolled, tied, and Addressograph-labeled newspapers. The newspapers all originated in a nearby city, but they were individually stamped with a Pitney-Bowes machine stamp and mailed from a smaller community about 30 miles from the city. Since newspapers usually come into the place in bulk, the guard thought this odd and opened one of the rolls. It contained a packet of heroin; so did each of the others. This had been going on for some time, but the addressees of the newspapers knew nothing of it; none of them had ever received any of the newspapers. The small group that had organized it all—with outside help of course—were intercepting the papers on their way through the mail distribution system, removing the heroin, and giving the papers to anyone nearby at the time.

Another incident involved two inmates, one black and the other white, who were running an illegal store during the evening hours. Prisoners, usually young men, get hungry in the evening when the prison commissary is closed. The entrepreneurs had a case of sardines stashed in one place, a case of fig bars in another, different candies in a third, all arranged for easy access. A hungry inmate could buy from them at about twice the normal price. (The ex-con who told the story commented, "There's a lot more capitalism inside one of those places than there is on the outside.") The white inmate had financed the venture, and the black man ran it for him. They split the take. Weekly there was an inventory, accounting, refinancing, resupply, and a split of the profit. But one hitch developed. The black man was hooked on heroin and began skimming the take to support his habit. There came a time when the venture showed no profit and the white man realized what was going on. He demanded his share, but there was none. He issued an ultimatum, "Come up with the money in two days or I'll get you." But the addict was too far gone, and no one would give him that much credit.

Our informant was present when the white man stabbed the black man in the neck with a knife. As the victim went down another black man yelled, "A red-neck stabbed a brother!" and a race war was on. In the next two months black men and white men were killed and seriously wounded in a rage of retaliatory stabbings. No one cut or cutting knew what had triggered it all.

Taking Care of Business

A resourceful addict going into prison may be able to take enough heroin in with him to tide him over until he makes the proper connections to get his stuff on the inside. A few swallowed balloons will do it for him. If he is dry, he usually has to locate friends and establish credit, but in some places the system of transferring prisoners is so slow, and the security so loose, that he may be able to make arrangements to have stuff waiting for him when he arrives. If he is known to be a good source of revenue, the dealers will know he is coming and will look him up.

It does not always work so well. One addict told us he had served 13 years for drug-related offenses at a small remote prison where he had no friends on the inside and no friends near enough to visit him. It took him a year and a half to set up a connection, and that was through turning a guard.

Friendships and a good credit rating are the two most important things in securing drugs. A well-liked man with good credit can usually make it in a couple of days. Things may be complicated in some places where the control of drugs is dominated by a strong faction. The faction may be racial, a group of trusties may run it, or it may be a strong-arm venture.

One informant who wore his hair long and dirty said that whenever he went into a county jail he took enough heroin in with him to last his stay. Usually he would carry a balloon high on the inside of each cheek, and two or three of them attached by bobby pins under the hair of the back of his head. He commented, "Man, those guards don't even like the *looks* of long dirty hair, much less want to run their hands through it."

Prison will usually have a credit rating system for cons who have been in before. One informant was an accountant who had done a bit of embezzling. He was a first-timer, a very intelligent young black man who was almost immediately assigned to the prison's budget section. Within a matter of months after his arrival he had become *the* Dun and Bradstreet for the place. When he first got started he had to talk with some of the old timers, men with 20 to 40 years in the place, to gain knowledge on how to go about doing the job, but he was soon selling credit ratings for a handsome profit.

The addict coming in for the first time, unless he has friends or has otherwise arranged a supply for himself, is hurting. If he wants to kick his habit while he is doing time, and not risk being caught as a user, prison is a fine opportunity. It appears that a high percentage of addict first-timers do this. If the man has not been able to keep himself supplied on his way into the prison, he has already gone through withdrawal; and he may elect to stay clean until he gets out. He knows that if he starts again and his source dries up, he has to withdraw again, and the recent memory of what he has just gone through may help him stop.

If the first-timer addict can bring enough money in with him, he is set. Money, several hundred dollars in large bills, can be swallowed in two or three condoms. Currency is easy to hide from the guards, and a con can leave fairly large amounts of money in his cell, well hidden. The cell is locked and other cons cannot get in to steal it. If there is no obvious reason for the cell to be searched, it will not be. The only problem is getting large bills changed down to usable sizes. There might not be change immediately available, and looking too widely for change may let the wrong people know that the new man has a large amount of money. A rip-off can occur in prison too.

The following interview is included to illustrate inmate attitudes and techniques. The man interviewed was not in prison at the time and was dry. After eight years as an addict he had heard the call of Christianity and decided to quit. He had been dry for about two months.

How do you get drugs when you are locked up?

Aw, man, it's simple. You just buy it. You make your contacts right in the compound. It is usually through friends, but anyone who uses drugs can tell anyone else who uses drugs just by looking at him.

How do you tell?

Man, when you look *at a dude you know if he's a user. I'm not fruit, but dopers find each other the way homosexuals find each other. If* you're *straight you can tell a woman when you see one, can't you? Fruits find each other the same way. And I know a user when I see one. I may have to open him up with a couple of questions about "action," but I don't very often ask the wrong guy.*

Well, what do you really look for?

Anyone who doesn't look as if he is neat, and well kept together, is probably going to be a drug user. But he can be too neat too. If he's too slick, along with being neat, he's a user. The neat "common" Joe isn't a user, it's the guys on the extremes. If you run into some guy on the inside who was dealing in the street, he's dealing in there too. And then, if you're standing watching new guys come into a place, and you see some one guy who is kind of popular or respected by the guys who are already in, watch him. *He's probably even bringing stuff in with him, and nobody's ever searched well enough by the guards. He'll be dealing in no time.*

What were some of the ways you've seen drugs come into the places you've been?

It's so easy to toss the stuff over the fence on most honor farms that you never have to worry about getting stuff in. You might like this too: I had a good friend in ———. I kept him supplied the whole time he was in there. I knew he'd be good for it when he got out, and he was. He was on heroin. I don't know if you know, but the Mexicans use the word "goat," "chiva," or sometimes "cabra," in their language for heroin. I would write him and say, "I know you miss the farm and all your friends. Here is a chiva to keep you company." Then I would draw a picture of a goat and color it brown with heroin and water color. All he had to do was to cut it out and soak it in warm water to get a couple of fixes out of it. The water color didn't seem to bother him. Sometimes I would draw pictures of flowers around the edge of my letter and I'd mix LSD in with the water colors I used. He'd just tear the flowers out and suck on them. Nobody ever stopped one of my letters. If I really wanted to get a

*lot of it in to him at once, I would write and say, "I'll see you next
Thursday. It's too bad I can't bring you some of those candy bars
you like so much." Then I'd go through the outer gate eating one
of those candy bars with a big bag of heroin in my cheek. Between
the outer gate and the visiting room I'd finish the candy bar, shove
the balloon into the wrapper with my tongue, twist it up and throw
it onto the ground. Man, nobody picks up anybody else's garbage.
They got trusties to do that. And a trusty had been told by my
friend what kind of wrapper to look for. It's that simple.*

How about outfits for shooting? Are they hard to get inside?

*Man, what do you mean "hard to get?" You could take a fine-
toothed comb and go through every institution, and there'd still be
enough left so that nobody would be hurting. They got so many
they don't need any more. Every user has two or three outfits
stashed away. And every time a doctor or anyone in the hospital is
the least bit careless with a needle or an eye dropper, swish, they
got another one. And then in a county jail, one of the biggest
sources of the stuff is the weekenders. You know, the guys the judges
feel sorry for and sentence them to do ten weekends or some deal
like that. The guards never search them well enough. Sometimes
they swallow balloons, and sometimes they carry it in their clothing.
It's easy to carry stuff sewn into lots of places in your clothes. A
frisk for weapons, or even for drugs, won't turn it up if you know
how to hide it. That bulge in the front of your pants zipper is great.
All pants bulge a little bit there. And in a belt loop is another good
place. I know a guy went weekends for a long time. He pleaded
with the judge that if he had to do a regular stretch he'd lose his
job, and then his wife and children would have to go on relief, and
that would cost the taxpayers a lot of money. Man, that judge
didn't know what a favor he was doing that dude. I think he had
to go twelve weekends, and he made more money dealing heroin on
the weekends than he did working all week. His wife even sewed the
stuff in for him.*

*Would you say that most of the drugs that go into a place go in for
profit?*

No, more goes in for friends. It's just one junkie helping another, and the trading back and forth of favors. But sometimes visitors, wives even, who are afraid to handle drugs will pass money instead of drugs knowing the guy can buy his junk on the inside.

If you were in and you wanted to try to turn an employee to bringing stuff in for you, what kind of guy would you pick on?

Shee-yit, man, you mean the people who work there? We got enough stuff coming in without them. I wouldn't go near one of them, they're poison. Why take a chance on someone you don't know when you're surrounded by people you do know and can trust?

If you were put in charge of a prison, how would you stop the drug trade?

The higher a position a prisoner has, the more he is trusted and the more he can get away with. Watch the guy who has the job most appealing to a prisoner, like a job with a lot of influence or authority and almost no work to do. Check this guy everywhere he goes. Shake him down all the time. He's the guy who's going to be moving the stuff around. But to really stop it would be impossible. It would be so rough on everyone, the guards, the prisoners, everyone, involved or not, that it would make everyone's life miserable. But still, there are some things you can do. A little more intelligence in examining the mail would keep the brown goats from wandering in. Then, watch the inmate in the visiting room who is scratching a lot. He's getting the guard used to the motion so he can receive a pass. The prisoners who are the happiest guys, who are the most condescending to the guards, who are always shaking hands, who know all the guards by name, who are most friendly, but not doing anything useful, dodging work and finding excuses for not doing things but still being real friendly, these are the guys who are dealing. Like, this guy's in on everything, he is popular, he's a hand shaker, the guards let him into places where he really doesn't belong because he's Jake, and everyone knows Jake, and he's kind of amusing to have around, and the guards are taken in by all this. The prisoners know what Jake's doing, but the guards never seem to catch on. Y'know, in a big jail where I had to spend a lot of time, the trusties had the run of the place. When visitors drove into the

*parking lot and blew the horn on the car that meant that a drop
had been made. The trusties just went over and picked it up. My
brother was in there for a while. I would put the stuff in the glove
compartment of the car and go to see my brother. When my brother
came to the visiting room, two of his friends would go over the fence
to the parking lot, find my car, get the stuff out of it and go back
inside.*

*Could you pay a trusty to be an informant and make much head-
way that way?*

*For little stuff, maybe, but for big stuff you're liable to get him
killed. But, y'know, some guys will do anything for money. It's
worth a try.*

Coercion

Threats and blackmail have been alluded to as devices used
to maintain narcotics traffic. Perhaps these are not unnatural tools
for men whose backgrounds in crime do not glisten with shining
love for their fellow men, nor are these devices incompatible with
the brutalizing atmosphere of prisons and the impotence of inmates
within them to bring about control of their destinies by fairer means.
Yet the extent of coercion in prison, as a major device for insuring
narcotics flow, is a matter of uncertainty. Administrators with
whom we spoke were divided on it; and, while inmates told many
a tale, one cannot overlook the drama in the telling or the justification that the claim of blackmail or threat can provide for people
searching for justification for what they have done. Like much else
in prison, such justifications rest on blaming someone else who was
more evil and had more power for what one has oneself done.
One of the most often heard tales was the use of coercion—
that is the threat of damage—just before a prisoner was due to
come up before the parole board, which would, if he were on in-
determinant sentence as most are, decide whether or not to give him
a release date. A man is understandably apprehensive before these
hearings and wants to put his best foot forward. It is claimed that
these are the times when others threaten him with "loss of his date."
Damage can be done, for example, by putting a hypodermic needle

in a pair of socks and tossing them into a man's cell while he is gone, then telling the guard about it. Telling an inmate what one intends to do works, so the cons say, among "susceptibles," to persuade them to bring narcotics in from their leaves or have their relatives bring drugs in to them.

Coercion is applied not only to inmates by inmates but, as the earlier story of the guard "in the trick" related, can be used by inmates against staff as well. One tale went as follows:

An upper-echelon employee in an institution had a faithful inmate clerk, one who did his every bidding to perfection, was always considerate, polite, and pleasant to be around. In addition, this clerk kept his freeman informed of everything that was going on, on a very confidential basis. This was valuable information to a man on his way up. A close relationship developed between the two of them. It went on for many months.

The inmate came up for a date before the parole board, the anticipation of which he discussed frequently and emotionally with his freeman. The inmate's wife was a "wonderful woman," and she came to the nearest town and stayed in a motel so she could visit her husband after he saw the board and could hear directly from him the joyous news of when he was going to get out.

He went before the board and they turned him down. He came back to his office job late in the afternoon the picture of dejection. He related to his freeman how he had seen his wife in the visiting room and lied to her. He just didn't have the heart to tell her the truth. He told her he wouldn't know until tomorrow. But, he said, he knew that she knew.

Now she was out there in that motel room with the terrible knowledge that he wouldn't come up again for another year, and he was afraid what she might do. She had taken an overdose of pills when he was first sentenced. Could the freeman just drop by the motel and tell her what a fine friendship they had here so she would be comforted and encouraged?

The freeman did.

She had obviously been crying, and she was obviously grateful. Her husband had told her about him. Also, she was more beautiful than her husband had conveyed. "Please come in and tell me about Carl." He wondered about the propriety of this as he stepped through the door, but his good intentions and his genuine feelings of sorrow quickly dispelled any sense of wrong. Besides, her perfume was just heady enough so that some of his actions were more instinct than intent.

He could see that she had been drinking a bit.

When he left at about midnight he was a little drunk. She "had not known for a long time anyone she could really trust. She was so grateful." He had not known for a long time such an evening in bed.

His conscience caught up with him the next morning. He had a little trouble facing Carl. But his conscience really overwhelmed him that afternoon when Carl came back from the visiting room. There were no hard feelings. "That's the way things go. . . . Just pick up the stuff tonight from her and bring it in tomorrow, and no one will ever know." And so he was "wired."

It was several months before the freeman was caught, tried, and started doing time himself. In the interim he had carried many, many thousands of dollars worth of heroin into the prison.

Pruno

Not all psychoactive drugs come in from outside. We have earlier noted the fermentation of pruno inside the walls. It is commonly made by putting slices of fruit, a bit of sugar, some yeast or uncooked dough from the kitchen, and some water into a plastic bag. A plastic tube, held in place in the neck of the bag with a rubber band, is poked down through the water trap of the toilet and shoved far enough up into the soil pipe so that the fermentation gases escape into the sewage system. The plastic bag then lies behind the toilet and is not visible from the cell door. Once started and going well, with a daily replenishment, this will provide an occasional nip, or a good drink before dinner. (The term "good" in this sense is intended to mean having a reasonably high alcoholic content, not by any means a beverage of fine character.)

Pruno is usually made for self-consumption, either individually or as a cooperative venture by a small group. In some places, it is a source of income for the makers, and therefore must be made in larger containers. One of these recently confiscated was a cleverly constructed tank, an artfully contrived flat box made of quarter-inch plywood. It was about 14 inches wide, 2 inches thick, and 5 feet long. The inside had been pruno-proofed with a plastic coating. The tank had been substituted for the regular shelf in the inmate-vintner's cell. It was not discovered for a long time because the shelf in each cell has a replaceable cloth that covers it and hangs down about 4 inches in front.

There was a hole about 1½ inches in diameter in the top at each end. The tank was resting on but not attached to the regular shelf brackets. The wine merchants would bring ingredients from the mess hall, introduce them into the hole in the left end, rock the tank gently back and forth a couple of times, then siphon some of the fermented liquid from the hole in the right end with a small plastic hose. Customer delivery was made in plastic sandwich bags, tied at the top and carried in an inside uniform pocket. When they were caught, the businessmen would not tell the guards what the going price was, but it was probably somewhere near a carton of cigarettes per pint. The tank was discovered because the design did not contain any method for getting rid of the odor of fermentation, and it became so strong the guards could not ignore it.

The use of a still to concentrate pruno into a crude brandy is relatively rare, since it requires a heat boiler, a heat source, a condensing coil, and a receiving container. Since its smell is so difficult to control, it invites confiscation.

Let us tell a true story.

There once was an inmate in a large prison, a highly edu-cated white-collar worker who had poorly managed a stock-juggling deal and had been convicted for it. He vowed to maintain his self-esteem and dignity in prison by having his usual drink before dinner. There was no place in the prison's educational system for him, since he was already well educated. He was assigned to one of the metal shops. There he designed and constructed a tiny still of exquisite perfection. It contained a boiler, a heat source (a half-inch candle stub), a condenser, and the receiving container. It would operate in his pocket! This man did not smoke, and he shunned the usual cigarettes, candies and cookies, sardines, and cigars in the inmate commissary. But he did use these items for trading purposes in the hospital for a type of athletes-foot medicine that contained 40 percent ethyl alcohol. Each evening before dinner he filled the boiler of his still with the green medicine, lit the candle stub, and put the device into his pocket. Within 15 minutes he had a pretty good little jolt to consume. With dignity, he went to dinner.

The whole affair came to an abrupt end when one night, lying in bed, he came to the sudden realization that if he were caught with this device it would probably cost him another year in prison. He turned it in to the guard captain, who was so impressed with his workmanship, his conscience, and his honesty that no complaint was lodged against him. His handiwork now reposes in the prison museum.

Glue-Sniffing

Glues and other volatile intoxicants were at one time popular; but recently their use has fallen off, primarily because toxicity has been recognized by the inmates. There have been a number of deaths, and most convicts want to die on the outside. There used to be salesmen in most institutions who had "glue routes" where they peddled their product. They worked in the paint shop, the shoe shop, the furniture factory, or anywhere else where some substance with a volatile fraction was used. As knowledge of liver damage became known, this traffic declined, with some exceptions. One guard, who conducts discussion groups with drug users in prison, stated that he was certain that all young Mexican convicts in his prison either sniff glue, a highly volatile rubber cement used in the shoe factory, or thinner from the paint shop.

Guards say they are relieved at the decline in sniffing, for the ones we talked to contended that an inmate intoxicated on glue was a troublemaker, reacting violently, they said, if threatened with seizure of his glue bag or bottle. They told us of men battling furiously with guards to retain their "sniffers."

Pricing

The cost of a fix in prison, as in any free enterprise system, varies with availability of the product and the current demand. The most readily available heroin fix is a weak $10 paper that has come in at about 3 percent and been cut twice before being resold. Three cartons of cigarettes will normally buy a fix. A straight $50 balloon will resell for $75 in the traditional three-for-two ratio of values for anything borrowed or sold in prison. Another late quotation for the going price of a $50 balloon in one large prison was 20 cartons of cigarettes. That many cigarettes constitutes a logistic problem in handling and concealment. Money is the preferred medium of exchange. The buyer takes his chances on the quality of the drug.

A recent heroin overdose death in a large institution was unique in that a sample of heroin recovered from the prisoner's cell was eight times the strength normally coming in. No one has been able to account for this.

Marijuana cigarettes may go at a rate of from one package of regular cigarettes for a joint, up to three cartons, depending on how much is coming in.

The cost of LSD varies widely. A single "high" will run the user from one to three cartons of cigarettes, sometimes $5 or $10 in cash. At other times, it will be given away, if the supply is right and friendships are involved, much as liquor is supplied by the host at a cocktail party.

A good glue bag, where it is still used, will bring from one to three cartons of cigarettes, but the new fast-setting water-mix glues and the fear of death have cut this trade sharply.

The price of methedrine, if it is made in the institution, will be low. If the convicts have access to a lab where they can conceal their activities and manage the raw materials along with the chemical knowledge to know what they are doing, they are in business. Rumor has it that "crystal" is so available in one penitentiary where it is manufactured internally that it is almost free. If there is no internal source, the price goes up sharply.

Prevalence of Psychoactive Drug Use

The "dark number" problem is considerably more difficult to solve in prison than outside, for outside one can gain confidence, do surveys, take personal and medical histories, and, if seeking accuracy, can employ tests such as thin-layer chromotographic analysis of urines, blood tests for alcohols, nalline, and the like. In prison where there has as yet been little reason to cooperate in such inquiries (the work of Kinsey on homosexuality in California prisons back in the 1940s is a happy exception), estimates are much harder to come by. We think it can be done by using prisoner-run surveys, but that will take some time to arrange.

Prevalence estimates are further complicated by the variety of substances used and the difficulty in distinguishing between placebos, psychoactive substances, and poisons. Inmates take pruno, nutmeg, mace, allspice, any drug from the hospital that is hoped to have central nervous system effects; they have sniffed a variety of compounds from insipid to lethal; and they seek smuggled alcohol, methedrine, morphine, cocaine, heroin, peyote, marijuana, LSD, and so forth. Further, they may drink anything from Ditto fluid (blinding or fatal) to topical remedies. Our best estimate, based on all of our interviews plus our own observations and experiences in the California prisons, is that half of the prisoners in adult institutions have used a psychoactive (nonprescribed) at least once a year and that between 15 percent and 25 percent use drugs other than alcohol, sporadically at least.

Overreporting rather than underreporting is, we think, the most likely direction of our error. Inmates enjoy the sense of beating the system through contraband and use, and they magnify their success. Staff may prefer to have a publicly acknowledged devil to fight so that they may, symbolically, get across to others the difficulty of their task. Administrators may prefer a high estimate to a low when they present their budgets that call for expanded staff and resources, for in these days of state funding cutbacks, raising the specter of heroin remains one way to get money when others are failing.

A poor estimate of prevalence derives from detected cases. Records of administrative action vis-à-vis drug users are not always accurate and complete—if they exist in retrievable form at all. Our recourse again was to figures given by administrative officers in charge of such action and records. They claim that official detection of use ranges from 3 percent to 7 percent of the inmates per year, or from about 6 percent to 15 percent of those believed to use once or more.

Prevalence estimates by group are risky. There was general agreement that younger men use more than older men, that Mexican-Americans use proportionately more, followed by whites, with blacks using the least. Most respondents also felt that Mexican-Americans were most likely to control the traffic, insofar as that is possible. Blacks more often than whites are said to work as dealers under Chicano control.

Pecking Order

There is disagreement on the status of users expressed both by staff and inmates. In general, older staff and older inmates, especially white-collar offenders, hold that users are a cut below the rest of the cons, being held in less esteem by most. They are likely to be the troublemakers, they bring on cell searches, cause mistrust resulting in disruption of normal routines, and threaten a nonuser with accidental trouble if he is an innocent bystander. The user, hurting for a fix, is a moocher and deadbeat who takes advantage of friendships. Most convicts, they say, would rather do their time and stay out of trouble; and drugs mean trouble.

Younger staff and cons are more sympathetic to users, elevate them to higher status, and are, of course, more likely to be users themselves or to have users as same-age friends. At worst, they are seen as other cons doing their time as best they can; they may even be objects of pity or, conversely, admiration if they are successful dealers who exercise skill and power. Younger men who are not users are said to be willing to help in contraband traffic more in the spirit of beat-the-institution, thereby aiding users, whereas older cons do their own time. The user who is a successful smuggler may also be feared, for he must have connections. This implies the solidarity of unknown others who can be dangerous if their interests, as, for example, a customer addict's safety, are threatened.

Control

Guards contended that it was difficult to control traffic in easily concealed substances when so few personnel had to watch so much going on. Inmates agreed. As one bull said, "Hell, we got a budget too, which means there are just so many of us. We can't search every truck, every box, and every ass-hole coming into this place. And we can't touch the visitors. We know we're surrounded by the stuff. The best we can do is try to keep it invisible."

One method of control is that which put the inmates there in the first place, punishment. An inmate who violates one of the Department of Corrections rules is subject to punishments that are prescribed by the department. These may be a simple loss of some privilege such as going to the movie, or up to as many as ten days in "the hole" (isolation). In addition, the inmate is "beefed"; a written report of the incident is placed in his file. When the prisoner comes before the parole board any beef he has is considered. A beef may keep a prisoner from becoming a trusty or achieving honor status.

If an inmate is drunk, he may get a simple "you can't go to the movie for a week." If he is so careless as to be discovered making pruno, and it is his first offense, it may mean a couple of days in the hole. The prisoner discovered with a pruno vat is also *assessed* (not fined) $1.00 per gallon for the contents of the container. The money is taken from the prisoner's own account. This assessment is based on the presumption that the contents of the vat were improperly used and cost the state that much, therefore the inmate must repay the state.

Any hard drug use or dealing is a felony. Felonies are handled by the county courts outside the prison. The penalty handed down by the court for a heroin dealer arrested in prison supposedly would be the same as if he had been arrested peddling on the main street in town. We have no figures on such referrals.

Control is also exerted on the staff by the threat of felony charges. In one institution with between 650 and 700 employees and 3500 inmates, the rate of arrests for drug offenses among the guards is about one per year and among the staff, about two. In another facility with 500 employees, the records show an average of three to four per year accused of involvement in contraband drug traffic. The rate of dealing among freemen guards and staff, averaged for the two institutions, is 5 percent a year. If we assume detection occurs at a rate half that of complicity, one guesses that

10 percent of the staff engage, at one time or another, in contraband drug traffic.

Benefits

When a staff member brings in contraband, he may do it as an act of friendship or kindness; in response to dares, threats, or blackmail; because he is "overidentified" with the downtrodden and is himself "antiestablishment" and "pro-drug" so that his own act is a symbolic one; or he may be acting out his own psychopathy vis-à-vis his employers and his own discomfort in an authoritarian role. Poor judgment may also be involved if the employee is tricked into carrying drugs when he believes his package is innocuous. Employees traffic for money of course; most often these are said to be troubled individuals who do not manage their lives or finances well and who are low paid on the salary scale. No doubt other motives can be identified, but these were the ones that staff and convicts mentioned most often.

There is, occasionally, a different kind of benefit that emerges not from the fact of traffic, but the fact of its knowledge and the ability of an administrator to manipulate it. We offer the following anecdote as told to us by a prison administrator.

A racial war had broken out, and there was a protracted series of stabbings of blacks by whites, and then whites by blacks. Each time a black was stabbed, a white was sure to be stabbed in retaliation, until a total of 19 stabbings had occurred, resulting in two deaths.

The prison administration had to stop the violence. There seemed only one solution: a complete lockup. In prison, a complete lockup means that prisoners are kept in their cells at all times except for meals, and in extreme cases this can include racially segregated feeding to minimize the opportunity for interracial violence. Lockup, under these circumstances, might have to go on for as long as two or three months or until the prison administration feels that the hostility has cooled to the point where interracial contact can be resumed with safety. This is very hard on the prisoners, and it is very hard on the staff. Everyone's morale suffers. It is a last resort.

In reviewing possible actions before turning to the unpleas-

*antness of a complete lockup, we considered the narcotics traffic. We
were aware that the Mexicans were in control of the introduction
of narcotics into the prison, its distribution and sale.*

*We were also aware that a complete lockup would paralyze
their business. So we used the narcotics traffic as a leverage to stop
the knifings. One administrator called the Mexican convict leaders
into his office. Four stony-faced influential Mexicans stood before
him. He explained to them that he was fully aware that the Mexicans were not involved in the interracial war, but that because of
it the prison was faced with a complete lockup. He also told them
he knew they were dealing heavy narcotics, and that a lockup would
stop their business cold. Did they understand each other?*

"Si."

"On this basis can you stop the knifings?"

"Si."

*For a full appreciation of this the reader should be aware
that the Mexicans are the most feared of prisoners. They have a
reputation among the others for incredibly fast and efficient knife
work.*

*For several weeks, each day during the exercise hour the
blacks had gathered in one corner of the yard, the whites in the op-
posite corner on the same side of the rectangle, and the Mexicans
lounged along the wall across from the other two groups. Later in
the day of the administrator's conference with the Mexican leaders
the pattern in the yard was the same. We watched the action.*

*Near the end of the hour there was a stir among the Mexi-
cans and the four leaders walked out of their group and directly to
the whites. They stood at the edge of the white group and called
three of them out by name. Then the Mexicans and the three whites
walked to the black group and similarly, three of them were called
out by name. This group of ten then went to the very center of the
yard. Even though there was absolute silence, we were too far away
to hear what was being said. One could see Mexican fingers pointed
at the whites and blacks. Some very precise instructions appeared
to be being given. The confrontation lasted about five minutes, at
the end of which the work whistle blew, and the inmates in the yard
went to their assigned jobs.*

There were no more stabbings.

*After a few days of careful arrangements one of us managed
to get one of the whites who had been called to the center of the
yard into his office to find out what had gone on. It was simple.*

*Mexican leaders told the black and white representatives,
"Look, we don't want our business screwed up. You dudes know
what we can do. The very next stabbing, we throw our weight behind the guy who got stabbed. One of you black dudes stabs a white
man we go to work on you. One of you red-necks stabs a brother,
we fix you. And if you think there's been some cutting going on up
to now, just try us."*

Peace. And prosperity in the drug trade.

Folktales, Heroin, and Evil

Consider the story related earlier in this chapter of the con servant who destroys his ambitious master. We would not be surprised
if that tale—like many others we were told by inmates—were apocry-
phal. These can be more interesting than true accounts, for folktales can be more revealing of psychological and social realities than
are accurate reports (Blum and Blum, 1970). Folktales exist because
they satisfy and what they satisfy are, at least, desires and morality
of tellers and listeners.

In the story, the clever con wins out over the high-status
employee, a supervisor; the con's subservient role is only a disguise,
for he proves to be a man of cunning and power. His apparent
obsequiousness and betrayal of all inmate secrets to the boss is false;
the real man behind the mask is masterful and is not in the service
of the prison administration after all, but is a dealer trafficking in
contraband on behalf of the inmate "system." Further, the con
forces demonstration of the venality, weakness, and naïvete—all
despicable—of the freeman who falls readily first for his obedient
servant's tales, secondly for his "wife," and thirdly for the blackmail that "forces" him to the ultimate evil, carrying heroin into the
joint. Furthermore, there is a lesson on ambition, for the freeman
"on the way up" is brought down whereas the con, not on the way
up, wins out. Relax, be satisfied with your lot, cautions the tale. The
further twist is also a moral delight, for there *is* justice of the kind
the con would like to see: all men *are* equal in degradation, for the

freeman ignominiously joins the inmate in prisoner status, but by implication as an inferior since he is less clever.

All such stories that prisoners tell—and sometimes staff, too —should be examined as folklore whatever one does with the facts. Folklore analysis of what we have heard in this study tells us, if nothing else, of the tremendous importance of narcotics traffic as *the* symbol for inmate power over the system that seeks to control them. Narcotics traffic and use, viewed symbolically, is more than a private escape from consciousness of oppression and degradation and is more than the successful achievement of private pleasure through drug effects. It is the means used by inmates (that is, those inmates participating in it) to stay the way they are against becoming the way the system of administration of justice wants them to become. If one accepts the popular view of heroin as an evil thing, destroyer and enslaver and the most taboo of pleasures, then inmates trafficking in it confirm their own evil, demonstrating their "badness" as opposed to the rehabilitated self that society claims it is seeking. It is as if they mean to say, "We are not just criminals and cons as we have been labeled; we are really bad inside and, like a convert to Satan, are going to make the most of it." The affirmation of badness is much like what Erikson (1968) described as "negative anxiety." With such an identity, bad becomes good; and the inmates in that condition revel, as we see from their stories, in knifing, in blackmail and extortion, in prostituting their wives in the service of narcotics traffic, and in betraying the staff who befriend them.

Narcotics traffic also has a social function, for it provides a community activity that binds together, at least the younger cons, into a working system that exalts cunning and ruthlessness in the service of inmate solidarity. Traffic in drugs is *their* chosen work —as is the making of shanks—as opposed to the "make-work" imposed upon them. As chosen work, it is for the inmate what hustling is on the outside (Preble and Casey, 1969), a way of centering one's interests, keeping life going at an interesting and busy pace, and, in doing so, continuing that which gives gratification—drug use itself, the company of like-minded peers, money-making, and the prideful demonstration of personal skill in the business. It is cool as well as bad, and its existence shows how hard it is to change people once they are in prison.

We feel heroin traffic—or traffic other than the morally acceptable one in pruno (neither staff nor inmates would call that evil)—must be viewed as more than a drug-related problem in prison. It is an exercise in the subversion of the straight world's morality and power. As such, it is a means for the inmate to continue to be himself, that is, to avoid being that which others insist he be. Instead, the trafficker concentrates on his ability to triumph with cunning devices, underplaying thereby his otherwise wretched status and self-esteem. Being a trafficker gives him power of the sort Faust enjoyed, and it offers the esteem of a man proud of doing evil to himself and to others.

This interpretation does not exclude the more mundane reasons for the use of drugs in prison, most certainly for their pharmacological effects and the altered mental states that boredom invites. We believe the interpretation does account for the intensity and pleasure in the traffic itself, which is otherwise not understandable since pharmacologically escape and euphoria can be obtained through pruno. Heroin, no doubt, is the more potent substance in theory, but given the highly diluted heroin in prison, one must await a comparative analysis of potency and clinical effects before arguing that prison heroin is, in fact, much stronger than fruit wine.

Temptation

In Blum and Associates (1972a) we observed different responses to temptation among adults; for example, faculty and narcotics officers. The data in this chapter allow us to comment on another respectable older group, prison guards and staff. One finds a rather high rate—if our 10 percent estimate is accepted—of dealing among a straight* group. Their exposure is most like that of narcotics officers (as opposed to pharmacists, faculty, and the like), for the relationship is as honest man *versus* a drug offender. In this at least somewhat antagonistic relationship, the offender, to protect himself, may seek to tempt or subvert the antagonist. It appears that the prison inmate accomplishes this with greater regularity among

* We do not have data on the criminal backgrounds of guards, culinary workers, and hospital employees, the three groups said to be at a higher risk of trafficking. We do know that, contrary to the rules, ex-felons do sometimes work as freemen employees in prison.

freemen staff than does the same offender, prior to incarceration, when pitted against narcotics officers in the region where we worked. It also appears that the rate of succumbing to temptation in the California prisons is considerably less than that which occurs among the police in some Eastern cities. One cannot account for these differences prior to research, but one assumes that the variables of personnel selection and training, of closeness of supervision, of institutional atmosphere, of quality of leadership, and so forth, would operate. Why one prison would differ from another, or one police department from another, is the enigma of the "corrupt ship" as the Navy calls it or the corrupted office as the Internal Revenue Service experienced in the mid-1960s, to their dismay. This differential institutional response to temptation remains a relatively untouched research area.

Interdicting Dealing

The data from prisons and juvenile halls (given in this chapter and in Chapter Seven) make it clear that one does not eliminate drug dealing simply by arresting and sentencing dealers to penal servitude. The dealers are moved from one place to another, thereby, no doubt, reducing the amount of their commerce and profits. Incarceration apparently does not substantially eliminate the interests of users in using or of dealers in dealing; but that proposition requires qualification, for we (Blum and Associates, 1972a) found that arrest does eventually deter some dealers from continuing dealing, upon release. We can understand how arrest and incarceration fail to deter dealing as we see that the attitudes of (some or most?) user-dealers are not, in fact, altered by the prison experience, but that, if anything, the experience may confirm their badness rather than their goodness. Further, it is evident that prison can give practice in cunning, which, as they continue dealing, ought only to increase the skills of the inmate user-dealers. The dilemma faced by society, if it seeks to prevent drug traffic by means of prison sentencing of drug offenders to existing institutions, is evident. Our inquiry does suggest that some user-dealers do stay clean in prison and, as indicated by our dealer study, stay clean afterward. Most appear not to clean up. Elimination of prison sentencing leaves still the jail experience before trial or after it; and, as allusions to jail by our inmates and dealers indicated, a jail can be a far worse place than a prison (see Blum, 1963). If such punishments are eliminated entirely, there remains the unresolved question of deterrence for others who have not begun to deal for fear of such dire punishment. We also do not know whether the rate of continuing in dealing would increase among those who after arrest and prison now clean up but without threat of unpleasant sequelae would not do so. These questions, of course, apply not just to dealers but to all those engaged in vice and, beyond them, to both the social philosophy of offender handling (to punish, exact vengeance, deter, cause penance, suppress only during incarceration, correct, rehabilitate, or any combination thereof?) and the actual consequences of the prison experience independent of social intentions. We raise them here as part of a contemporary chorus of questions to which all of us, as citizens, are well advised to pay heed.

Drug-Dealing and the Law

John Kaplan

Most of the other work in this study of drugs, reported here and in *The Dream Sellers* (Blum and Associates, 1972a), has been concentrated, in one way or another, upon the direct or indirect influence of the law upon various aspects of drug-dealing. In this chapter, we will reverse the process. We will look at aspects of drug-dealing to see how they are affecting the law. Of course in one sense—a static one—the law exists, and the behavior of its subjects does not change its written terms. This view, however, is much too simple, since the law is a dynamic process; even though the behavior of its subjects cannot change the words in the statute books, the behavior of those affected by a law exerts an enormous influence on the law in action—how the law is enforced and applied by legal officers.

In a larger sense, moreover, the response to a legal measure exerts a powerful influence on the development, over time, of the formal law. More specifically, the nature of both drug use and drug-

201

dealing will be major factors influencing the measures society will take to cope with the problems of the use and abuse of drugs.

It is impossible in one short chapter to assimilate for this purpose the vast amount of information revealed in the entire study. As a result, we will not discuss the "medical" drugs. It is true that the areas of our study involving detail men, pharmacists, and physicians are replete with information that might be invaluable in framing a rational policy. For the most part, however, the medical drugs are not the urgent problem that the illegal drugs are. Here we will concentrate our attention on the illegal drugs.

Effectiveness of Criminal Laws

We can set out in very general terms some of the major results of the entire study. First, the deterrent effects of the criminal law upon dealers of illegal drugs is by no means weak. The figures on those who have left drug-dealing as a profession because of fear of criminal punishment or because of the strains of the dealer's life—caused in great part by its illegality—show that the criminal law has a substantial effect on them as individuals.

Second, in a broader view, this effect is not very important. For laws aimed at deterring armed robbery or drunken driving, each offense deterred (regardless of how many are not deterred) represents a saving in risk to human lives and property; deterrence of drug-dealing is quite different. If the supply of drugs is sufficient, the fact that many dealers are deterred is not of great significance, as long as many others take up the slack and the would-be drug user can find an available source.

This situation obviously holds with the drug dealers in our sample. As a practical matter, there is, in general, no shortage of illicit drugs, although particular drugs may be in short supply at any one time; and when a shortage does occur it is, for various reasons, often of dubious pharmacological benefit.

The next aspect of drug-dealing documented by the overall study is at first very hard to grasp fully—the enormous number of drug dealers. For instance, in one high school the study located 129 dealers and in a large private university found no fewer than 700. (We must remember that the university sample includes only regular dealers for profit and takes no account of what may be a substantial number of either one-time dealers for profit or regular sources that supply but not for profit.) The same university, which utilizes more than 700 drug dealers, is served by only three retail liquor dealers of the immediate vicinity. These figures doubtless overemphasize the disparity, since in addition to the "big three" of the liquor trade a number of other retail liquor dealers farther away are certainly patronized by some students and since students consume a sizeable amount of alcohol in the bars and restaurants of the area.

On the other hand, the disparity in the numbers of dealers in alcohol and dealers in illegal drugs who serve the campus is nonetheless enormous and, if one thinks about it, is obviously an effect of the drug laws. As long as drug-dealing is made criminal, the cautious dealer will prefer to deal only with his friends and those whom he can trust. In order to cover a drug-using campus in a period when people just do not have that many friends, an enormous number of dealers is necessary. The liquor dealer, however, does not have to worry whether his customers will talk to the police about his dealing and hence can sell to anyone of legal age with no concern about security against detection.

In short, one effect of law enforcement is to atomize the illegal drug-dealing industry to a point at which the deterrent effects of the criminal law—which of course increase significantly as one deals with more distant acquaintances—reach a balance with the desire for profit and the other rewards of drug-dealing.

The deterrent effect of the law seems at its most effective at the very lowest retail level since these dealers generally are easiest to catch and, at least at this level, the profits are lowest. The higher up the dealer hierarchy, the greater the profit (though perhaps not the other rewards of dealing), and the harder the dealers are to catch—both because they have the incentive to take much greater precautions and because, as individuals, they are much more con-wise than the retail dealer. Of course, law enforcement can be expected to attempt to compensate for this inversion of the deterrent effect by allocating more effort toward apprehending bigger dealers. Obviously, this attempt is made by the federal and state narcotics bureaus, though we must remember that the locals make most of the dealing arrests. In any event, the effort pays off to some extent since the bigger dealers of our study were more likely to be arrested than were the lesser ones. However, it is most doubtful that the relatively slightly greater danger of apprehension does more than balance the greater financial and status rewards of big dealing. Nor can we hope through enforcement to put enough big dealers out of circulation to disorganize the market for any length of time. On this point, another finding of the study is relevant. Just as the arrest of even a sizable percentage of illicit retail drug dealers could not be expected to have an enormous effect on the market, simply because there would be so many of them remaining at large, the effect of an arrest of a "Mr. Big," or indeed of several of them, would also be easy to overestimate. Even if there are not so many at the top of the pyramid, there are more than enough lieutenants just a bit below who know enough about the operation of the business and stand ready to step in and take over.

Dealing in Marijuana

At this point, let us narrow our focus somewhat and examine the marijuana situation. Of the illegal drugs, marijuana is by far the most commonly sold; and, regardless what else they sell, most of our dealers sell or have sold that drug. It should be clear that, despite successes here and there, our present laws covering drug-dealing are not really doing much good relative to marijuana. As long as the law cannot discourage a high percentage of potential users (and other studies reveal that it seems to be unable to do this among the solid majority of young people)' and so long as we cannot shut off the drug at its source (the government is devoting great amounts of energy to this goal in what many observers think is a futile quest) we must look elsewhere if we are to cope with the problem of illegal dealing in marijuana. With respect to at least this particular drug, the study clearly reveals the imperative need to search for alternatives to the criminal law for solutions in the dealing area.

This study of drug dealers documents a number of facts that demonstrate our need for alternative solutions: (1)' Beginning users tend to get marijuana from their friends. '(2)' This marijuana is generally the first illegal drug they have used. (3)' Some users, among those who like the drug most, go on to selling marijuana.

(4) Marijuana typically is the first illegal drug our dealers have sold. (5) A majority of marijuana dealers use, and a sizable fraction deal in, "harder" drugs.

The process, basically, goes something like this. Many young people are exposed to marijuana at a fairly young age, typically in high school but often shortly thereafter. Some get the drug from a friend, try it, and, in simple terms, like it. They get "turned on" to the drug and tell their friends about it—perhaps even bragging about their experience in part because there is a "forbidden fruit" aspect to marijuana use even though the practice is now quite common. The new user's friends hear about the experience and, perhaps more important, that their friend has access to a safe supply. They, too, want to try the experience and ask their friend for his help. Initially, it is a friendly matter—he merely makes part of his supply available to his friends. Perhaps the gains in status among his peers are more important to him than money at this stage. Assuming some of his friends also take a liking to the drug, they will want more; and very soon, as a matter of economics, he will have to insist that they pay their share (it is doubtful, too, that they want to be spongers). The next step down the road to marijuana dealing is an equally small one. The user keeps buying his supply but now divides most of it among his friends; and he prices it so that, for the service he performs, he gets his own marijuana free. He can still regard himself as not really making a profit on the transaction. From that point, he may gradually slide into selling to a larger number of friends— who are not *such* good friends that he cannot, in conscience, make a profit from them. Reinforced by this profit and perhaps his growing status as a "big man," he can gradually go on selling more to a somewhat widening circle of friends and acquaintances until he enters our category of regular dealers for profit.

Dealing in marijuana, in other words, can sneak up on a young person by a gradual series of steps, each one too small to produce any feeling of crossing the Rubicon. Indeed, a sizable percentage of dealers—not only in the legal sense but under this study's much more restricted definition—do not consider themselves dealers at all.

Obviously, the progression from initial use to regular dealing does not happen in every case. After initial trial of marijuana, many users do not like the drug that much, and many others do not feel that the status and profit of the dealer's life is worth the risk. Nonetheless, for a significant proportion (approximately 6 or 7 percent), the sequence described above does happen. The theory that a certain percentage of users are, for some reason, vulnerable to the seductions of the dealer's life is bolstered by perhaps the most often repeated finding of the study—that the simple user of marijuana occupies a position on a large number of dimensions intermediate between the dealers and the nonusers; or, in other words, the dealers are just like the users only more so.

From Marijuana to Other Drugs

In any event, one cannot read the pages of this study without being made aware of the harm that is done by the dealing career not only to society at large but also to a sizable percentage of the large number of dealers themselves. As far as the dealers themselves go, it is true that a certain proportion of them tend to be criminalistic or at least sociopathic to begin with. Nonetheless, even for them the hardening effect of violence and other aspects of the dealer's life is a serious problem.

With respect to the rest of society, the study documents the contagion spread by drug dealers. Of the sample of 480 dealers, 270 had introduced between 1 and 19 persons to illicit drug use while 124 had introduced more than 20! Moreover, dealing in marijuana is an entry to dealing in other illicit drugs. Even though less than half of the marijuana dealers deal in other illicit drugs, the number is so large that obviously the temptations to branch out are extremely strong. By the time the marijuana dealer begins to contemplate the sale of LSD, pills, or the like, he already has a regular clientele. Furthermore, being like the users only more so, he is likely to be drug-oriented and to spend a sizable proportion of his life thinking about drugs not only from the business but from the personal point of view. His own source of supply for his marijuana dealing is likely also to sell other illegal drugs—indeed, the higher one is in the dealing hierarchy, the more likely he is to sell a variety of drugs. The small marijuana dealer then forms a ready-made conduit to supply other drugs to users who are not so deeply enmeshed in the drug culture as he. Is it possible that all he does is circulate the word among his clientele that he has other wares for sale? However, if he is indeed dealing with his friends, and if, being more drug-oriented than they, he does think highly of his other illicit wares, it would hardly be surprising if he touted them to the clientele in the same way he began with marijuana.

It would be interesting to compare, in this regard, the likelihood of a progression from dealing in marijuana with that of a progression from dealing in "special substances." Although sniffing glue, solvents, and the like, is dangerous and often illegal (and certainly the juvenile court tends to take an interest in it), it is hard to find any evidence for a progression from dealing in these substances to becoming any other kind of drug dealer. Like marijuana, these substances are widely available, and the laws attempting to restrict their availability are by and large ineffective. Although substance abuse may be a serious health problem to some users, the serious consequences of dealing seem less evident. This is true not only as far as the dealers themselves (who by and large seem to be legitimate businessmen) are concerned, but also in the case of the users. Whatever their other problems, substance abusers seem less likely to form a ready market for additional drugs.

Alternatives to Criminal Laws

If the issue then is how we are to prevent the harm caused by marijuana dealing, it seems clear that there is only one practical way. The criminal law has shown itself unable to do more than atomize drug-dealing, thus increasing the number of dealers and the likelihood that they will act as conduits for more dangerous drugs. Moreover, the trend is toward an even lesser deterrent effect of the law. Some time ago, the penalties actually imposed for drug dealing were much more severe, the police were more interested in the issue, and there were many fewer dealers. Now, if our studies of Comfort and Steinville are in any way typical, discreet dealers are really not very much bothered by the law.

As a result, barring a massive and suddenly successful crackdown on all dealers, there are but three ways to reduce the massive social costs of marijuana dealing in society. There must be a change in the ability of our government to choke off the source of supply, a change in the tastes of the drug users, or a change in the law. The first two changes are extremely unlikely. The possibilities of choking off the supplies of the drug at their source have been discussed elsewhere and been found meager. Although we have heard for several years that marijuana use may be a passing fad and about a year ago the reports of a massive switch from marijuana to beer were widely circulated, there is no evidence to support either contention—nor, for that matter, much reason for such an expectation. To be sure, marijuana use probably will eventually reach a steady state even with no change in the law. Not everyone in the population will be willing to try the drug, because of personal beliefs, health fears, religious convictions, or fear of the law; and there may well come a time when the number of new users exactly balances those giving up the drug. Indeed, marijuana use seems already to have peaked in some areas that have been characterized by heavy use, such as the campuses of the elite universities on the east and west coasts. In these, one-time marijuana experience hung at around 70 percent from 1969 through 1971, with about 45 percent who used on a regular though sometimes infrequent basis. These figures showed no sign of dropping substantially, however; and, in those much larger areas of lesser marijuana use, where the introduction of the drug into the middle class has occurred more recently, the percentages continued to grow.*

The final method of coping with the social problem of drug-dealing is one that the dealers themselves have pointed out as the only way to put them out of business—turn over the market to legitimate businessmen. Designing such a legal system, however, is an extremely complex task. Although a prohibition on sale that does not work provides no control at all, the licensing of legitimate dealers

---

* It is interesting to note as a sidelight that the sharpest increase in marijuana use seems to occur in a community of young people of the most susceptible ages when one-time use reaches about 20 percent. In a very short time, it doubles; and thereafter the rate of increase in use tends to slacken. We can speculate about the causes of this phenomenon. One may lie in the structure of the dealing market—that is, once 20 percent of a community try the drug, enough dealers among them are called into being to supply a substantially greater number. Alternatively, it can be argued that once about a fifth of a community have used marijuana, about as many others can be expected to observe them and decide that the physical, mental, moral, and legal dangers of the drug are not so serious as they had believed.

in marijuana allows for the enormous range of methods of control that become possible only when the dealers are known and regulated by law. It is indeed an irony that what appears to be the most stringent method of control of sale—flat prohibition—can exert only the kinds of control that we have previously discussed—an atomization of the market, a high initial status for dealers among their peers followed by their progressive alienation from our society and a growing incentive to deal in other illegal drugs. As long as dealing remains widespread, criminal laws prohibiting the activity cannot produce any of the more beneficial aspects of control, which we would desire in order to reduce drug abuse.

Proposed Statute for Marijuana Control

The following draft statute would implement control of marijuana comparable with control exercised over alcoholic beverages.

Section I. *The Department of Alcoholic Beverage Control is hereby renamed the Department of Social Drug Control and given administrative authority to regulate marijuana in addition to alcohol. All presently existing agencies subsidiary to the Department of Social Drug Control shall carry the name Social Drug rather than Alcoholic Beverage.*

Section II. *The Department of Social Drug Control shall provide by regulation for the treatment of marijuana in a manner as similar as possible to that of distilled spirits. Such regulations, however, must provide: (a) that sufficient numbers of marijuana growers be licensed to meet the projected needs of the marijuana distribution system, and that reasonable security precautions be required of growers to prevent the diversion of licensed marijuana into illegal channels; (b) that marijuana wholesale distributors be licensed to purchase marijuana from licensed growers, package the drug in one-ounce containers, and sell or consign such containers for sale by any retailer authorized to sell marijuana; (c) that each container of marijuana carry a short statement of the medical and scientific dangers of the drug drawn up by a committee of medical experts to be selected by the Department of Social Drug Control;*

*(d) that two grades of marijuana be packaged, one containing
1.5% and the other containing 4% tetrahydrocannabinol, each
plainly marked as such; (e) that should a method of marijuana
potency more precise than its tetrahydrocannabinol content become
available, such method be used instead of the tetrahydrocannabinol
content in defining the grades required by Section II (d); (f) that
should the Department of Social Drug Control find that the licensed
grades of marijuana are so potent as to create a serious public health
problem and that such potency may be reduced without causing an
even greater degree of social harm, the Department may reduce the
degree of potency in either or both licensed grades; (g) that the
licensed wholesaler of marijuana be held responsible for collecting
from the retailer a tax of $6 per ounce on the weaker grade of mari-
juana produced and $15 per ounce on the stronger grade. However,
should the Department of Social Drug Control at any time find that
illegal sales of marijuana have become so competitive in price with
legal sales as to capture a sizable fraction of the market, the Department may reduce the tax upon marijuana until illegal channels no
longer represent a significant fraction of the market. Similarly,
should the Department determine that a higher tax might be collected on either grade of marijuana without seriously impairing
control of the drug or diverting a large percentage of the traffic into
illegal channels, it may raise the tax on one or both grades; (h) that
if the Department of Social Drug Control determines that marijuana use involves a serious hazard of dangerous operation of a
motor vehicle, it may require that some biologically inert material
be added to packaged marijuana which material can be measured
in the blood, urine or other body fluids so long as the presence of
marijuana or its metabolites in the body gives rise to the danger in
question; (i) that any seller licensed to retail packaged distilled
liquor shall be licensed to sell marijuana provided that the marijuana be purchased from a licensed wholesaler; (j) that, in any
event, no marijuana may be sold to anyone under the age of eigh-
teen; (k) that individuals be licensed to cultivate marijuana in
reasonable quantity for their own personal or family consumption.
If at any time the Department determines that such private cultivation has created a serious law enforcement problem or has deprived
the state of substantial tax revenues, it may impose additional license*

fees on a per plant basis which yield an amount approximately the tax upon an equivalent purchase from licensed retailers; (l) that no advertising of marijuana—or of any brand of marijuana—aside from that in trade publications directed solely at those licensed to sell marijuana, shall be permitted, except that advertising may be displayed wholly within the establishment of licensed retailers of marijuana.

Section III. *All monies collected under this statute in the form of license fees or taxes shall be used, as a first charge, to pay the administrative costs of the licensing system provided for in this law. All monies over and above this first charge shall be divided by the legislature among programs for the rehabilitation of, and medical services for, drug abusers, including those who have abused marijuana or alcohol; education concerning the dangers of abuse of psychoactive drugs, including marijuana and alcohol; and scientific research on the effects and use of psychoactive drugs, including marijuana and alcohol.*

We can speculate about the effect of such statute upon marijuana dealers, as their characteristics were revealed in our study. First of all, insofar as many dealers claim ideological justification for dealing by their allegations that the drug control laws are "unwise if not immoral," this justification would disappear. (To what extent behavior would change in consequence is another matter entirely.) On the more concrete level, we may reasonably assume that, under the pressure of economic forces, the marijuana trade would become very much like that involving alcohol. Younger people would of course have some access to marijuana, in part from parents and older siblings; but such "contributions to delinquency" would be leakage from the licensing system rather than floods from illegal channels of supply. The drug so acquired would have the same potency and purity as legal marijuana and, if illegally sold, would have to carry a price enough higher than the taxed price to afford the seller his profit and to compensate him for his risk of detection. The rewards of illegal dealing in marijuana would to a greater extent than now have to be financial, since it is hard to imagine any young man acquiring much status among his peers merely because he can get hold of a product that is legally available to everyone over 18, and it is perhaps even harder to see how he could make much money at it. If, indeed, status among one's peers and extra money are the crucial elements in becoming a marijuana dealer, a licensing system might effectively prevent these inducements from enticing the young into the dealer's life.

More important, if the sources of marijuana illegally sold to the young would be leakage from the licensing system, such sources would no longer be the same as those that provide LSD, amphetamines, and the like. It is of course possible that a group of intermediaries might come into being to purchase marijuana legally and then sell the drug to young dealers and that these intermediaries would also handle more dangerous drugs. On the other hand, it is hard to imagine that this development could occur under a licensing system to anything like the extent to which it has occurred already. Indeed, since our study fails to indicate any serious connection between illegal alcohol dealing and dealing in other drugs, it is likely that it would not occur to any significant extent at all.

In short, our dealers probably spoke with less than complete prescience when they asserted that the only way to put them out of business was to legalize the drugs they were dealing in. It is likely that the chain need not be broken at every one of its links. Should only marijuana among the illegal drugs be licensed for sale, the damage to the pattern of socialization of new users and dealers might well be sufficient to cripple a sizable segment of the marketing of "harder" drugs.

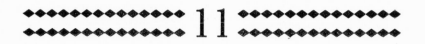

11

Corrections and Treatment

Jared Tinklenberg

Since widespread illicit drug-dealing is a new phenomenon in our society, an analysis of corrective intervention must be a tentative and speculative commentary. Present data, as collected in this volume and in *The Dream Sellers* (Blum and Associates, 1972a), illustrate that dealers are a variegated lot ranging from college students who sell off a few lids of marijuana to pay for their own drug supply, to professionals who do a volume business in a variety of drugs and make their living exclusively in the criminal world. In order to predict the success of various approaches to intervention among this complex group of drug dealers, it is useful to focus on their common traits.

Two characteristics of drug dealers described in these two volumes may have prognostic significance. First, most dealers use drugs extensively, and many could be described as drug-dependent;

213

in fact, the more extensive their dealing, the more probable their dependence. However, is the converse also true? Does increasing drug dependence enhance the probability of drug dealing? There are data suggesting this may be the case (Goode, 1970). This is obviously an important question, for in terms of maximum benefit to society, it may be that intervention and prevention of drug *abuse* would be the most productive solution to dealing. If heavy drug use correlates with dealing and the consequent spread of drug abuse, a primary aim of intervention should be to reduce the overall incidence of drug abuse. In this chapter, the terms *drug abuse* and *drug dependence* are used interchangeably to refer to the nonmedical use of psychoactive substances that result either in behavior that is specifically detrimental to others or in physical or social damage to the individual user. The term *addiction* is used to connote an extreme behavioral pattern of compulsive drug use, characterized by overwhelming involvement with the use of a drug, the securing of its supply, and a high tendency to relapse after withdrawal (Jaffe, 1970a).

Extrapolations from the various forms of drug-abuse intervention attempted in recent years may be useful in proposing methods of intervention with drug dealers as *drug abusers*. Although the following sections of this chapter will focus on the treatment of heroin addiction, it should be emphasized that drug abusers tend to be multiple-drug users. Therefore, one need not focus exclusively on the specific drug a dealer may be taking at a given time; subsequently he is likely to abuse other drugs.

A second characteristic of drug dealers is delinquency. Many dealers may be termed delinquent, not only as violators of drug laws, but also as violators of other criminal codes (see Blum and Associates, 1972a). Extensive drug-dealing often correlates with many forms of criminal behavior, including violence, the carrying of concealed weapons, and the like. Although minor delinquent behavior usually antedates drug use and dealing, the risk of extensive criminal involvement increases markedly with increased participation in the drug-dealing subculture (see Blum and Associates, 1972a).

Drug abuse and delinquency appear to be interrelated. In part, this interrelationship may stem from the fact that the same controls systems, usually penal, are applied to both of these behaviors. In any event, previous long-term studies have demonstrated positive correlation between criminality and drug dependency (Robins, 1966, 1970; Guze and others, 1969, 1970; Goodwin and others, 1971). Rates of recidivism among ex-convicts increase if drug use persists. Thus, for purposes of exposition, in this chapter an obvious oversimplification will be made: Drug dealers will be characterized as drug-dependent, delinquent individuals. In terms of this generalization, dealing with drug dealers may be considered not a new problem but rather as another facet of a very old problem of dealing with deviance of all types.

Problems in Assessing Approaches

A realistic discussion of methods of intervention among drug dealers requires a long-term perspective because dealing, like drug abuse and delinquency, may involve chronic behavioral patterns that persist over time yet demonstrate episodic changes. Unfortunately, we lack pertinent, longitudinal information on drug dealers. For example, if drug-dealing is interrelated with drug abuse, dealing may wax and wane with the characteristic drug-abuse patterns of exacerbation and remission. Episodic changes in drug abuse entail not only variations in quantity but also shifts in preference from one drug to another (Manheimer and others, 1968; McGlothlin and others, 1970a; Devenyi and Wilson, 1971). Following dealers over time may determine whether or not dealing patterns correlate with drug-abuse patterns. We may then be able to answer such questions as "Do shifts in drug preference correlate with shifts in the drugs a dealer handles?" and "What is the risk that 'psychedelic dealers' may become 'hard-drug dealers'?"

In addition to the paucity of long-term data, it is important to remember that some drug-dependent or delinquent persons fulfill the diagnostic criteria of the sociopathic or psychopathic personality. This personality disorder involves recurrent tendencies toward deviance in many areas of life regardless of the immediate circumstances or the social context. These individuals seem unable to maintain loyalties with any other person, group, or code; and they are predisposed toward both criminal behavior and drug abuse. Such people are notoriously difficult to treat by any therapeutic method, probably due to their notable lack of consistent motivation toward changes in attitudes or behavior (Hare, 1970). Furthermore, many dealers are in the 19 to 25 age group. Individuals in this age group who demonstrate drug-abuse problems, sociopathy, or delinquency are often unresponsive to any form of intervention. Yet, with age, the same individuals may show spontaneous improvement and may abandon deviant patterns of behavior without any treatment (Moore, 1964; Drew, 1968; Hare, 1970; Waldorf, 1970). Thus assessments of intervention effectiveness are confounded by the changing course of drug abuse, sociopathy, and delinquency, with relative immutability until age 25 or 30 and an increased tendency toward improvement in the thirties or forties (O'Neal and others, 1962). Many forms of intervention are likely to appear beneficial with drug-dependent delinquents in their forties (Diskind and Klonsky, 1964b; Rathod and others, 1966); but the same therapeutic efforts with these individuals in their teens or early twenties are much less likely to be successful.

Regardless of the personality characteristics of the individual drug dealer, it should be recognized that any intervention will confront a number of forces that encourage continuation of drug-dealing. These reinforcing factors, which include a number of personal and social variables as well as substantial economic incentives, necessarily change over time and further complicate the assessment of treatment endeavors.

In addition, treatment goals or outcome criteria for drug dealers have not been clearly defined. In assessing treatment success, different observers assign different degrees of importance to such outcome factors as drug abstinence, noncriminal conduct, improved physical health or psychological function, reintegration into a stable family situation, and ability to assume a self-supporting role. It seems reasonable to evaluate the success of any intervention approach on the basis of individual improvement along all these parameters. However, how does one evaluate the effectiveness of a program when there is marked improvement along certain outcome dimensions and little or no improvement in other areas? Should one emphasize the elimination of drug-dealing as the primary consideration in determining the effectiveness of an intervention approach or focus on total drug abstinence and social stability? The importance of making outcome criteria explicit and preferably standardized is apparent.

In addition to the limitations already mentioned—lack of longitudinal perspective, the difficulty of treating the sociopathic personality, changes in individuals with age, variable forces that encourage drug-dealing, and the lack of clearly defined treatment goals—assessing drug-abuse treatment programs is further complicated by the difficulties one encounters when investigating institutions, which usually contain vested interest in their survival. Problems in assessing the effectiveness of various forms of individual intervention are not unique to the treatment of drug dealers, but apply to the analysis of all therapeutic endeavors directed toward any type of persistent behavioral problem, for example, delinquency, psychiatric disorders, alcoholism, and other drug abuse (Blum and Blum, 1967; Robison, 1969; De Long, 1972).

Intervention for Treatment

This section will rely heavily on available data on the treatment of drug-dependent individuals, especially heroin addicts, as well as treatment approaches used with delinquents. The term *treatment* is used here in a broad sense to mean any form of intervention, even if the primary intent is the alleviation of suffering rather than the modification of behavior.

Several treatment approaches are available, and most of them have been well reviewed (Blum and Blum, 1967; De Long, 1972). These approaches will be arbitrarily categorized into the following five groups: medical-psychological, pharmacotherapy, communal, legal, and community-based. It should be emphasized that most efforts at intervention with drug abuse and delinquency use combined techniques derived from several of these categories.

Medical-Psychological Approach. The medical-psychological approach is based on the assumption that delinquent, drug-dependent individuals suffer from psychological and physiological disorders. Intervention by skilled professionals is required, often in a hospital setting. After an initial diagnostic phase, followed by detoxification or stabilization, the individual may receive one or more forms of psychotherapy. In many institutions, actual therapy is minimal and "treatment" consists largely of regular diet, rest, and time away from the individual's usual environment. For many decades, this form of intervention conducted in large public hospitals characterized treatment of drug abusers in the United States. Programs that entail primarily detoxification and medical management with little or no systematic after care or concurrent psychotherapy definitely do provide some benefits: (1) the amelioration of medical complications, (2) at least a transient reduction of drug consumption for the user who needs a respite and thus a short-term protection for the community against drug-related crimes, (3) accommodation for the 10 to 20 percent of drug abusers who at any given time voluntarily seek abstinence, and (4) contact with many drug abusers and hence the possibility of initiating other forms of treatment.

Psychological-medical intervention does seem to be effective for the small percentage of individuals whose drug abuse or delinquency is associated with certain specific psychiatric disorders. For example, an individual who excessively uses illicit drugs may be doing so in a futile attempt at self-medication for manic-depressive illness, schizophrenia, or severe anxiety. These disorders can be effectively treated with specific pharmacological agents such as lithium and antipsychotic drugs. As the level of distress subsides, the abuse of illicit drugs may dramatically decline. However, the vast majority of individuals who require drug-abuse or delinquency intervention do not demonstrate these disorders; thus other forms of treatment are required.

Recently, considerable emphasis has been placed on psychological intervention, especially therapy in group settings. Traditionally, these therapies have been oriented along psychodynamic lines. The use of transactional analysis represents one modification of this approach (Berne, 1961). Transactional analysis emphasizes helping individuals to become aware of their characteristic interpersonal behavior patterns by a systematic analysis of their transactions with others, particularly the responses they are seeking and eliciting from others.

Psychological intervention may also entail "therapeutic community" principles such as deemphasis of the usual hierarchical structure and dichotomy between patients and staff. Patients may assume responsibility for each other's care and participate in decisions affecting the overall community. In these intervention programs, there is usually emphasis on group meetings and on directly mirroring to the individual his own behavior (M. Jones, 1953).

However, such insight-oriented techniques usually require rigorous screening of applicants to insure adequate motivation and capacity for the required verbal participation. Unfortunately, many drug-dependent, delinquent individuals lack verbal skills and consistent motivation. In fact, some intervention programs based on verbal interaction and insight orientation are less effective than programs that do not emphasize verbal therapies (Craft, 1966; Carney, 1971). Even highly intelligent drug abusers who verbalize "insight" into their problems do not necessarily have a favorable prognosis (Tamerin and Neuman, 1971).

Another development in the psychological treatment of drug-dependent delinquent individuals is the use of behavioral-modification techniques (Schwitzgebel, 1971). Behavioral modification is a general term that refers to the application of experimentally established learning principles to the treatment of maladaptive behavior (Ford and Urban, 1963). The essential proposition of behavior modification is that overt behavior can be altered by explicitly defining the desired behavior and then recognizing and reinforcing approximations to this behavior. Positive reinforcements consist of pleasurable rewards, such as praise, privileges, status, or even money.

Behavioral-modification techniques seem especially useful in altering discrete, circumscribed behavioral abnormalities such as phobias. These techniques appear more difficult to apply when disturbances involve many aspects of the individual's characteristic modes of behavior—as in the case of drug dealers. It is difficult to replicate the complex set of antecedents and reinforcers that operate in actual drug-dealing. In the real world, drug-dealing is a very complex phenomenon that inherently entails the interactions of many psychosocial forces. These forces cannot be brought to bear and hence cannot easily be changed in any other setting.

Success with psychological therapy requires strong, consistent motivation on the part of the individual to change himself. After the initial impetus to seek help subsides, most drug-dependent, delinquent individuals have difficulty maintaining motivation to change. Similarly, the therapist finds it difficult to maintain patient motivation toward the long-term rewards of therapy in competition with the immediate pleasurable rewards of drug-taking. These problems may account for the lack of consistent data to demonstrate that any type of medical or psychological intervention, within an institution or within a traditional outpatient setting, significantly alters the long-term prognosis of most drug-dependent, delinquent individuals (Diskind and Klonsky, 1964a; Brill and Lieberman, 1969; O'Malley and others, 1972). Similarly, no reports indicate that therapeutic communities are more consistently effective than lockup treatments in restoring drug-dependent individuals to normal functioning, due in part to the fact that very few adequate treatment studies have been completed (Joseph and Dole, 1970).

Inpatient programs are limited by the difficulty of transferring newly learned behavioral patterns back to the community. Many people markedly change their ways by conforming their behavior to the demands of the institution while cloistered, only to revert to their former deviance when they leave the structured program. Another limitation of medical-psychological approaches is that unless legally coerced, a significant percentage of patients leave against professional advice (O'Donnell, 1962; O'Malley and others, 1972).

Medical-psychological programs, especially those based in hospitals, are expensive; they usually cost $10,000 to $14,000 per person per year. There is always a shortage of resources, especially of adequately trained, skilled therapists. However, medical-psychological programs may be useful for some individuals, especially juveniles who have not yet been extensively involved in the drug-delinquent subculture.

Pharmacotherapy Approaches. There are two basic pharmacological approaches in the direct treatment of drug dependency: maintenance and chemical antagonistic or blockade therapy (for review, see Jaffe, 1970b). Maintenance therapy entails the legal use of chemical substances that induce a sense of well-being in addicts without appreciably interfering with daily activities. The treatment of opioid addicts with methadone is an example of maintenance therapy. A variant of maintenance therapy is the legal use of addicting drugs per se on a continuing basis; this method is exemplified by the British system in which registered addicts receive inexpensive heroin or cocaine on a regular controlled schedule.

Addicts maintained with appropriate drugs are less likely to focus their lives around compulsive drug-seeking and other behavior intrinsic to the illicit-drug subculture. They are more resistant to the impulsive resumption of drug abuse, usually become more amenable to other forms of rehabilitation, and often resume law-abiding, productive behavior (Joseph and Dole, 1970). Currently, various forms of chemical maintenance, especially with oral methadone for narcotic dependency, are extensively used in the United States with apparent success (Goldstein, 1972).

The second type of pharmacological therapy is the use of chemical antagonists that either block the pleasurable effects of certain specific drugs or induce an unpleasant reaction when the specific drug is taken. Examples of chemical antagonists would be cyclazocine or naloxone for opioid addicition and disulfiram for alcoholism. When these agents are used appropriately, the individual's tendencies to resume use of the specific drug for which the antagonist is being taken is curbed. Also, since the positive effects of drug use are not experienced when the drug is taken, extinction of drug-seeking behavior may gradually occur. However, antagonists must be taken regularly, and rigorous patient selection is usually required to assure adequate cooperation. Many patients do not like to take antagonists; some amount of coercion is often necessary. Unfortunately, drug abusers tend to be multiple-drug users. Although pharmacotherapy may reduce or eliminate the abuse of specific drugs for which the therapy was intended, some drug-dependent individuals simply shift to other psychoactive agents.

The side effects of these chemical therapies are largely unknown, and there are virtually no data on long-term consequences of their use. The history of pharmacology suggests that the cumulative use of a drug is likely to exact a greater toll than expected; for example, heroin was first used as a substitute for morphine. Long-term costs to the individual and society may turn out to be considerable if our programs focus on maintenance to the exclusion of gradual withdrawal.

In addition to these long-range concerns, the use of pharmacological agents requires continuous systematic monitoring in order to detect possible relapse or the simultaneous use of other psychoactive drugs, and diversion of the chemical substitutes into the illicit market. Many observers feel that pharmacotherapy alone is not enough and that other ancillary services are required. Most programs emphasize vocational counseling as the single most important service to be offered in addition to pharmacological therapy. However, additional services add to program costs and may not significantly alter the success rate, especially among individuals with long criminal records (De Long, 1972). Since the cost of methadone maintenance programs without ancillary services and frequent urine testing can be kept as low as $500 to $1000 per addict per year, determination of the effectiveness of ancillary services is required for the efficient allocation of scarce resources (Wieland and Chambers, 1970). At present, few cost-effectiveness analyses are available to assist in these decisions, with the notable exception of the excellent report by McGlothlin and associates (1972)'.

Communal Approaches. Communal approaches usually emphasize (1) mutual support and aid; (2) the concept of continual catharsis and confession; and (3)' in the case of drugs, the concept that there is no such thing as an ex-addict, only an addict who is not using at the moment. Synanon, Hilltop, and Phoenix House are examples of communal programs that provide living facilities in which the individual initially spends most of his time (see, for example, Sharaf, 1971). The social structure of these settings demands maximal sustained contact so that the drug-dependent individual's behavioral patterns, his values, and his expectations may be altered by a complex system of punishment and reward and replaced by the values and mores of the group. Other communal approaches do not entail 24-hour living arrangements, but instead offer day-care facilities (Reality House)' or frequent meetings and other social events (Alcoholics Anonymous)'. Communal approaches may have an intense religious or philosophical orientation or may focus on interpersonal skills and vocational improvement. Rather than conventional professionals, treatment personnel may be former drug abusers who have been successfully adhering to the tenets and procedures of the group.

One of the difficulties in evaluating the effectiveness of communal intervention is obtaining the necessary data. Some programs are openly resistant to any type of analysis, keep only minimal records, and are content to justify their existence on humanitarian grounds. None of these communal approaches has been adequately studied.

On the positive side of the ledger, communal interventions are helpful for some people. Alcoholics Anonymous would be the best known example of an organization that is extremely beneficial for certain people not amenable to other forms of treatment. Communal intervention may also be helpful in ameliorating the life of the individual, especially in reducing criminal activity, even if the individual does not complete the entire prescribed course of treatment (De Long, 1972). Drug-free communal approaches may also offer modeling, hope, and inspiration to drug abusers and residents of neighborhoods having a high rate of drug dependency by demonstrating that drug maintenance programs or closed institutions are not imperative for all drug-dependent delinquent individuals (Lennard and others, 1972).

On the other hand, many individuals seem incapable of successfully joining these intense, demanding groups or of remaining in treatment for sufficient time to achieve benefit (Kaufman, 1972). Communal approaches are limited by the constraints of all treatment approaches that require specialized environments such as hospitals or prisons—often the individual does well as long as he remains in the treatment setting but is vulnerable to relapse when he returns to his old community. Many such programs, especially those with 24-hour facilities, are costly—anywhere from $3,000 to $10,000 per resident per year. Other programs that utilize primarily volunteer help and the assistance of their members are relatively inexpensive.

In summary, communal approaches seem to help a few people a great deal, and others to some degree. The problem of predicting in advance which individual will benefit from communal methods remains unsolved; adequate data are simply not available.

Legal Intervention with Confinement. Two basic types of legal intervention have been used with delinquent, drug-dependent individuals: (1) various forms of incarceration, and (2) noninstitutional legal controls, such as probation and parole. For many years,

criminal imprisonment has been the most extensively used intervention with drug dealers. Proponets of imprisonment argue that a
punitive approach prevents recidivism in former offenders and
deters potential delinquent drug abusers. This argument is hotly
disputed by those who point to recidivism rates as an argument
against imprisonment. Other proponents of incarceration cite the
importance of quarantine. If deviant individuals are isolated from
the rest of the community, as one might segregate infectious-disease
carriers, then rates of delinquency and drug abuse among the general population might be lessened by reducing opportunities for
learning these aberrant behaviors by observing, imitating, and
modeling. There are insufficient data to buttress or refute this contention.

Legal intervention may include the various types of psychological therapy discussed in the previous section, especially group
therapy, the use of behavioral-modification principles, transactional
analysis, and other methods. Unfortunately, many inmates view
these attempts at therapy as merely game playing, that is, it is not
wise to be good at first because then you are unable to show subsequent improvement. At present, there is no firm evidence that the
rate of recidivism is affected by these techniques, perhaps because
few adequate studies have been conducted. At present, the California Youth Authority is systematically investigating the relative
efficacy of different treatment modalities within an institutional
setting; hopefully its data will provide useful information on institutional intervention.

Civil commitments, a recent form of legal intervention pat-
terned after treatment programs for the mentally ill, place individuals in institutions for various periods without criminal proceedings.
However, in California and New York, states with the longest
experience with civil commitments of drug abusers, the basic structure of most civil commitment programs is predominately penal
rather than therapeutic despite the intentions of those who established them (Kramer, 1971). The committed individual tends to be
concerned with the amount of time he will spend in an institution
rather than how he might be "treated," his behavior changed, or
the like. This orientation differs from voluntary psychological
therapies where the mutual focus of therapist and patient is not on

the length of time in therapy but ideally on obtaining shared goals —relief from distress, change in behavior or attitudes, and so forth. The orientation of the committing institution tends to be toward its own smooth functioning, with strict adherence to rules and policies, rather than toward flexibility in meeting the needs of the individual.

The Narcotics Addict Rehabilitation Act (NARA) is a federal program involving civil commitment for addicts. The NARA program seems to be more successful than either the New York or the California civil commitment system (De Long, 1972) but has not been operative as long nor has it been as extensively evaluated. The success rates of institutional programs tend to decrease on closer, longer-term analysis and as enthusiasm for the novel program wanes.

At present, there is no evidence to support the claim that intervention by incarceration—either by criminal or civil proceedings—significantly prevents the drug abuser's return to drugs or alters an already criminal way of life (Brill and Lieberman, 1969; Lerman, 1968). Similarly, there is no evidence to support claims that one correctional program or the use of a particular psychological therapy has more rehabilitative effectiveness than another (Robison, 1969; Martinson, 1972), or that civil commitment results are significantly different from those of penal systems (Kramer and others, 1968; Kramer, 1970, 1971). The lack of demonstrable overall effectiveness should be weighed against the expense of these programs—$4000 to $12,000 per year per individual while he is in an institution. On the other hand, as is becoming increasingly apparent in the field of mental health, there will inevitably be some individuals who require prolonged incarceration for their welfare as well as the protection of society. Not everyone can be treated in a community setting; some secluded institutions will always be necessary for the small percentage of deviant persons who require around-the-clock supervision.

Legal Intervention without Confinement. Probation and parole are forms of noninstitutional legal intervention that do not entail confinement. Under the usual format, the individual is continuously susceptible to either civil or criminal sanctions—most often incarceration—unless he faithfully fulfills certain conditions. These conditions may include participation in methadone maintenance or other chemical treatment, regular attendance at group, family, or individual therapy—as well as periodic checks for illicit drug use, the avoidance of known delinquents or drug dealers, regular employment, family support, and so on. It should be noted that the coercive approach to treatment is antithetical to traditional views of psychotherapy as entirely voluntary. However, coercion does militate against the tendency of drug abusers and delinquents to drop out of therapy programs. In addition, the judicious use of probation and other interventions that avoid incarceration may serve a preventive purpose; lawbreakers whose deviance is not well established are not exposed to the influences of greater sophistication in delinquency and drug use inevitably present in institutions.

Unlike other forms of intervention already discussed, where evidence of effectiveness is slim or lacking, data from several sources suggest that noninstitutional legal intervention does enhance rehabilitation in drug abusers and delinquents (Diskind and Klonsky, 1964a, 1964b; Vaillant, 1966; Vaillant and Rasor, 1966; Bowden and Langenauer, 1972). In the recent cost-effectiveness analysis of opiate addiction control alternatives by McGlothlin and his coworkers (1972) interventions that combined civil commitment procedures and emphasized nonconfinement programs, with other treatment modalities, especially methadone maintenance, demonstrated the greatest potential for reducing street addiction at the lowest overall social cost. Theoretically, this combined approach, albeit coercive, would offer the best possibility for reducing the demand for illicit heroin to a point at which dealing ceases to be a profitable activity. However, these noninstitutional approaches are not a panacea. The rate of recidivism remains high, especially with young offenders and those who are well entrenched in deviant patterns. In addition, citizens and officials who prefer to have the drug dealer isolated from the community may not tolerate interventions that do not entail prolonged confinement.

Community-based Approach. The community-based approach emphasizes that delinquency and drug abuse occur within a specific social context and therefore, treatment efforts should be directed at changing the individual within his community rather than in the isolation of an institution. A wide range of treatment modalities, including counseling, group therapy, vocational training, job placement, pharmacotherapy, and half-way houses, may be utilized while the drug abuser remains in his community. Focus is often on the practical aspects of daily living rather than on delving deeply into the individual's past or analyzing the nuances of his interpersonal behavior.

Community approaches may entail (1) a combination of treatment modalities, the multimodality program, or (2) separate programs for each modality, the unimodality program, for example, methadone maintenance. The advantages and disadvantages of the two approaches are not well established. Multimodality programs have been criticized for conveying contradictory messages, for example, abstinence is best and methadone treatment is second-rate. Unfavorable comparisons within multimodality programs occur despite valiant efforts to convey the idea that there is no absolute best way, only what is most useful for a given individual in terms of what he needs and what he can do. Since morale and motivation are essential to successful intervention in any type of chronic behavioral disorder and given the unfortunate fact that drug abuse and delinquency are very difficult to treat, it seems wise to structure programs along lines that minimize demoralizing comparisons. Another limitation to the effectiveness of the community approach is the drug abusers' lack of motivation to participate in community treatment programs except during times of crisis. For this reason, many observers, including myself, believe that community-based therapeutic programs are most effective if the drug abuser is subjected to a judicious amount of coercion. For example, the addict's status of probationer or parolee can be used to hold him in a program long enough to permit the desired behavioral change (Brill and Lieberman, 1969). The treatment therapist and the probation or parole officer operate in concert toward various shared goals. With the rational use of coercion, the therapist has a chance to reinforce other positive forces affecting the drug abuser. In some cases, significant people in the drug abuser's life, especially girl friends, spouses, and sometimes parents, exert considerable pressure on the drug abuser or delinquent to abandon his deviant ways. It may be possible to form an alliance with these positive forces, perhaps with conjoint meetings. On the other hand, it should be noted that in the criminal dealer category described in *The Dream Sellers* (Blum and Associates, 1972a, Chapter 7), individuals continued to deal despite fear of arrest because of the need to support their own habits or as a negative reaction to persuasion or coercion. Again, the theme of no single treatment approach being effective for all types of drug dealers/abusers is illustrated.

In summary, preliminary reports indicate that community-based programs can alter the behavior of some individuals—especially in terms of criminal arrest rates (Shin and Kerstetter, 1971). Community-based programs also offer the advantages of not requiring costly facilities and of permitting the individual to maintain employment to support himself and his family. Community-based programs offer the advantage of intensive early intervention, optimally before the first arrest. Effective first intervention is important; maximum long-term success appears to be positively related to the efficacy of the first intervention; and, with some individuals, chances of success decrease with each subsequent intervention (Diskind and Klonsky, 1964b; Kramer, 1971).

Comment

In surveying these five categories of intervention with the individual, drug-dependent delinquent, it is apparent that most approaches have some success but also are ineffective for a significant number of individuals. Certain programs are more therapeutic than others in treating particular subgroups of drug users. If we view drug dependency and delinquency as an extremely complex phenomenon involving an intricate interaction of pharmacological, psychological, and social forces, it is not surprising to find individual responses so varied and no one form of intervention effective for all. Some dealers may be amenable to several forms of intervention, for example, the psychedelic dealer (see Blum and Associates, 1972a, Chapter 7), who is less involved in both drug dealing and criminality may be more easily rehabilitated regardless of the method of intervention. Many campus marijuana dealers may revert to drug-free, law-abiding behavior without specific intervention as their life-style changes with time. Other subgroups of dealers, for instance the criminal group, may be more or less immutable no matter what the method of intervention may be. We must also expect that there will be a few individuals for whom no form of intervention is effective; this is true of all chronic behavioral disorders.

Selection of the appropriate approach for the individual is a major problem. How can we predict which modality or mixture of modalities is most likely to be effective with a specific individual? The difficulty of matching treatment to the individual applies to all efforts to modify complex behavioral disorders and is an increasing problem in the behavioral sciences where multiple therapeutic options are available. It is especially perplexing in the topic at hand—drug-dealing—since descriptive data are too recent and too limited to form a sufficient basis for prediction.

Selection of treatment modes raises the question of cost-effectiveness. Resources are limited and requests for funds to cope with drug-dealing must compete with other equally pressing societal needs—education, health care, pollution, and so forth. Rational allocation of these funds can best be made if analyses of the various forms of intervention are made and data on treatment effectiveness are available. Attempts, such as those of Fujii and Lind, to systematically evaluate the relative effectiveness of various treatment programs using formal economic criteria are essential steps toward accountability (Fujii, 1972; Lind, in press). However, sophisticated mathematical procedures require more accurate and extensive information than is currently available. Some programs do not keep detailed records; and most do not maintain continuing systematic evaluation of treatment effectiveness. One obvious method of insuring adequate assessment would be to designate a given percentage of a program budget for ongoing monitoring of intervention effectiveness and make subsequent funding contingent on adequate assessment. Monitoring might be done by an independent research team from outside the program, analogous to the external auditing of governmental and business operations. Evaluation of programs should be made over a prolonged period in order to assess the value of internal changes made in response to monitoring feedback. In addition, a program that seems ineffective on a short-term scale might ultimately prove more beneficial if assessments are continued over a prolonged period.

Assessments of various treatment programs would be greatly facilitated if standardized criteria for intervention effectiveness were established. As suggested earlier, value judgments are intrinsically involved and must be made, for example, the relative value of a totally abstinent individual on welfare compared with a person who shows some drug use but satisfactory job performance. One must weigh the relative benefits to society and to the individual and then establish an order of priority; the evaluation is then made on the basis of rates of change within the established priorities. These priority judgments should be made explicit; perhaps we should formulate several sets of criteria that would depend upon specific problems at hand (see Jaffe, 1970b). For instance, one would expect different rates of effectiveness between a program designed for the rehabilitation of long-term heroin addicts and one directed toward a less deviant subgroup, for example, moderate drug-using delinquents. The important point is that a standard should be established and made explicit; otherwise rational assessment of effectiveness is difficult if not impossible.

Since present methods of intervention can claim only limited success, continued research in drug abuse, drug-dealing, and delinquency is urgently needed. Some initial investigations suggest promising avenues of exploration. As outlined by Blum and Associates (1972b), characteristics of high-risk candidates for drug abuse can be identified. Prevention or at least early intervention before deviant patterns are firmly established may become possible. Similarly, Wolfgang (1970) found that repeaters accounted for the greatest number of crimes among a delinquent group and emphasized the importance of the first intervention in reducing the overall rate of crime by reducing the number of repeaters. The early application of intervention in drug abuse and in the related phenomenon of drug-dealing is promising but more research is needed.

Summary

The widespread drug-dealing in our society cannot be treated simply as a disease easily altered within an individual by a specific treatment. Instead, drug-dealing is a multifaceted phenomenon that entails dynamic, complex behavioral interactions of drug use, drug abuse, and delinquency. Although a range of interventions for drug-dealing is available—medical-psychological, phar-

macotherapy, communal, legal, and community-based approaches
—no method is uniformly effective. On the other hand, each approach seems to be successful with some individuals. The problem becomes that of predicting the modality most suitable for a given individual. Unfortunately, at this time there is little accurate information that would help one to make this prediction.

12

Social Response to Drug Problems

Richard H. Blum, Sanford Kadish, Milton Luger, Arnold J. Mandell, Patricia Wald, Norman V. Lourie

There is uncertainty as to what is meant by the terms *the drug problem* and *drug abuse.* We call attention to a wide variety of (specific pharmacological) outcomes from the use of various drugs —or from use of the same drug in various persons under different conditions. We call attention to the probably greater variety of behaviors associated with drug use, behaviors that are not due to specific pharmacological effects. In considering drug use and drug abuse, one must realize that a range of benign, neutral, and malignant outcomes occur and further that judgments as to outcomes are colored by the stance of the person making judgments. It is not unusual for estimates of benefit or abuse to contain hidden assumptions about the intentions of the user, about the nature of the drug, about stereotypes as to outcomes given certain circumstances, and about prevailing beliefs about the social significance of use.

Among societal responses, the legislative response commands particular interest among those associated with government. The legislative response to drug abuse is essentially political, but it is likely to contain strong elements of belief in the "silver bullet" of either control through repression or behavior change through treatment. The current trend, in statutes and in practice, toward merging enforcement and treatment requires examination and justifies concern. Insofar as the merging of these two "silver bullets" constitutes a compromise (as, for example, when arrest is followed by disposition to treatment), that resolution may serve to obfuscate issues and to delay informed decisions. Questions regarding intervention by means of the law and efficacy of procedures labeled as treatment may not be faced.

Although most public concern is with the present, with some analytic attention paid to the past, we suggest that the future holds some of the most severe problems of policy that will have to be faced. We expect development of more powerful behavior-shaping drugs, some of which will be very attractive either to users or to social controllers. In the face of this likelihood, it is compellingly important that we adopt a workable stance. Our present response styles, which are demonstrably insufficient, are a frozen posture inherited from the accretion of habits, statutes, and views that in United States and international law are at least 50 years old. There are pressures further to freeze policies into this mold through uniform state laws and new international treaties; these pressures occur at the same time that many scientists and administrators sense an urgent need, not for hardening old ways but for identifying new models that can be adapted to likely drugs and drug problems of the future as well as those of our present.

Drug problems occupy a special place of interest. However, we should realize that the issues surrounding either the development or distribution of drugs as commodities and the "deviant" behavior of persons who use them or sell them are essentially similar to other public policy problems. Whether considered in relation to the regulation of research and commerce, the labeling and shaping of deviant behavior, or the analysis of the response process itself, the drug arena is not unique. Rather, it is a peculiarly powerful illustration of the complexity of judging and responding to any conduct in others that troubles a large segment of our society.

Inherent in the issues that surround societal response are matters of both law and philosophy. We call attention to the importance of drug cases that have come before the courts and of societal responses to drug use in the identification of constitutional issues in the law. Beyond that, however, we must face questions of developing legal interpretation, of moral beliefs, and of social values: Shall society decide that there is a "right" to treatment for persons involved with drug problems? Is there a "right" for people to use their own bodies as they see fit? Is it wise for society to set forth criminal sanctions that punish persons for acting in ways that are detrimental solely to their own welfare and not that of others?

In any heterogeneous society, there will be a variety of definitions of drug "abuse" and of appropriate societal responses to that abuse. Each of us could benefit from examination of his own beliefs about drugs, drug abuse, and preferred interventions, for each of us reflects in his views his own membership in social groups. Policy recommendations are, we believe, the outcome of covert as well as overt forces that shape our values and emotions, which in turn contribute to our definition of disorder and deviance. Moving beyond reflection and, hopefully, beyond insight, we might profitably consider the various responses social groups offer and seek to understand the process by which diverse programs and/or uniform central policies emerge. That understanding should teach us much about our assumptions and limitations, factors that bear strongly on the success and failure of any and all community or governmental actions that are proposed as desirable responses to drug problems.

There are strong pressures to alter and to expand existing programs and policies in the drug field. We ask that a sense of caution permeate drives toward the adoption of new policies, especially those that create rigid and continuing laws or institutions, until we have some assurance that reasonable estimates of impact and outcome are available. Much social action is undertaken without regard for impact and outcomes—this, no doubt, under pressure of morals, emotions, politics, self-interest, and other immediate factors. Nevertheless, the long-term effects of actions must be considered and restraint must be exercised when there is evident paucity of impact estimates that are empirically sound. Historical/administrative/ scientific data do exist in other areas that are close enough to the drug arena to allow transfer of information; for instance, in the educational field the conditions for efficacy of teaching with regard to tobacco and alcohol are partially known. Likewise, data from driver education or venereal disease programs might bear on estimates about the impact of drug information. For many years, statistics on recidivism have shown us the difficulties of correcting or rehabilitating certain criminals, among them groups of offenders who have much in common with drug traffickers. Insofar as any major programs are proposed in the drug field and impact estimates are inadequate, we counsel against overoptimism, unjustifiable urgency to act, and undue expense in creating institutions when pilot projects might better serve.

It is unrealistic to require a consensus either in the larger society or among specialists in the drug field at this time. Given the immense domain of the drug arena, the variety of experience brought by differing individuals to their interpretation of disparate sectors of this domain, the changing nature of drugs and drug-use conduct, and the absence of long-term data on many forms of intervention, disagreement is to be expected. That disagreement is useful, for it identifies issues and generates fact finding. To the extent that proponents of one or another interest area (for example, health, law enforcement, political enterprise, community organization, religious life) are effective advocates, their resulting actions, reactions, and interactions should provide opportunity to learn about the efficacy of one or another kind of response. Diversity then is an opportunity and constitutes a natural laboratory for learning. Lest observers too readily accept the rhetoric of advocates, we call attention to the possible similarity of underlying processes in what various people do—as drug users, as experts called in to help, or as administrators and policy makers. Likewise, we note the likelihood that these various domains and the workers and institutions in each do have impacts on one another; for example, pastoral counseling is affected by developments in psychiatry, while the criminal law incorporates alternatives developed in medicine and administration (that is, mandatory treatment).

We believe it is helpful to call attention to two diverse processes, which are occurring simultaneously and in which a potential polarity and conflict may needlessly occur. On the one hand are proponents of centralization, coordination, and rationalization of controls and services. Usually these advocates call for concentration of power in governmental hands and the use of criminal and regulatory law to accomplish this control. On the other hand are those advocating—or practicing—decentralization, diversification, and immediate local responses to what are viewed as local needs and opportunities. Insofar as a variety of community endeavors now exist side by side with governmental centralization, no current conflict exists. There is, however, the possibility that extreme centralizing might vitiate diverse community efforts—if, for example, increasing availability of funds were used as a device for requiring conformity or if professional standards were imposed to eliminate lay change agents from responsible contact with drug users. We express our hope that centralism—which is obviously underway—will not take on repressive functions within communities. We ask instead that policy makers consider how central coordination might facilitate local response without gradually assuming power over its spontaneous development.

As we examine present and past response patterns to the "drug problem"—be that dealing or using—we are in fact studying the phenomenon of social adaptation to a "problem." Insofar as diversity of response occurs in communities, this is a "multimodality" adaptation, whereas those community innovations now may be viewed by those in government as an "administrative problem." The paradox is that those with a central administrative interest may view diversity and experimentation as "uncoordinated" (or chaotic), thus denigrating that diversity while at the same time their perspective simply reflects (or upholds) their own administrative modality. It is possible that sociocultural factors and existing institutional matrices dictate both forms (diversity and centralism) of social problem solving. A better understanding of response capabilities is thereby achieved if one includes both diversity and centralism as objects of study and develops a catalogue of nonexclusive alternatives that can be considered.

Another conflict and polarity within it may be both unrecognized and unhelpful. On the one hand, there is what may be referred to as personalized (individualized, humanized) intervention, essentially informal one-to-one activities that conceive of drug programs as serving persons who deserve respectful service. On the other hand, there are operations that conceive of themselves as administratively efficient and equitable in which emphasis is placed on the manner of delivery rather than on the recipient. Sociologists have made useful analyses of the evolution of such points of view (see, for example, Reiss, 1971). Respectable values exist in each system, and advocates may become unduly harsh with one another if they fail to see the reasons for the other's development. It would be regrettable if the administrative/bureaucratic perspective—which tends to be that found among those holding power (that is, not rendering direct person-to-person services to uncoercized clients)—becomes dominant simply because of the exercise of administrative power. Both perspectives probably are inevitable and valuable; it would be unfortunate if they were so much at war that the rendering of service would deteriorate during the combat.

We should acknowledge that we do not now know how drug use is best evaluated, how drug problems are best defined, or what actions in response to identified drug problems—including dealing—should be undertaken. This is not to discount the value of work that is being and will be done; it is to ask that we all tolerate uncertainty and ambiguity during this phase of our pharmacological and social development. In many other areas of life, especially those that involve so-called social problems, there is confusion and conflict. We call for patience, for respectful hearings, and for a commitment to administrative and scientific experimentation and flexible posture.

All of us who are involved in drug concerns are likely to have views that we hold strongly but that are not buttressed by data (even if they are buttressed by righteous certainty), and such moral/emotional positions are probably inescapable when one confronts the drug-problem arena. We suggest the desirability for each specialist (researcher, teacher, healer, officer, administrator, prison worker, policy maker, and so forth) to confess his bias publicly in his reporting to others. Putting bias "up front" allows readers and listeners to separate the person from his data and, we believe, will quicken the identification of social solutions as well as underlying issues.

The problems to be solved in the drug arena do, we believe, transcend the issues of drug production, drug distribution, drug use, the outcomes of such use in users, and, in society, the response to users that characterizes most of us. Basic values and styles of life are at stake. In what do communities take pride? How much individuality or communality does society seek?

How do communities create and use social problems, for example, drug abuse, as a means for conducting political life or generating moral change? Do social issues that affect relatively few people (for example, heroin addiction or drug dealing) achieve prominence because, like neurotic symptoms psychodynamically, they are functional and indirectly express feelings and issues that profoundly bother many citizens but that, at the level of the average man, simply are not faced? (See Zinberg and Robertson, 1972.) For example, is the approach in the United States to illicit drug dealers and drug users reminiscent of Puritan times (Cook, 1970), reflecting a preoccupation with demons?

As we consider governmental or other intervention, dare we ask concerning the limits of any deliberate policy action in shaping the conduct of any particular citizen group? Can a nation admit that its institutions and concepts have failed?

How often are we intent on spicing our rhetoric with genuine action? Consider some of the sensible recommendations made about American prisons by American Friends Service Committee (1971). Dare we act on these? Consider the eminently practical recommendations made for crime control by Morris and Hawkins. Has anything been done to follow through?

The lack of follow-through is illustrated by recent cases. In 1967 the President's Commission on Crime and the Administration of Justice made recommendations for drug policy changes. Detailed proposals were set forth by that commission's Task Force on Drunkenness (1967) and its Task Force on Narcotics and Drug Abuse

'(1967). Now only a few of the recommendations have been acted on, although many are under debate. In 1969 the National Commission on the Causes and Prevention of Violence addressed itself to drugs and violence. Studies were made, information disseminated, and recommendations offered. One has the impression now that the information gathered is not yet widely acknowledged. Certainly the commission's many recommendations have not been implemented. In 1970 the President appointed a Task Force on Drugs, giving it a year to prepare for the decennial White House Youth Conference. Unlike most task forces and commissions it had a membership that was remarkably heterogeneous: a Republican Presidential staff assistant, a Republican governor, the director of the Bureau of Narcotics and Dangerous Drugs, youthful white radicals, black militants, Spanish American activists, proponents of store-front treatment centers, even youth who had dealt drugs. The chairman was the coordinator of the Democratic Party's Policy Council drug subcommittee. That eclectic group, two thirds of them under the age of twenty-four, came to unanimous agreement on what should be done, except on the degree to which marijuana penalties should be lessened. Again there was no response, even though one may assume that most opinions were encompassed by the task force membership.

If we take the foregoing as illustrative, are we not deluding ourselves in thinking we intend to act? Or is it that we are simply slow to act because new information and informed opinion diffuse but slowly among leaders and citizens? Have we faced in the drug field the fundamental questions: Are we, as a society, so organized and constituted that we can distribute and apply people, money, facilities, or other resources in support of *any* effort that will actually bring about benefit to the community (as, for example, reduction in drug-associated crime) and to the individual (as in diminishing of addiction-related distress) as opposed to the already demonstrable benefits (salaries, prestige) accruing to those who operate the service or control apparatus?

Change and uncertainty have strongly affected most persons and institutions involved in the drug arena. As priorities, concepts, and fashions have shifted, program shifts have followed. Probably some (or much) of what is heralded as "breakthrough" or even "progress" reflects simple change or less simple opportunism or intolerance for long-term effort. Fashions in response modalities (from store-front help centers to revisions in the law to new crackdowns on drug peddlers) may be followed by rationalizations that become righteous in tone; thus, paradoxically, defensive rigidity may occur simultaneously with or consequent upon quite accidental changes in drug-intervention methods or goals.

The action of change must be noted in other ways; for example, most persons now in the drug field are newcomers who acquire their "expertise" in ways that may not depend completely on careful instruction, familiarity with the scientific literature or social/political history, or on supervised experience. We thus have a cadre of "experts" who are ill prepared but are flattered by sudden eminence. Insofar as people are asked to take on new roles or are catapulted to eminence and responsibility, we face, not just a challenge to knowledge of career development, but an unknown influence on policy and programs that will be exerted by such sudden and widespread career changes. We do not know, for example, to what extent some specialists simply change labels without changing their old behavior and thus do not respond to new phenomena. We do not know to what extent the creation of a new class of experts has led to specialists who have a vested interest in particular definitions of and responses to drug problems that will keep these specialists in control even if the methods they employ—or the policies they espouse—may be, in fact, inefficacious or counterproductive. Given these questions, all of us in the drug field may offer our best service through an awareness of limitations.

An important question arises as one considers how solutions to social problems are to be attained. On the one hand are those who argue for massive action, governmental responsibility, and citizen protection. On the other hand are those who expect that neither social nor individual problems can be avoided or, once at hand, can be solved either completely or without agony and struggle. These positions are partly set forth by Brown and Savage (1971). We believe it may be helpful to examine advocates for their commitment to either (1) the assumption of technological/administrative efficacy directed from above, which can intervene to affect (control or direct) lives without involving lives or (2) the assumption of development in lives only through individual/communal struggle requiring increased inner complexity, self-discipline and a sense of the tragic. These are profoundly differing views of the role of government and change agents vis-à-vis drug dealers and users. The position taken by policy makers will affect all proposals for drug programs.

Insofar as any program involves public services, certain public requirements must be met. These include constitutional safeguards to ensure against arbitrary or capricious rejection of clients who apply for service. The requirement for public accountability and for external evaluation as a requisite for that accountability is stressed. In approaching evaluation, one must recognize the problem of criteria definition, that is, the impact of services will necessarily be measured by standards that incorporate moral and social as well as health, legal, economic, and administrative standards.

We remind service proponents that the creation of programs, institutions, and services in no way guarantees either utilization or efficacy. Analysis of any system designed to have impact upon drug dealers and drug users must identify the total population of "problem" persons, determine what portion are officially identified (whether as arrestees, patients, or other), follow their processing and experience with service to learn which outcomes attend which kinds of experiences among which groups of clients. Insofar as all interventions will have hits and misses all along the lines, it is useful to think in terms of cost/benefit analysis, of comparative impact evaluation for alternative services, and of diversified services tailored to population groups so as to optimize outcomes.

We believe that the foregoing analyses imply at least three things. One is that the actions taken in response to perceived drug problems are important in themselves, not simply because they may be failures or solutions but because they reflect powerful forces at work in the minds of participants and in society. Therefore those who are at work in the drug arena are well advised to contemplate their own roles and reasons as well as to evaluate the results of their recommendations or commitments. A second point is that drug use itself as well as those associated outcomes and life styles which cause concern are remarkable "tracers" which aid the persevering observer in coming to grips with fundamental issues in human biology, in behavior, in morals, and in politics. In this way, the issue of drug abuse has much more importance than do drugs themselves. Perhaps a corollary phenomenon accounts for the intensity with which persons and communities address themselves to that drug use, for in their beliefs and action they are mobilizing those same forces which the observer, using drugs as a tracer, comes to meet. A third point is that, given the great complexity of the matter, the search for understanding is most strongly justified. Scholars think of this in terms of research; yet that is but one form of inquiry. Whether it be reflection, discussion, observation, or some other means, benefit will occur by taking advantage of drugs as tracers—as well as responding directly to drugs—and of people problems to enhance knowledge and from that, one hopes, the ability to undertake effective and humane personal and public action.

Future Research and Policy Action

Peider Könz

It is apparent from data currently available that drug traffic is not the exclusive domain of structured, well-managed, and well-financed dealer organizations. The user-proselytizer-dealer, often beginning with modest transactions and motivated by the need to finance his own consumption, emerges as an essential link in the distribution chain.

These findings are significant in several respects. To the policy maker and to the law enforcement officer, they provide a typology of subjects that may require different control approaches. While there is probably no alternative to strict regulation with regard to the pharmaceutical industry and medical practice and to strict repression where organized illegal traffic is concerned, such measures are not necessarily effective—and may indeed be counterproductive—in dealing with the subculture of user-dealers who are at the same time victims, carriers, and profiteers of the drug habit.

It is to be expected, for instance, that user-dealers will be less sensitive than professional traffickers to the deterrence effect of criminal penalties. Once referred to the criminal justice system, on the other hand, user-dealers are likely to be particularly vulnerable to the harshness of labeling and imprisonment—a harshness that, as is apparent from available case histories, tends to confirm their dealer role upon release.

This pattern of drug consumption and distribution involving user-dealers carries particular implications for the future. In fact, a plausible 1990 scenario, based on projections of current trends in science, technology, and social responses, is characterized both by the availability of a wide range of mood- and behavior-affecting substances and by the virtual elimination of organized illegal traffic, large-scale illegal production, and lax prescription practices through a combination of improved detection, supervision, and repressive measures at the national and international levels. It cannot be assumed, on the other hand, that controls will be as successful in coping with user-dealer circuits. Quite apart from the fact that small and unplanned transactions (including artisanal production) may defy detection, effective controls must come to grips with subcultural characteristics and motivations, which are more complex, and probably far less responsive to straightforward law enforcement, than those of profit-seeking entrepreneurs.

If these assumptions are correct, and if future patterns of drug abuse will increasingly involve user-dealers, then it should be obvious that social engineering directed at this phenomenon and based on solid and specific data is urgently needed. The purpose of this note is to formulate some suggestions for research in this area, keeping in mind the possibilities of cross-cultural inquiries.

In general terms, an action-oriented research program on the user-dealer phenomenon should provide information, including trend data, on the following: (1) profile of the user-dealer subculture, (2) proselytizing and dealer roles, and (3) responsiveness to particular social controls.

Profile of User-dealer Subculture

Evidently, research on the subcultural profile of the typology of user-dealers should draw from and be placed in the context of general epidemiological data regarding drug abuse and its etiology, incidence, prevalence, and trends. Who are the drug users? What substances, or combinations of substances, in what frequency, form, and degree of purity do they consume? And why? What determinant or contributing roles do value and identity conflicts play?—cultural and cross-cultural influences?—the general availability of legal mood-altering drugs (medically prescribed or over-the-counter) and their advertisement in mass media?—alcohol and tobacco?—educational systems, with their achievement orientation, often dysfunctional curriculum, and extensive leisure time?—socioeconomic or family backgrounds? Surprisingly, answers to these questions are still fragmentary and often unreliable.* Yet deliberate efforts to fill this information gap are both possible and needed if effective social responses are to be developed.

Meanwhile, some specific data with regard to user-dealers, focusing on their progression from addiction to proselytizing to drug sales, may nevertheless be obtainable. In fact, the referral rate of user-dealers to the criminal justice system (arrests, prosecutions) and thus their accessibility for purposes of research are likely to be higher than those of simple, and often occasional, users. Correlations and rough etiological data can be derived even from limited sample surveys, matched-pairs research, and in-depth interviewing, involving identified user-dealers.

Apart from a general profile of the user-dealer in terms of his value systems and attitudes, drug-taking habits, family structure, age, sex, residence, and general psychological characteristics, a few specific correlations involving variables susceptible to remedial actions should be explored.

One is the correlation between school or professional performance and drug use/dealing. It may be hypothesized that, as for juvenile delinquency generally, there is a clear correlation between drug addiction and dealing on the one hand and school dropout, school failure, and poor professional performance (reflected in absenteeism rates, disrupted career patterns, or chronic unemployment) on the other hand. Confirmation of this hypothesis would not

* Police and court statistics reveal only the top of the iceberg. In fact, much of the drug use is either undetected or deliberately tolerated even in societies where use and possession are punishable. Surveys—for example, of high school populations—are frequently not representative or are conducted with unreliable survey methods. Longitudinal research is particularly spotty.

only provide predictive indicators, but also would identify the educational system as a major area for remedial policy action.

Another important correlation concerns the criminal record and the record of referrals to other social control agencies (for example, to various types of therapy and community action). Are recidivism and relapse rates particularly high among user-dealers? If so, why? It has been suggested that criminal labeling and imprisonment of users hardens their drug habit and, generally, results in social ostracism and reduced employment opportunities. Since hardened drug habits, isolation from "normal" social patterns, and economic necessity appear to be among the conditions upon which user-dealership is thriving, this would point to a major dysfunction of most control systems, not only those that penalize simple use or possession, but also those that—while not punishing users—consider user-dealers as ordinary traffickers.

A third group of correlations concerns the illegal-drug market structure and prices. It can be surmised that user-dealers are most active in market conditions in which drugs are not freely available, but in which the level of official tolerance, profit margins, or the volume of consumption are not such as to attract organized illegal entrepreneurs. Such market conditions are likely to occur with new drugs, at least during an experimental phase, and also upon the introduction of more effective controls and prohibition-type legislation. It is evident that specific information in this area should be available to those charged with the planning and implementation of drug-control policies.

User-dealer Roles

A somewhat different perspective must be adopted for research on the roles—as contrasted with the profile and typology—of user-dealers. The principal setting in which such research is to be conducted is that of the subculture of drug users, including occasional and experimental users, and not that of the user-dealers themselves. In such a framework it would be significant to check out a number of key assumptions:

that proselytizing (gratuitous distribution) and trafficking constitute sequential, though possibly overlapping, phases of a single career that proselytizing is generally conducted within small, well-defined, culturally homogeneous groups to which the user-dealer "belongs" (for example, same age, school, socioeconomic background)

that within these groups the user-dealer is accepted and frequently enjoys an image of prestige, experience, and worldliness (which may relate to his previous brushes with the law)

that in some instances proselytizing serves the purpose of inducing future sales, much as the distribution of free samples by the pharmeceutical industry is designed to encourage prescriptions by physicians

that sales are conducted within a wider and less homogeneous circle than proselytizing but still in a limited setting (a town or section or street, a school system, a club)

that user-dealers are instrumental in introducing new substances and thus in promoting "shifts" and multiple-drug use

that within their circle of customers, user-dealers tend to play other illegal or socially deviant roles (prostitution and procuring, gambling, organized crime, and the like)

All these assumptions, if validated, would carry direct implications for control policies. This is of course equally true for any data on the user-dealer's motivation. In that connection, economic factors are likely to be paramount, though prestige-seeking may, at times, provide a contributing or alternative motive. The most disturbing hypothesis (or finding, since considerable evidence is already available on this point) is that the progression from drug use to user-dealership may be largely attributable to conditions inherent in the very control policies introduced to curb drug abuse, that is, the high black-market price of drugs in prohibition systems; and the social and economic ostracism that surrounds drug offenders—especially those who have undergone criminal punishment, but also (for example, in terms of employment opportunities) for individuals who have been labeled as users and referred to treatment.

An addict, possibly one who has already been in prison for use, possession, or sale of drugs, stands very little chance of supporting the cost of his addiction at illegal market prices, except by selling drugs; prohibition and criminalization systems breed the most effective agents of the drug contamination that they seek to prevent. It is evident that there is no simple answer to this dilemma; however, accurate data on the economics of user-dealership in function of possible variants of prohibition systems, as well as approaches to treatment, punishment, and social reintegration, may point the way to control policies that would minimize the very real hazard of user-dealership.

Lastly, the relationship between organized drug traffic and user-dealers should also be explored. There are some indications that user-dealers are only occasionally connected with organized traffic and that the two circuits operate separately, with different types of drugs, sources of supply, and clienteles. If this is correct, enforcement and preventive measures directed at organized traffic, for example, international detection networks and major seizures, are not likely to have much of an impact on user-dealers; if, on the other hand, user-dealers are cogs in the organized production and distribution system, action affecting the former would have an impact on the latter, and vice versa.

Responsiveness to Social Controls

A third area of research concerns the responsiveness of user-dealers to particular social controls, with emphasis on treatment and rehabilitation. Recidivism and relapse rates may provide some rough indicators, but they are notoriously inaccurate and fragmentary. It might be more rewarding to explore the impact of particular policy instrumentalities—treatment, maintenance, educational and community action, rehabilitation programs—on the basis of selected case histories. In keeping with the general profile of the user-dealer, success and failure of these programs must be measured by a multiple yardstick:

Has the dependence on illegal drugs been eliminated?

Has the subject been reintegrated, socially and economically, that is, does he have a reasonable alternative to drug dealing?

If not, or if the subject remains vulnerable to relapse and the temp-

tation of illicit trade, has he been isolated from the likely targets of his proselytizing and drug sales?

Quite possibly, major differences will emerge, some relating to the characteristics of the user-dealer, some to the therapeutic and referral approach (for example, voluntary as compared with involuntary referrals), some to environmental variables. Such differences would, of course, be most significant in devising effective control policies.

Transnational Research Programs

Having suggested some of the areas in which future action-oriented research on drug dealing seems most desirable, there remains the problem of selecting significant, and practicable, locations for the proposed inquiries, so as to ensure impact on effective policy planning and implementation.

It is recognized that remedial policies in the drug area are most feasible and most likely to succeed in a local or national setting. Indeed, the effectiveness of international controls depends, to a very large extent, upon responses within individual countries. Also, the cross-cultural transferability of research data cannot be taken for granted; profiles and modes of operation of drug dealers may vary considerably from country to country, and so do control policies and their effectiveness.

Nevertheless, much could be gained by a well-orchestrated international research program in this particular field. In the first place, it would provide a wide coverage with relatively limited resources. By conducting research in a variety of cultural and epidemiological settings and in locations representing different patterns or levels of socioeconomic development, it would be possible to obtain trend data, at least in the form of working hypotheses to be checked out by selected longitudinal research. Lastly, it is evident that drug production-traffic-use circuits are not limited by national boundaries. Nor are the cultural patterns and trends that condition drug use and attitudes toward drug use. Transnational research is clearly required, for instance, to understand the role, structure, and behavior of the itinerant youth subcultures, which acquire their drug habits or purchase cannabis or opiates in the Middle East, Southeast Asia, or Latin America and import both habit and drugs to their home countries. Are these subcultures breeding grounds for user-dealers? Certainly the opportunities for profitable, if small, transactions exist, and there is every reason to assume that occasional smuggling and resale ventures, whether or not detected and punished, lead to confirmed trafficking roles. And what impact do these itinerant subcultures have on the foreign countries which they visit and from which they operate? It appears that while the incidence of drug use among the American and European hippies found in Afghanistan, Nepal, Mexico, or the Mediterranean area is very high, they remain isolated from the local population. On the other hand, there have been instances of local impact and cases in which new substances, for example, hallucinogens and stimulants, have been introduced by foreign visitors.

All this calls for a joint or coordinated research effort at the international level. A first step in that direction was taken in 1971 by the creation of an International Research Group on Drug Legislation and Programs, which pools the efforts of a variety of scholars and research institutions, private, governmental, and international. Among its efforts, the country-studies program undertaken by the United Nations Social Defense Research Institute in Rome appears particularly significant as a model—or framework—for the proposed research on drug dealers. The Rome Institute, in collaboration with members of the International Research Group and several United Nations agencies, is seeking to generate a series of parallel but coordinated systemic studies in a dozen countries, covering quantitative data on incidence, prevalence, and trends in drug use and production; attitudes toward the drug problem; as well as an inventory and assessment of the effectiveness of control policies. At least some of the issues proposed for future drug dealer research will probably also be included in these studies. Based on the work in progress and planned, information useful for improved international policy-making and collaboration should emerge. Since it is my thesis that effective policy and action internationally require a factual base, I believe one can expect, if sufficient understanding and support for research is forthcoming, much improvement in legal and social action focusing on drug dealers and drug dealing by the middle of the 1970s.

14

Responsibilities of the Pharmaceutical Industry: A Personal View

C. R. B. Joyce

First one must separate the way in which attitudes toward drugs are spread through the community or nation and the way in which drugs themselves are disseminated. Drugs are disseminated by their inventors, manufacturers, distributors, pharmacists, physicians, patients and—in the case of social, self-medicating, or illicit users—by nonpatient users. Attitudes toward drugs are disseminated by all these people and by friends, relations, the mass media, politicians, and others who possess strong views even if they do not happen to be in possession of strong drugs. When we consider policy—that is, what any institution (be it industry, government, schools, etc.) might do or ought to do—we realize that attitudes or opinions as facts in themselves can be more important in shaping events than the facts about drugs or drug dissemination. We must also separate those drugs and those acts in regard to drugs that are lawful and those that are unlawful. The unlawful drugs (for example, heroin in the United States, alcohol in Moslem lands) and their distributors and users generate an especially complex body of attitudes—and particularly unascertainable facts—because they are underground. Consequently, we face incomplete knowledge—slowly building up through work of the sort reported by Blum and Associates (1972a, 1972b)—and strong but possibly invalid opinions as we consider what ought to be done with regard to illicit traffic, even if it begins as licit dissemination that somehow becomes illicit.

Causal Chain of Availability

Drug misuse requires drugs; the initial responsibility in the causal chain of availability lies with the inventor or, in the case of natural substances (cannabis, morning glory seeds), with the discoverer. It is natural then for those who attempt to control misuse at first to think of inventors and producers: the pharmaceutical industry, for example. On the other hand, once an individual has used any drug himself, whether legally or illegally, he himself is in a sense its discoverer, for he has discovered its effects upon himself. Thereafter the "discoverer" may become his own inventor or producer as well, planting cannabis, for example, or installing an illicit amphetamine laboratory.

One regulatory mechanism for the actions of these potential inventors and producers in making drugs available is their own personality, training, and experience. A new drug or, for users, a new drug experience is considered in the context of one's other knowledge—about drugs in general and their likely effects on people. If the discoverer and potential producer has rational data at his disposal, for example, knowledge of pharmacology and epidemiology, he is likely to exert certain precautions. Even if he has merely not been caught up in romanticism, mythology, fads, or psychopathology, a discoverer can be led to caution by his common sense. Lacking both empirical data and common sense, he may be unduly enthusiastic and convert himself into a producer of potentially dangerous substances. Individuals and industries have acted in this fashion. In doing so, they have become critical links in a chain of unwise if not illicit distribution.

As far as legal drugs are concerned, the inventor is only one item in the producer's black box. Usually the company (invention these days is usually corporate enterprise) decides that work upon a particular compound or range of compounds will be done for reasons that may be in part altruistic but are largely dominated by commercial factors. The best of these may be that there has previously been no treatment for an illness with a sufficient market potential to merit the necessary investment. Research is undertaken to protect a patent that is on the point of expiring or to secure a share of a market that has already been proved in the hands of other manufacturers. Although it is a major objective to produce for therapeutic uses new drugs that are devoid of the disadvantages (unwanted effects) of existing ones, nevertheless, the mere existence of a drug promotes the invention of others in the same category. This is not necessarily a bad thing; a good product with a new action may result—many monoamine oxidase inhibitors, diuretics, and antidiabetic agents were found in this way.

Control Measures

The measures that may be adopted to control the undesirable use of drugs are usually classified under the headings of education, prevention, punishment, and rehabilitation. The inventor is perhaps the most educated of all those participating; his very education should make it possible that he will end by inventing other substances that are less unsatisfactory. But it is unfortunately not unknown for inventors to make their results available to others, or at least to be careless in guarding them. At such an intellectual level, disasters can perhaps be prevented only by extremely careful selection of collaborators—never an easy task—but not by placing a total embargo upon the manufacture of certain classes of compound, a technique the results of which have not been particularly encouraging. The effect of blocking legal production can well be a shift, if an adequate demand already exists, into illegal sources that are less easily controlled.

During manufacture and transport of the finished legal substances to their eventual outlets, there are possibilities for diversion. Ordinarily diversion is theft, although unauthorized purchases or even authorized ones that intend to take advantage of differing national laws also contribute to diversion. Opportunities for illegal synthesis also arise during the manufacture and transport stages. At once the problem of control descends from the licit development of new drugs to the elimination or reduction of theft or deceptive purchase. There are many motives for theft and possibly other kinds of diversion; and attitudes toward theft differ too, on the part of both thieves and their beholders. If there is high recognized intrinsic risk in the materials, as for instance in radioactive substances, explosives, or rattlesnakes, the knowledge of risk in the potential thief probably reduces the likelihood that he will steal. In that sense, educating thieves to intrinsic risk is an important control measure. When such intrinsic risk is not so evident, at least to thieves and diverters, then there must be education to another kind of risk, that of apprehension and immediate and certain punishment (or other reproof). Such education, like propaganda, cannot be effective if it is false, that is, if the risk does not exist. If they lack this knowledge of intrinsic risk or are uncertain of apprehension and punishment, those whose desires and character make them liable to be thieves will be deterred only by the physical security of the drugs themselves during their manufacture, transport, or sale. Physical security is expensive; so is education, apprehension, or punishment. Nevertheless, these days the most popular method of attempting intervention appears to be education to intrinsic risk, seeking to convince potential distributors and users—all of whom are therefore potential delinquents —that drugs (for example, stimulants or hypnotics) are as dangerous to those for whom their use has not been medically (or in some cases religiously) prescribed and controlled as a dose of radioactive gold, cobalt, or iodine would be. Given the data presented earlier in *The Dream Sellers* (Blum and Associates, 1972a) on the low risk of arrest for users or dealers, it would appear foolhardy and even counterproductive to attempt to educate anybody about the improbable risks incurred under the criminal law. As for physical security, this appears to be a feature that could be considerably improved, although how the costs should be borne is uncertain. The data on pharmacists presented by Blum and Smith (1972) show that all the pharmacies sampled in San Francisco had suffered burglary and shoplifting. Can we make these pharmacies (and, presumably, others elsewhere) more physically secure? The data on physicians (Blum, Wolfe, and Lewis, 1972) show that the security with which they habitually store their drugs varies with their own attitudes toward drugs and their own drug habits. How can we, knowing something about these relationships, nevertheless increase their security consciousness?

The pharmacist in particular is in a difficult situation. The physician has the right to prescribe—and overprescribe. He may even prescribe certain prescriptions for himself—and overprescribe these too as we see from the data of Blum, Wolfe, and Lewis (1972)' and others. The pharmacist is the passive agent of both physician and customer, submitting to their instructions. But physicians, too, may be manipulated by their patients into prescribing when they would not have done so on their own initiative. One must not overlook the instructions to or demands on those who dispense drugs that create unwise or illicit dispensers. Thus, to examine the characteristics of those who do divert, dispense unwisely, or deal illicitly is only part of the task; one must understand the psychological and market demands upon them that may change them from possible to actual and improper disseminators of drugs.

The behavior of the cautious and controlled physician, the detail man, and to a lesser extent the pharmacist is inversely proportional to the commercial interests of the manufacturer. The manufacturer needs proselytizers and believers, people who will prescribe or use drugs with the conviction that drugs are useful. On the other hand, to prevent unwise use, society requires people to act in conservative and skeptical ways toward dispensing and using drugs. The physician data (Blum, Wolfe, and Lewis, 1972) suggest that one feature in physicians who prescribe widely is their low opinion of the potency—of either values or dangers—of drugs. It would be reassuring if one knew that such physicians prescribed widely only when the drugs were, by outside evaluation, merely ineffective and not actually harmful. It is of little consolation to learn only that the skeptics do prescribe widely. Questions about the physicians' own views of the potency of drugs in relationship to their degree of control and their dispensing practices are important and need to be answered by further reliable studies.

Here, as elsewhere, we have to ask the right questions. We have clearly not been doing this so far. As Gertrude Stein is reported to have said as she lay dying, "We know all the answers, it is the questions that we do not know." Personally, I do not know any of the answers either and am so ignorant of the questions that I can only propose, very diffidently, some ways of looking for them. Let us call them models and motivations.

Models

James Joyce once said of the 80,000 words in (then)' current English use, "They are all the wrong ones." There may not yet be 80,000 models, and not all of them are wrong, but it may be worth inventing some new ones. For example, by considering other kinds of dependency than that upon drugs; or by looking at the problem in terms of ecology; or by inverting the customary relationship of experimenter and subject to ask, not "How can we stop this happening?" but "How can we make it happen all the more?"

Suitable models may be found by considering the spread of drug dependence as a kind of environmental pollution (Joyce, 1970) or as a response to overpopulation. It is noteworthy, incidentally, that most programs for research (Drug Research Report, 1970) continue to be framed in terms that take drug dependence as causally related to social phenomena, such as crime, whether as cause or effect of a complex process. There are exceptions: Messer (1969) has suggested that the use of marijuana is a valuable predictor, or sensitive *independent* variable, in its own right.

These three approaches cannot easily be discussed in isolation from each other. It has been pointed out that 99.5 percent of American males are dependent upon their trousers, and that 51 percent of married American males are dependent upon their wives (the remaining 49 percent may be dependent upon someone else's). Other examples abound: 5 percent of former alcoholics are dependent upon Alcoholics Anonymous; 7 million American women are dependent upon the oral contraceptive; a much larger number of Catholic women, however, are dependent upon the advice of their priest. Dependence is part of the human condition. Some kinds of dependence are permissible, others are impermissible. On what grounds are they distinguished? The grounds are continually changing. What would be involved, what would be gained, and what sacrificed, if dependence upon drugs were recognized as one of the permissible dependencies?

Of course, as far as certain drugs are concerned, permission has already been given; the so-called social drugs are in this class, but the idea of "dependency" on tobacco or caffeine is seldom mentioned except in a strictly technical context. In view of the mounting evidence that many people can use even opioids as mind-altering drugs intermittently and that the overwhelming majority of those who use cannabis in any of its forms can take it or leave it alone, should we not consider the possible gains and losses of admitting those who use drugs in this way to membership in society after all? Conservative estimates suggest that at least a million people living in Britain are dependent upon placebo, which is a "respectable" medical treatment (Joyce, 1969a); 14 percent of people sampled at random in the street have ingested a centrally active drug within the previous 24 hours; 25 percent of American adults are "currently using" centrally active substances (Parry, 1968). It is a large number to deny the vote. It may even be the tranquillized majority.

The usually held belief that man is the only animal that manifests spontaneous drug dependence is not valid. Of course, it is well know that many animals can be experimentally addicted by human intervention, sometimes in quite sophisticated situations set up to model as far as possible those in which human dependence may be expected to occur (Thompson, 1968). But there are also at least two species of ant that become spontaneously dependent and the same may apparently be true of at least one species of bee. To take one species as an example, it appears that *Lasius flavus* cultivates another kind of animal, *Claviger,* which it feeds and from which it receives a secretion, which is so important that in times of danger *Lasius* will save the *Claviger* in preference to its own eggs (Nilsson and Lindroth, 1959; Emerson, 1964). The interesting point in the present context is that the ant's behavior is taken by some commentators to indicate a kind of depravity (the word is not theirs, but it is definitely the meaning). There is an assumption that in such circumstances the animal should seek at all costs to preserve its own offspring, although it is conceivable—and has not, so far as I am aware, been proved otherwise—that the offspring might not survive at all in the total absence of *Claviger*. It is the Pathetic Fallacy again. Perhaps our attitude toward dependence, even in our own species, evinces a comparable pathetic fallacy?

Let me put the question more boldly: Whom, in terms of benefit either to the individual or to society, should we be actively striving to addict? Two years ago, a senior British politician appeared to have heard some interesting suggestions in New York that heroin dependence in *carefully selected individuals* might be preferable to the aggressive and criminal psychopathy shown by such individuals if the drug were withdrawn from them or if they had never used it in the first place (Joyce, 1969b). A brief and congratulatory broadcast comment was followed within 24 hours by an angry denial from the politician concerned that he had ever said or meant anything of the kind. But why not? Was he ashamed of his own intuitions, or his own research services, or of his own eyes and ears?

To go even further—let us define not only those individuals we should actively strive to addict, but also, since most attempts to prevent people from becoming dependent have notably failed, how might the number of drug dependents be indiscriminately increased? What methods of propaganda to this end would be most worthy of adoption? A successful examination of the problem from this point of view might enable us to turn it back into the negative form, so clarifying the form of propaganda most likely to be effective in the contrary sense.

To put the same argument in another way: *whatever* measures are adopted to change the incidence of and traffic in illicit drug use, illicit drug use and traffic will remain at a certain level above zero. The level of tolerance must be decided, after which the necessary partition of social effort and resources can be made to maintain the agreed level. Tolerance must also involve a definition of the characteristics of the group affected, since it is unlikely that any conceivable measure will secure a homogeneous distribution of drug misuse throughout society as a whole. On the principle that no assumption should be allowed to pass unquestioned, however, we might inquire what kind of propaganda campaign it would take to ensure that the sample of those misusing or trafficking in drugs was in fact a randomly drawn sample from the population as a whole, instead of, as at present, only the underprivileged, black, high school dropouts; lonely housewives; white, overprivileged college graduates (Sapol and Roffman, 1969); peace-loving soldiers in Vietnam; and oversocial Madison Avenue executives (Malabis, 1970; Margelts, 1970).

To define the problem in terms of tolerated probabilities rather than in absolute prohibitions is more constructive. It is also usually less time-consuming and therefore likely to be more acceptable. This is, after all, what we do (admittedly often by default or by pragmatic necessity) about road accidents, suicide, most crime, the escape of lethal materials from chemical and biological warfare establishments, atmospheric levels of toxic industrial and other substances including radioactivity, pulmonary and coronary disease due to smoking, and so on. Why make an exception of drug dependence?

Motivations

Motivation is also a major variable in drug dependence. I am not talking about the motivation of the drug user, a field that has been very thoroughly ploughed and furrowed without yielding much in the way of a harvest. I wish to draw attention to the motivations of those of us who are concerned with drug dependence in any way at all: as worried parents or spouses, journalists, broadcasters, legislators, lawyers, policemen, or research workers. What, in fact, are the kicks that each of us gets out of being involved in this murky scene? Very often, and not only for the professional pusher, there is a financial motive: I admit to this myself, having written and broadcast about drug dependence from time to time for a fee, an ambiguous fact that I justified by the claim that it was in the public interest to do so. Perhaps to work in the drug field at all at someone else's expense, usually the taxpayer's, is another kind of villainy, not so far removed from that of the "venal" dealer we all so righteously if not rightly abhor.

Villains or not, there are at least two reasons why we should study our own motivations and persuade others to do likewise. First, some of us might then go away and do something more important, such as interfere with overpopulation, venereal disease, or other natural disasters. Second, we might compare what we say we intend to do with what gets done, which would allow us to assess our impact as well as to question our sincerity. Consider studies of the success rates of individual physicians in persuading addicts (usually to nicotine) to give up their habits. Most professed evaluations are of change agents who are successful, but it is at least as interesting, perhaps more so, to look at those who are particularly unsuccessful in improving the behavior of their patients. Why are they bad? Can it be because their actions are downright inefficient, ambiguous, diametrically opposed to what would be effective, or actively proselytizing for that which they claim to be anathema? Consider the data in *The Dream Sellers* (Blum and Associates, 1972a) on police departments intervening, so their public policy states, to "get the dealer." Even assuming the true risk of arrest for a dealer is above the estimated 0.02 percent per year per region, is not almost everyone aware that the level of risk is still low? And if one is arrested, what then? Look at the more solid data on the disposal of offenders by police and the courts. Get the dealer indeed! Consider the descriptions of adult prisons and juvenile detention centers. Is their purpose really to correct sentenced dealers? If not, what are the dealers there for? What are the prisons there for? Consider industrial regulation. There is a host of regulatory agencies and codes, including those pertaining to the pharmaceutical industry. Do they protect the public? Which public? Or do regulatory bodies, as has been suggested (Kaplan, 1970; R. Lind, 1971 personal communication), simply protect industry from competition, the commissioners from having to find other work, and the general public from having to worry about regulations? The attempt by certain European countries to control the misuse of stimulants by virtual embargos on legitimate import has merely substituted a legitimate source of supply by illicit manufacture and has made the drugs unavailable (indeed, has prohibited their use) for legitimate medical purposes. It has had no noticeable other effects except to increase the costs of governmental control (Goldberg, 1968). The intention of the Vienna Treaty on the Control of Psychotropic Substances and its probable consequences, whether or not it is implemented, are to bring about the same so-called control everywhere. Can it be that no one has been looking at costs and outcomes?

But this has taken us away from the consideration of individual motives. Most of us, especially doctors, seek to avoid admitting our complicity, despite the greatly increased use of mind-altering drugs by physicians (Vaillant and others, 1970), the increased risk that they run of becoming dependent (Farnsworth, 1970; Watkins, 1970), and their generally conceded tendency to overprescribe (Balint and others, 1970).

In the study by Balint and colleagues (1970), of 1000 patients treated by ten general practitioners, 30 to 40 percent of whom were given "repeat prescriptions" (that is, medication continued for a long time without any attempt at change or further medical investigation of the condition), the doctors participating believed that such prescriptions were usually unsatisfactory from the medical point of view and had been started by other practitioners than themselves or by consultants. In fact, more than two-thirds of these prescriptions had been initiated by the general practitioner himself. Without access, there is no dependence. Without overprescribing or prescribing of even reasonable quantities of drugs on inadequate grounds, there would be very much less access to drugs that are at present only manufactured legally. Of course, the cessation of manufacture of drugs on inadequate grounds would be a major contribution as well. But society gets the drugs the effects of which are reputed to be those that it desires—freedom from pain, from anxiety, from depression; all of them drugs designed to restore function to a normal level that is often painfully, fearfully, depressingly unambitious. We have to decide what drugs we need. *Are* these the ones? Is it not also time to take a closer look at "normality" itself? (Lilly and Stillwell, 1965; Stevenson, 1970; Wallace, 1970.)

It is a safe prediction that our attitudes toward drugs, like our attitudes toward normality, are conditioned by our previous experience, knowledge, and expectations, much of it unconscious. An alarming feature of this process is the extent to which an "authority" in one field is accepted as an authority in another on the basis of his authority in the first and not of knowledge in the second. A request for references was made to a noted and very quantitatively minded British basic scientist who has expressed himself on drug dependence frequently and vehemently but with very little evidence and a statistical approach that is open to more doubt than is the case with his major work. The request produced only an apology that he had no references, but he gave a recommendation to make contact with an equally eminent American specialist in another but related basic field who was said to have a great amount of documented information at his disposal. The "information" that was sent turned out to be a number of letters to editors and talks to parents, policemen, high school and university students, with only one quantitative statement in 70 pages of text. True, the statement was illustrated by a graph, but the provenance of the figures upon which it was based was nowhere stated.

This criticism is not merely an academic exercise in psychodynamics in view of the impressive demonstration by Rosenthal and his collaborators (see Rosenthal and Rosnow, 1970) that the expectations of the research worker greatly influence the nature of his experimental (and this presumably includes clinical) findings, even when the work is carried out at one or more removes by intermediaries. There is no doubt that the reviewer also finds in the literature the evidence he requires to support his contentions (Farnsworth, 1970; Weech and Bibb, 1970; Louria, 1970; Freedman, 1970). It seems very probable that the policy maker does the same thing. Unless, therefore, my picking is in some sense "better" than that of others, it is fortunate that no one has asked me to be a policy maker.

However, I have been invited to suggest what the pharmaceutical industry might do to reduce drug abuse. I have noted some of the complexities and paradoxes that make such recommendations difficult. If one admits that drugs are overused and that they are powerful, that they can damage as well as help, it follows that conservatism in production and use should be encouraged. Caution rather than enthusiasm should also inform influences, such as advertising, rock music, or movies featuring idyllic drug-use scenes, upon prescribers, patients, and other users. That remedy is coming to be adopted by industry itself. Each promotional campaign, whether mediated by the detail man or made directly to the pharmacist or physician, is likely to insist that any drug be prescribed only when it is strictly necessary and only in amounts that are needed for the purpose at hand.

Ideas about "purpose" for use, either in the mind of the

physician, the self-medicating individual, or the social/private user, would benefit from an attempt to separate demonstrable efficacy from merely hoped-for effects and to separate specific (drug-related) from nonspecific (environmental and personal) factors (Rinkel, 1963). When this has been done, instruction as such can become more effective. That means having facts, of course, and communicating them to dispensers and users. Here members of the pharmaceutical industry should and can function even more than at present as drug educators. Economic self-interest can be modulated by long-range social interests.

However, education alone is not likely to be wholly effective in controlling either diversion or unwise use. Other measures are needed, including the straightforward but costly one of physical security. Security means careful selection and supervision of people with access to drugs or to ingredients necessary for their manufacture. It means careful record keeping and independent, regular, and complete audit of records, at all stages in manufacture, transport, and distribution. Security also requires the physical means to make theft difficult and to increase the risk of capture for thieves. It should go without saying that responsible (and not merely big) pharmaceutical companies are already doing a great deal in this direction without national or international obligation to do so.

If, as suggested here, the motivations of inventors, manufacturers, narcotics officers (see Blum and Associates, 1972a), physicians, patients, users, and researchers also contribute to drug misuse—whether as the motives of proselytizers, profiteers, and social gainers or those simply of escapists and euphorics—one should also attempt to influence motives. Individuals should learn about their motives or, better, what they are really doing. Most people have incompatible motives or values; that is, few are wholly in favor of poisoning others or themselves even if some of what they do leads in that direction. Thus it is possible to demonstrate to the individual contradictions in his own behavior and to guide him down the presumably more civilized path. Detail men, pharmacists, and physicians should be subject to selection and training procedures that would increase the chances that those who are unable under stress to handle discrepancies between their beliefs and conduct are helped to learn to do just this. If that cannot be done and they cannot be helped in other ways, those who are unable to control their drug-dispensing or drug use must be denied opportunities to visit the consequences of their limitations on themselves and others.

Rules that are internalized are far more effective and harmonious than those that are external—compare the studies on pharmacists and faculty in *The Dream Sellers* (Blum and Associates, 1972a). This is as true for industry as a whole as it is for the individual. External rules require coercion to produce conformity. They may also encourage the art of discreet violation. Since the resources for coercion are rarely sufficient, they may also be either inequitable, lax, or corrupt in relating the members of an industry to its regulatory body. This may lead producers to demand a "laissez-faire" policy, or the public to demand disciplinary measures the costs of which exceed the benefits. Instead of all this, an effort resembling that proposed and demonstrated in other settings by Kurt Lewin (1951) might achieve higher standards if leaders of public interest groups and of the pharmaceutical industry were to participate in continuing mutually self-influencing groups. Such an experiment in the encouragement of self-regulation through programs of continued social intercourse might have some merit. The proposed awareness or conscience creation sessions would not replace systems of regulation entirely but, taking place entirely outside the framework of law, might make them easier to implement by emphasizing human rather than bureaucratic or legal mechanisms. Those outside industry tend to blame it for a variety of sinful deeds, ranging from outrageous profiteering to willful blindness about diversion, yet righteous demands are more likely to bring about righteous denials than desirable changes, whereas informal discussions would not allow for stylized claims and responses, but might moderate and even humanize the usual ritual and political posturings.

The report (Palo Alto Citizens Task Force, 1972) of a citizens' council from the same community in which several of the studies of drug users and dealers were made states: "Drug advertising by pharmaceutical companies, particularly through the television media, is by far the most powerful factor in creating and perpetuating harmful drug use attitudes and behavior. The constant repetition of drug messages plays a direct and significant role in creating and maintaining harmful and irresponsible attitudes toward the use of drugs." The council recommends that "pharmaceutical companies and the mass media cease irresponsible drug advertising practices" and also "police their own distribution practices more carefully so that products will not be diverted into illegitimate channels." I could not agree more, despite the failure of British and American research units and official commissions on violence and on pornography to demonstrate that exposure to such influences has an effect upon behavior (McGuire, 1970). After all, the work of Zajonc (1970) and others suggests strongly that merely to expose animals or human beings to repetitive stimuli, a reiterated word, or the repetition of a certain kind of music, without emotion or any kind of evaluation, increases the likelihood that these stimuli will subsequently be selected from an array of proffered alternatives. Such work suggests that exposure to violence would not make one more likely to commit violence, but only more likely to accept it. If exposure creates not aggressors but victims, the frequency of crime is increased, but not the number of criminals. In any case, let us have less repetition.

We might also produce fewer useless or merely repetitive drugs; but then we would have to accept lower levels of profit, and physicians and citizens in their turn would have to learn to accept discomfort as part of life rather than to seek in chemicals immediate but transient comfort and symbolic reassurance. I do not believe that resounding calls of the sort made by this citizens' council help to change these attitudes. Indeed, it is questionable whether that is their purpose. They may be intended, instead, to disguise an inability to change on the part of the authors, while requiring it from their readers. Would these citizens be willing to forgo owning a television set if advertisers refused to forgo the revenues of drug advertising? Would they be willing to go to a doctor and not demand, even silently, that they be "given something" when they hurt, are nervous, or are otherwise indisposed? And with regard to traffic, would they be willing to join in controlling diversion by not passing around pills to friends and relatives? Instead of clarion calls to battle, a more domestic music might have those citizens sitting down, say twice a month for dinner until further notice, with pharmaceutical company executives, doctors, and pharmacists to explore problems and possible solutions. In such a way they might give help to one another, developing in each other new standards for drug production, advertising, prescribing, and use; and, above all, for civilized discussion and factfinding.

For in the final analysis, we have to decide rationally what drugs we need, what drugs we will tolerate, and how strongly we will turn our feelings into action against those that are unnecessary and intolerable, if we are not, as T. S. Eliot fears, to "die of . . . absolute paternal care."

15

Action in the Schools

Jasper Woodcock

Education might be relevant to the prevention of drug-dealing in two ways. It might indirectly reduce drug-dealing by reducing drug usage, thus shrinking the dealers' market; and it might directly reduce drug-dealing by dissuading some who might have become dealers.

In suggesting a possible role for education in the prevention of drug-dealing, we will no doubt be seen as having too soon thrown in the sponge. For we tend to turn to education as an instrument of social policy aimed at specific kinds of deviant or delinquent behavior, or specific forms of ill health, only after experience (bitter sometimes for those on the receiving end) has convinced us that neither direct deterrence, in the shape of the law, nor curative measures, in the shape of medical care, can exercise effective control. Had we an effective cure or prophylaxis for dental decay, would we spend so much time teaching children to brush their teeth? In the case of drug *usage*, especially that by children and adolescents, we seem to have begun to accept the ineffectiveness of law or medicine and have duly begun to turn to education. Though this may be an

267

indication of our growing ability to love the sinner, our need to hate
the sin is not abated. As our espousal of an educational approach
has deprived us of the average drug user as an object to be alienated
by legal or medical means, so we have turned on the drug dealer,
the "trafficker," as a recipient of our thwarted sense of outrage. Is
it a coincidence that, in both the United States and the United
Kingdom, a growing emphasis on drug education as a preventive
weapon has been accompanied by an increase in the severity of the
legal penalties for dealing? The United Kingdom Misuse of Drugs
Act, 1971, for example, introduced simultaneously two new features
into British drug legislation: preventive education, and "possession
with intent to supply" as a new offense, distinct from simple possession of a controlled drug and carrying much harsher penalties.

To deny, however, that education may have a role in the
prevention of drug-dealing is to ignore our belief in the role of
education as a road to the achievement of socially accepted lives
and values and, particularly in the United States, as a means of
homogenizing the population. To want to use education as a means
of establishing desirable behavior and values vis-à-vis drugs is thus
an expression of our confidence in the schools as molders of citizen-
ship and inculcators of a kind of conformity.

If we hold that education can have this kind of positive
impact upon drug use, then recently established findings of the
characteristics of drug dealers (Blum and Associates, 1972a) should
encourage us to expect that it could have a similar impact upon
dealing. For dealers, particularly at the commencement of their
dealing careers, are not significantly different from heavy users. The
sharp distinction between use and dealing drawn by the law and by
enforcement agencies is not paralleled by sharp dissimilarities between the user and the dealer. Insofar, then, as we adopt an educational approach to drug use based on our belief in its own positive
contribution, rather than on our despair at the failure of other
instruments of social policy, then we shall have no reason to suppose
that education that is effective in diminishing drug use will not be
effective in diminishing drug-dealing.

In essence, then, the premise of this chapter is that if education in schools is an effective way of diminishing problems deriv-
ing from drug use, then it is likely also to influence the prevalence of

dealing. Is education effective in this way? If it is not, what are the prospects that it can be?

Deciding on Drug Education

Preceding the adoption of education, there has been a debate, not about its efficacy, but about the direction of its impact. The question usually asked is not whether drug education in the schools has any effect, but whether it will lead to more rather than less drug use and, correlatively, greater or fewer drug-related problems, dealing included. It is thus apparent that the potency of the school as a force for affecting drug conduct is assumed. Although the debate has been resolved in the United States by assuming a favorable impact, the World Health Organization Expert Committee on Drug Dependence (1970) has concluded to the contrary and recommended against drug education. Inspection of the decision process indicates that drug education will be suggested only when the known prevalence of illicit or otherwise disapproved drug use among school-age youngsters has reached a level at which one need no longer worry that education will itself promote interest in use. This argument was made explicit by the chairman of the United Kingdom Health Education Council who stated in Parliament during a debate on the (1971) Misuse of Drugs Bill that the development of policy guidelines for schools on drug-abuse education must await the results of social surveys on youthful drug use (Birk, 1971).

Even in the absence of studies showing high prevalence, that is, illicit experience among the majority, for those nations where there is any indication that illicit use is occurring, there are pressures for the schools to take some action. Since direct education is forbidden until high prevalence levels are reached, the interim measure adopted most often appears to be an indirect one: the education of teachers so that they will at least be knowledgeable about drug problems and will be able, presumably, to intervene informally in special cases, as, for example, when children themselves raise questions about drugs or when a child is found to be a drug user.

There are conditions under which, even in the absence of high prevalence of use among school-age children, it is proposed that a second form of interim measure is required. These circumstances occur when it becomes apparent, either from scientific studies or official records, that adult use of illicit drugs occurs, that adult use is expanding, and that there is fear that children upon leaving school will be exposed to previously nonexistent drug-taking temptations. In such situations, proponents of education propose that the schools must intervene to forestall that possible future use. The formula most often advanced is that factual information about the effects and dangers of drugs will suffice to retard later experimentation.

The foregoing suggests three areas of decision. One is the level of risk of future use by adults, the second is a band frequency of unknown width when some children's use is occurring but is not yet deemed great enough to justify direct education, and the third is when a critical point of prevalence among children has been reached such that the risk of arousing interest is more than offset by the risk of not intruding to stabilize, if not to reduce, current use. Yet the prevalence is often a subjective estimate in the mind of the decision maker rather than the product of reliable data on levels and patterns of use determined scientifically. Thus if one introduces the notion of a critical mass of use required to produce pressures for drug education in schools, the mass may not be that which is found in the population itself but that which exists in the perceptions of those who influence school activities. The sources of such beliefs are varied; but, at the very least, they include highly publicized cases in the mass media, police alarms, parental anxiety over changing conduct styles among children, and school concerns over their institutional reputations for moral soundness. All these events occur on an international stage where the backdrop consists of the very active demons of popular drug mythology. Faced with perceived threats and such demons, the average citizen feels compelled to take some action. One of the most convenient pressure points is the school. As one English citizen wrote, after hearing a debate on the pros and cons of drug education, "I am sure we must educate our young people about the dangers of drugs. At least we will have done our duty."

Bureaucratization

Once a decision has been reached to introduce education, be that indirectly of teachers or to deter future use or more directly to affect present student habits, drug education itself becomes institutionalized and subject to the usual snowballing of bureaucratization. This means that there will be pressure for the ever-increasing appropriation of funds, the emergence of a cadre of experts, the definition of sets of proper and improper techniques, including demands for personnel training and certification, competition with other subjects for the time of the school-child audience, competition among educational suppliers for the new market in teaching aids, and the growth of vested interests dependent upon the continued expansion of this particular industry. Bureaucratization very early reaches the point at which, given the current politics and demonology of drugs, it is irreversible.

Philosophy

What is done by way of drug education will reflect how teaching is conducted generally in a society. This in turn rests upon views as to the nature of man and the particular nature of children. In those fields of instruction bearing on social conduct and self-control, as does education in the drug field, it is pertinent to ask if the society regards the child as inherently sinful or angelic, as a tabula rasa, or as a prize or chattel.

In the Western world, certainly England of yesteryear, the view was that children were born bearing the sins of the father and thus had devilish potential (not unlike current Balkan peasant beliefs to the effect that the unbaptized child is a *drak,* or demon). Education therefore had to instruct for enlightenment and to control the powers of darkness. It was consequently moral in tone, civilizing with respect to aims, and repressive or controlling in classroom practice. Drug education in such cases should be in the context of ethics, an exhortation to elect nonuse as good and godly, the warning that use is evil, and the practice of strong punishment should the discovery of drug use be made.

Belief in the child's nature as essentially neutral, that is, a tabula rasa, pretends to be an areligious doctrine. From it one would expect the educator to assume the child pliable and in need of molding, probably through facts and by good example. Bad influences such as the "wrong" information or bad companions are to be avoided lest proper development be impaired. The term *proper* is probably defined by community norms, religious though these may be; but the educator, preferring to be "objective," elects to see himself as a pragmatist working to avoid harm. That concept of harm can be described in physical, social, or mental terms and, like the mental health movement, it conveys much that is conventional under a scientific disguise.

The angelic child, lineal descendent of the noble savage of Rousseau, seems to be growing in popularity, especially in America, although Summerhill in England is a prototype. The modern belief may represent in part some misreading of Freud, an adaptation of the psychodynamic commentary on repression as a dangerous force leading to neurosis, the result of which must then be avoidance of repression, currently expressed as aversion to control. For Freud, of course, the savage was not so noble, discontent being, for him, a necessary outcome of the forces required to build a working conscience. Nevertheless, the current interpretation would see oppressive society as the source of discord juxtaposed against the child's innate harmony with nature. Parents do wrong to destroy this natural harmony through coercion; so also do educators who thus sense that they must instead beckon rather than compel. The drug educator proceeding according to this assumption must be sure not to restrain or antagonize; such actions as he takes must aim only to arouse and channel the natural interest of the child or, in the extreme form, pander to his desires.

Approaches

The Health Approach. There are several alternatives by which drug education may find its niche in school systems. By far, the commonest is to consider drug education a form of health education. The assumptions here are that drug use is a health problem, that is, its occurrence represents some form of illness—mental or physical—and that this illness is preventable by supplying appropriate information. A similar model is venereal disease education. Accident and dental caries prevention programs are also similar. Such health models may be employed even if it is recognized that some forms of drug use are not in themselves evidence of illness; casual cannabis smoking can be an example. However, such drug use is always held to present the risk of a future health problem so that the health model approach is sustained.

Both assumptions underlying the health approach are of course in doubt. The contention that ill health is demonstrable simply by the fact of drug use is strongly questionable. Whether or not preventive programs work in any area of health education is also dubious. Controlled studies of such programs are rare and their results tend to be discouraging, even when the chosen objectives and target populations would seem almost to guarantee success. For example, Schlesinger and others (1966) used intensive programs involving discussion groups, specially appointed block leaders, visiting experts, and monthly newsletters—all aimed at teaching parents of children under seven how to protect them from accidental injury —with no discernible effect whatever. Similarly, Adams and Stanmeyer (1960) found that, in a group of United States servicemen in Antarctica, films and lectures had no significant impact on dental self-care; only close individual supervision by a dentist made any difference. Neither of these studies was aimed directly at children, but dare we build upon the hope that children will respond more rationally to health education than do their elders?

The Delinquency Approach. Illicit drug use among children is necessarily a matter of delinquent conduct; it is a failure of children to be law-abiding. Search reveals remarkably few programs designed to inculcate law-abiding conduct as such, leaving aside recourse to punishment or corrections after the fact. One such teaching program in California employed in grades 7 and 8 seeks to instill understanding of the basis and nature of the criminal law. In the United Kingdom, Hauser (1963) has sought to encourage a sense of relationship to society and the law among adult offenders, and recently to inaugurate similar programs preventively in the schools.

Were such programs to be employed more widely, the outcomes might be in doubt. An intensive effort to prevent vocation, school, and law-abiding failure has been reported by Ahlstrom and Havighurst (1971). The study began with socially disadvantaged youngsters in the seventh grade for whom the prognosis for vocational, school, and lawful adjustment was lower than ordinary (given statistics on their predecessors and peers). The investigators worked with the group through high school, studying their total environment and trying out a work-study program. A control group received regular academic work whereas the experimental group received considerable extra vocational and counseling services. The extra effort made no difference, measured statistically, although one-fourth of the boys were presumed to have profited in one fashion or another. The majority of the experimental sample ended up socially and educationally maladjusted and with a record of continuing delinquency. Drug use as such was not recorded, but it is reasonable to expect that this group that was so widely involved in crime—including homicides and rapes—would not have overlooked pharmaceutically derived peccadilloes.

Social Learning. In communities in which drug use by children has become so widespread as to be statistically normal and, to some extent, accepted as inevitable by authorities, one can distinguish another approach, one that is less well elucidated because it does not subscribe to the traditional health or delinquency definitions of drug use, although it may incorporate these. In California, for example, where in metropolitan areas the majority of youngsters over age 12 admit to at least experimentation with cannabis, several school systems experiment with programs based on the assumption (empirically supported) that most drug use by children cannot be demonstrated to have immediate or long-term health hazards (for example, cannabis experimentation) nor need it be associated with nondrug delinquency (R. H. Blum, 1972, personal communication). Since the origins of this behavior are complex, arising from child-rearing styles (Blum and Associates, 1972b), and are dependent upon opportunities for access to drugs among peers, the goals for school intervention are limited. It is assumed that education cannot affect the on-going illicit drug behavior (including alcohol and cigarette use) that is normally learned (from peers, from advertising, in consequence of parental values and conduct, and the like) but that it may conceivably either prevent or reduce the unusual drug use that has demonstrably greater risks for health, arrest, social adjustment, and so forth (for example, self-injection, glue-sniffing, unsupervised drinking of hard liquor, and barbiturate use). One goal is to create among children new group norms that operate to control these abnormal uses; another is to deflect whatever emotional or symbolic processes may lead certain children to unusual, dangerous-drug use.

Again there is as yet no evidence as to efficacy, although in the case of the San Mateo County schools experimental program, there is in progress an evaluation that includes control groups and objective measures of outcomes based on children's self-reports of drug use over a two-year teaching and testing period.

Techniques. What goes on within the classroom depends not only upon the model employed for describing drug use and upon the goals set (prevention, encapsulation, reduction; general for all drugs, specific for drugs or manner of use) but also upon the teaching methods believed to be most efficacious—or perhaps simply most convenient. Techniques vary as to the intensity of application—whether one hour per year or one hour per week—and the teaching materials and styles employed. It appears that at present there is great reliance on teaching aids—manuals, films, and other teacher-supplementing devices. Perhaps some of the popularity of teaching aids may be attributable to the uncertainty of teachers themselves as to how or what to teach, given their own lack of training in this field, the alternative models, and the frequent absence of clearly explicated goals.

Whether or not the uncertainty one postulates for teachers in this difficult role also arises from doubt about the efficacy of traditional didactic approaches is unknown. Certainly the teacher called upon to give just the facts may be expected to have some doubts about it, if only because the two groups of people most knowledgeable about drugs also seem to have very high risks not just of use but of demonstrable poor outcomes. These are, among the "respectable," physicians, and, among young people, the drug dealers themselves.

As soon as teachers consider moving away from a traditional didactic approach, they are also likely to be assailed by doubts, this time about their competence in this more ambiguous situation to handle matters of values, symbols, emotions, and social rather than school learning. Most are equipped neither by training nor by disposition to set foot in this poorly charted terrain (Aubrey, 1971).

One development, which seeks both to replace didactic method with one allowing more feedback from the consumer himself—the school child—and at the same time to provide a modicum of structure for the teacher, is variously called group counseling or process education. It is one of the components of the drug education experimental design in San Mateo county. At its very simplest, it substitutes give-and-take discussion for information-giving by the teacher. At a more complex level, it can be seen as a method using group dynamics to instill new group norms regarding drug use; while, as counseling, it may be expected at least to divert individuals with demonstrable maladjustment away from symbolic and emotional investments in dangerous forms of drug use as "solutions" to their difficulties. But again, if all the evidence for psychotherapy over these many years is so equivocal as to success, dare the schools hope for better through process education?

The Moral Approach. Whether explicitly considered a matter of health, crime, social learning, or what-have-you, it has long been evident that moral judgments play a strong role in describing drug use. The word *abuse* makes that clear enough. Similarly, such studies of the etiology of illicit use as exist make it clear that values and beliefs do have strong predisposing functions. It can be assumed that regardless of the label under which the schools present their endeavor, all parties to it recognize that drug education is partly a moral endeavor. The explicitness with which this is acknowledged varies with cultural context and, one suspects, specifically with the religious orientation of school and community. Had there been drug education a hundred years ago, it is likely that the moral approach would have been primary, as indeed it usually was in education about alcohol at the time. Today, in countries in which traditional religious morality is taught in the schools, we may expect that drug education will be subsumed under religious ethics. Under these circumstances, disapproved drug use is bad—and, in Christian lands, sinful. The educational prescription is to say No. For the young children, that formula is not only appropriate in terms of Piaget's observations on the moral development of children but, given an integrated and supporting community, probably effective as well. On the other hand, under conditions of social change or of family or individual psychopathology, one would expect that the cost of repressive moral education can include some extreme counterresponses. If, for example, as with sex, there is a powerful natural urge toward altered states of consciousness—attainable perhaps most readily through drugs—then one would expect unhappy long-term consequences from the simple repression of drug use unless other rituals existed for producing altered states or unless sanctioned situations for ritualized drug use were present.

Accepting Altered States. The thesis that altered states of consciousness are widely sought and enjoyed and constitute natural biological as well as perhaps spiritual phenomena is advanced by Weil (1972). In support of Weil, one may observe the propensity of cats to get stoned on catnip, of children to engage in the Valsalva maneuver, and of almost all cultures so far described to use one or another psychoactive drug for nonmedical purposes. Weil, along with Meher Baba, William James, Saint John of the Cross, and Lord Buddha, would maintain the necessity as well as the value of the experience of altered states of consciousness. Weil proposes that, insofar as drug use is an attempt to satisfy this human potential, either drug use or alternatives for reaching altered states should not only be condoned but should be actively taught to children. Should his proposals be put into effect, drug education would consist of teaching meditation and, insofar as drugs were involved, the safe use of drugs as ancillaries. Such drug education or its prototypes may already occur in certain spiritual communities or in those hippie families where children are early initiated into drug use. Since the Manson "family" may also be taken as an illustrative case, we trust that the proponents of Weil's scheme would attend to suitable support and control structures.

Community Centers. Schools can be the center of drug education efforts while shifting their emphasis from the teaching of children—or teachers—to that of becoming a community resource. In such a situation, the school becomes a center for activities as well as learning, a place where parents come for drug information or counseling, where cases of unusual or dangerous forms of drug use by children are identified and referred to professional or other helping sources, and where outreach programs begin. In the community survey conducted by Blum and his associates (1972b) as part of their family studies, parents and drug-responsible professionals not only nominated education as the most desirable form of intervention with regard to drug problems, but seemed most willing to use the school as the central community resource.

Focus

For the most part, existing and planned drug education programs have focused on the illicit or exotic drugs, have been aimed at all rather than some students, have opted to present information but not to handle cases, and have remained safely obscure in offering general goals (drug-abuse prevention) rather than specific ones. Each of these quite understandable developments may be taken as a problem in its own right or, put differently, as an opportunity for future development.

The emphasis on illicit and exotic drugs is to the exclusion, in many places, of those most widely employed substances, alcohol and tobacco, with their quite noticeable burden of immediate and long-term adverse effects. Yet, whether one is concerned with the prevention of these effects (alcoholism, assault, road accidents, upper respiratory infections, heart disease, and lung cancer) or on the very specific prevention of that drug problem par excellence, drug dealing, it would appear that the focus must include alcohol and tobacco. Consider the finding in *The Dream Sellers* (Blum and Associates, 1972a) to the effect that the earliest and most widespread admission of anxiety over a drug problem on the part of the young dealers was in connection with their drinking. Even if these already or soon-to-be drug-peddling youngsters were using cannabis, LSD, amphetamines, or opioids, it was their alcohol use that they could first see—or admit to seeing—as presenting a problem to them. This being so, it would follow that drug education in schools might well consider safe and unsafe forms of drinking and, in essence, teach the safer uses (at home, under supervision, with meals, wine or beer rather than spirits, and so forth) before as well as during adolescence.

The danger signals for alcohol problems might also be taught, not just for self-recognition but for helpful use with friends and family as well. Indeed, this option gives to alcohol and tobacco a most favored place in education, since inquiry about and discussion of them in class need evoke no fear of the police or of the narcotics laws operative in all nations that subscribe to the Single Convention. Some students, beginning most often in the mid-teens if the data of Blum and his associates (1972b) are generalizable, will recognize themselves as already in the danger-signal category. Clearly, the giving of information will only affirm what they fear, and that affirmation must be done in a way that allows constructive action to be taken. The question, for these youngsters who identify themselves as cases, is: What is to be done?

At this point, the general focus of the schools might well be replaced with a more individualized one, and the information-giving function might be supplemented by systematic case finding and referral. Such steps imply considerable expansion of the facilities for helping children and adolescents. The needs for personnel and facilities in the United States are well documented by the recent report of the Joint Commission on Mental Health of Children (1969) and their inadequacy in the United Kingdom has been described by Payne (1971). Lest the drug-using youngster be given attention to the exclusion of the child who suffers other problems of living and lest the latter be forced into taking or pretending to take drugs in order to qualify for treatment, it is imperative that such child-care facilities be general rather than drug-specific.

The foregoing focuses imply specification of goals in drug education by drug, by individuals, by developmental status, and by community as opposed to the amiable but simplistic drug-abuse prevention now advocated. Such tailoring is predicated on the existence of and knowledge about diversity of forms of drug use among children and youth as well as follow-up data that enable one to say which forms of drug use are likely to be benign and which dangerous. It also assumes the availability of different approaches to individuals or groups of users depending upon their stage of life and their drug habits. It further assumes some knowledge about the relative efficacy of one or another form of intervention to be applied in school to these different consumers of school drug programs.

Evaluation

The extent of drug education has tended to be inversely related to the degree of evaluation. This is perhaps not accidental, given the degree of disquiet that evaluation efforts can arouse in the hearts of those with vested interests. Indeed, any demonstration of the inefficacy of drug education could hardly be welcome by anyone who has dedicated hopes or career to drug education for itself. Yet a note of optimism may be injected. In the United States, there is massive drug education with now, belatedly, the small beginnings of evaluation. In the United Kingdom and Holland, there is some drug education with proportionately much more (though still not much) accompanying outcome evaluation. In Australia, drug education evaluation precedes, in pilot-project form, any commitment to drug education per se. This progression, temporal and geographical, in the emphasis placed on evaluation is welcome evidence that the voices crying in the wilderness for education based on demonstrable results are finally heard. Nevertheless, insofar as evaluations that are under way are examining only attitudes and intentions, not drug use and outcomes, such efforts are insufficient. Perhaps direct measures are allowable only in those communities in which drug use has already achieved a high level of prevalence. That being so, this constitutes an argument for the correlation of attitude and intention measures with actual manner of drug use and their outcomes. It also is an argument for concentration in education and evaluation on the prevention (and individualized case referral) of dangerous alcohol and cigarette use. Such programs should also be accompanied by research in a variety of environments on the relationships between such approved drug use (in Western countries) and disapproved use including the particular related problem of drug-dealing.

Let us assume that reliable large-scale research were to tell us that drug education in the schools is essentially worthless as far as affecting the drug use and drug-use outcomes of children. What then? The most likely answer is that drug education would continue, the evaluators would be fired, and whatever methods they used to achieve such calamitous findings would be ridiculed. Such an eventuality may be taken as just retribution on the evaluators for having taken a narrow view, construing the purpose of their evaluation to be to pronounce moral judgment of a yes/no variety on the goodness of education rather than to use evaluation as an opportunity to learn more about the impact of teaching and to feed back this knowledge into schools, teaching them how better to proceed. The firing of evaluators may also be taken as just retribution for their having assumed the major motive of drug education simply to be to change drug behavior of children, rather than comprehending it as an expression of the intense need of people to act "for the good" despite uncertainty of how that good may be achieved. One has in mind the insightful work of E. and J. Cummings (1957) showing how the best-intentioned community mental health program defeated its own ends when it failed to understand the dynamics of existing institutions, processes, and beliefs in a community.

The more evaluation can be seen as an integral component of drug education rather than a one-shot alien process, the more likely it will be to yield insights applicable to achieving the several ends implicit and explicit in drug education. Educational evaluation must be akin to engineering developmental design with its continuous process of feedback and modification. It must not use as a model the laboratory test of the null hypothesis whereby the observing scientist, uninvolved, negates the life work of his fellows.

It will be seen that two further opportunities lie herein. One is that insights developed through evaluation may be used to assist citizens over time to think through their goals for their children and for their schools and thus refine them, perhaps making constructive use of that contradiction inherent in much of the current scene. The other opportunity is for research personnel to treat this scheme as a clear invitation to join the ever-growing pyramid of bureaucrats who justify themselves on the basis of their existence and not their accomplishments. This dilemma has yet to be resolved.

16

Taking Action

Richard H. Blum

There is consensus among the contributors to this volume that drug dealers, drug trafficking, and societal response thereto are indeed complex. The evidence, limited as it is, does indicate that whatever the law enforcement effort, illicit international drug traffic is a burgeoning big business. One presumes that without the enforcement of criminal sanctions, it would be an even bigger business. It is a business immersed, as McCoy has shown (1972), in national and international politics. It is, as Joyce notes, immersed in international trade as well. McGlothlin shows us that it is intimately linked to the growing demands of consumers and involves tens of thousands of these as dealers themselves. Enforcement does have an impact, but it also has a cost. International traffic is not, as our earlier data (Blum and Associates, 1972a) and the work of Tartaglino and others here show, simply a matter of a few mysterious mobsters running an export-import trade. Depending on the geographical region, it involves tourists, migrating laborers, business travelers, students, transportation workers, and others from many walks of life. Through them and through more commercialized trade routes, illicit drugs cross many boundaries and involve many nations. Further, it is not a matter of drugs alone, for the smuggler is not bound to one commodity; an auto built to conceal drugs may carry drugs on one leg of its journey, but on its return the same secret compartment may carry guns, gold, jewelry, currency, liquor, or some other profitable item. Nor is illicit drug traffic a matter of smuggling alone, for it is linked with purportedly honest commerce, can rest on licit agriculture or chemical production, and can be tied in with major financial enterprises. Indeed, this simultaneously licit (in one place) and illicit (in another) aspect poses some of the most important international questions as far as cooperation in drug policy is concerned. There are sanctuaries for production, for warehousing and transshipment, for business operations, for holding cash and real property returns, and for safeguarding persons who are elsewhere wanted as criminals.

These rather obvious features of international traffic constitute but a portion of the complexity. We have seen that those institutions that are set up to combat traffic or to interdict dealers are themselves vulnerable to that which they oppose. Prison guards and the narcotics police are vulnerable to corruption, including trafficking. Institutions intended presumably to deter if not to correct drug offenders become centers for drug use and dealing. Even juvenile facilities, where some might hope that the myth of innocence might once again invest the wayward youth, show themselves—depending on their clientele and milieu—to be active trafficking centers. Indeed, we have seen prisons (although not herein described) in which international drug trafficking operations are run from the inside.

The corruption of prison and police personnel is no small consideration in weighing the risks and gains of one or another societal response to dealing. Given the data at hand, these personnel appear less thoroughly immunized against temptation than those in other vocations that we have examined, as for example physicians, drug salesmen, college professors, and pharmacists described in *The Dream Sellers* (Blum and Associates, 1972a). One must say that it is risky for civil servants to fall in with evil companions, that is, to be so close to all those drug-dealing criminals. How the narcotics officer in one city but not the next, the guard in one prison but not another, or the judge in one town but not the physician in the same town becomes corrupted is a question for further study as well as for administrative concern. Our limited evidence on prisons and police suggests that matters of differential personnel selection and training, a different regional or "cultural" milieu in which to work, a different administrative atmosphere, and perhaps simple opportunity are operative. We do have some peripheral data coming from inquiries on deception—work with confidence men, police informants, industrial spies, and political defectors (Blum, 1972)—that may be relevant. On the basis of that work, we suspect that corruptability is enhanced when persons suffer serious difficulties in their work or in their personal lives, when the job situation is characterized by inept management or a dysfunctional organization, or when individuals have characterological problems of the sort that make them unconcerned about the rights and welfare of others. Perhaps corruptability can be enhanced by the individual's secret fantasies writ large but not yet acted out, by having learned models of transient rather than solid loyalty in family relations, and by a life not easily committed to boredom and convention. Also, vanity does play a role in other deception as does the usual human search for vengeance, power, and material gain. If one is part of an already untrustworthy or corrupted environment, it is all the easier to follow that road.

In addition to learning to be concerned about prison and police corruption as a complication of the criminal law applied to vice, we have learned something about vice squads themselves in relationship to police policy, at least in the local departments studied. In both of these departments officers told us frankly what they were about, as opposed to what the law was about. In both situations, what officers did was to arrest few of the estimated available population of users and dealers. Those whom they did arrest were young, male, and visible—either the hippies of the town we called Comfort or the delinquents of the city we called Steinville. No rhetoric, no big dealers, no crash efforts, no large dent on drug use or trading, no corruption, and no incompatibility with what one deems the local taxpayers—and judges—wanted. This is the reality we should keep in mind when politicians talk big, for on the local level where the users live and the dealers deal, the police are not a potent intervening force. They are inactive if not invisible if the dealers enjoy sanctuary. We have learned that sanctuaries exist, not only in other nations with other laws, but also on a campus or in a given socioeconomic circle within a town. The police in the two departments reported here claimed to be nothing more than they were; and, in Steinville, they sought to do no more, for they had set their sights on crimes with *victims*. Neither drug use nor drug-dealing qualified for that priority in their eyes. What is to be done?

We sense among the contributors to this volume agreement that the criminal law is overworked, at least in the United States, and would better be administered in sparing but potent doses rather than those so capricious and diluted as now. There is the sense, too, that we had best abandon apocalyptic visions of final triumph over human ignorance, frailty, or ugliness—be that drug-dealing, delinquency, or dependence. Instead, perhaps we should settle for using a variety of imperfect systems and interventions that may allow us better tailoring, and thus better fits, to particular drugs and people as information is gathered. As for particulars of what might be done, *none of the recommendations made by our contributors dare go unexamined,* for in a world of noisy troubles the thoughtful solution, gently put forward, deserves welcome.

Subsequent policy decisions, insofar as there ever are decisions—as opposed to the slow evolution of practice and consent in a democracy—rest only partly on questions of fact—and rarely on the details—but are heavily loaded with pragmatic, moral, and political considerations. Because policy setting does rest on matters partly extraneous to scientific query, one cannot assume that scientific investigators have unique competence in policy making beyond gathering facts and trying to clarify issues. Such recommendations as an investigator may make as a result of his work usually encompass only a small portion of the world of dealing and a smaller portion of the considerations upon which policy is based.

At this point then we offer certain propositions that go beyond our data but are consonant with them. Among these are several not already set forth by other contributors to this volume.

1. Planned intervention to inhibit drug traffic cannot be

considered apart from the origins of that traffic in the consumer, that is, apart from the extensive existence of life styles that center on the use of illicit substances.

2. Planned intervention to inhibit drug traffic cannot be considered apart from knowledge that some traffickers do proselytize and, although there is no evidence in our work for the seduction of the innocent, we must acknowledge that "missionary" zeal, personal and ideological appeals, and commercial gain figure in the expansion of the user-consumer base.

3. Planned intervention cannot proceed on the assumption that users and dealers are different people. Specifically, laws passed to affect dealers only are laws that affect those users who are also dealers. One may posit a continuum from abstainer and nondealer through major dealers with an accompanying continuum of abstainer and nonuser through the completely drug involved person. In various locales one would want to know the degree of correlation between the two. Beginning with that position on the scale where occasional illicit use occurs, there are also simultaneously violations of laws that aim to interdict supplying. As involvement in drug use becomes more extensive, with certain qualifications as to skills and environmental constraints and to the generalizability of our data, the likelihood of the user and dealer being the same person increases.

4. Planned intervention must proceed, cautious of rhetoric. The "righteous" or "holy" dealer is a fiction if one asks of these "righteous" souls that they are, in other areas, honest and constructive citizens. Our data suggest that they are not, for they do not pay their taxes, they are likely to be delinquent in nondrug areas, and they may profit from the sale of substances they know to be adulterated or harmful. Likewise the dealer as "fiend," "enslaver of souls," or otherwise demonically possessed—whether as superhuman or subhuman—is myth. Dealers are ordinary mortals, neither more nor less, and neither their motives nor their persons nor their powers are extraordinary. Rhetoric also beclouds rather than clarifies when particular modalities for intervention are romanticized. There is no evidence that law enforcement crackdowns can eliminate either internal or international traffic. Medical treatment, methadone, or maintenance psychosocial rehabilitation programs do not have the

capability of "curing" most of those who are drug-dependent or of vastly altering those who are drug-involved without being dependent. Improvements do occur, but none so certain or dramatic as nature herself offers in the process of maturing, that is, growing older and wiser.

5. On the basis of its long history but limited planning, experimentation, and evaluation, intervention is advised with limited goals: not total elimination of drug use or traffic but suppression by means of enforcement and not cure of all those disabled by drugs but only improvement among them by means of treatment. In the overall situation today even these aims can be achieved only to limited extent and only through costly endeavor.

6. Planned intervention should proceed with the knowledge that drug use and drug-dealing begin, at least for most Americans so far studied, in adolescence and are at least partly predictable on the basis of family values and parental conduct, plus individual idiosyncrasy and, later, peer association. In consequence, if we are *serious* about prevention, we must engage in it before adolescence and, over the long haul, by changing child-rearing styles, parental conduct, and youthful environments. If children come from those pathological families in which the criminality and drug-dependence of parents bode no good at all, the "neatest" solution would be to persuade such persons not to have children at all or at least not until they are themselves reformed, secure, and mature. For the many more children who come from less dramatically disabled families— or ones that simply predispose to drug use—we recommend those experiments in the restoration of family strength and happiness that the findings reported in *Horatio Alger's Children* (Blum and Associates, 1972b) suggested. Primary prevention is the ideal.

7. With regard to intervention by means of law enforcement, there is evidence that arrest does reduce the risk of later dealing for some, but not for all, arrested dealers.* From the data, we can infer

---

* Zimring's (1971) review is relevant. He suggests that "apprehension and conviction may substantially reduce future criminality" but, contrariwise, "those subjected to punishment for major crimes commit many more crimes after their release than other groups in the population but fewer perhaps than they would if they had not been caught." We call attention to Zimring's additional conclusion from his literature review that there is no evidence that severity of punishment (time served) is associated with reduction in recid-

deterrent effects as well, but these, too, differ depending upon the background, personality, and circumstances of the dealer. Simultaneously the "cost" of drug arrests includes exacerbation of dealing among some as a consequence of incarceration.

8. With regard to legislative change for any one psychoactive drug (for example, marijuana) or for all, so as to "decriminalize" use, any such change that sets age limits, whether 18 or 21, for use will not affect the legality of conduct at the ages at which inception of use and dealing most often begin, that is, the adolescent years.

9. With regard to intervention, there is such a variety of dealer "types" within the dealing population that any form of intervention must be expected to be limited in its results to success with particular persons, at particular ages, released to particular environments.

10. Regarding forms of intervention and their costs, our data show that one risk associated with enforcement and incarceration is the corruption of the enforcement officer and prison employee. Perhaps these risks are less for personnel in other modalities—for example, those in community agencies, probation, responsible medical/psychological care, and work with families. If so, one benefit of the other modalities is the reduced risk of corruption among personnel working in them.

11. Reviewing possible modalities for intervention, we find that any that utilize existing facilities or resources immediately share in the problems that already characterize these facilities. Thus, to rely on the criminal law and the administration of justice is to know that the dealer processed through that system is subject to the same ineffectuality and that society perpetuates the same encumbered system as now exists. Similarly, psychiatric hospitalization or other residence in mass or in "total" institutions confront the dealer-patient with the same misadventures that other inmate-residents face and adds to the costs and inefficiencies that large institutions already present to society. Consequently, we should consider modal-

---

ivism. He concludes that there is "an impressive case for the reduction of the present scale of major criminal sanctions in the United States." To this one adds Banfield's (1970) conclusions after review that immediacy and certainty of punishment, rather than time-served severity, are critical components for the reduction of recidivism.

ities that do not rely on mechanisms already known to be overtaxed or inefficient. In considering new approaches, lest these become soured investments, the principles of management learned elsewhere should be applied. These include the requirement of systematic evaluation of costs and consequences.

12. An explicit concern with the drug dealer and an emphasis that makes prevention or reduction of dealing per se the major criterion of success (presuming evaluation) overlook the great variety of other personal and social disturbances that may be problems for those who are dealing or who are at risk of dealing; other delinquency, violence, school problems, and the like characterize them. Interventions that aim at only one aspect of conduct to the exclusion of what the person is like—his problems and potentials —are at best superficial and ineffectual if not ludicrous or mischief-making.

13. A large number of our young people are passing through a drugs and dealing stage. The attributes that identify them, in contrast to persistent dealers, appear to be a lesser and later involvement with delinquency, drugs, and drug users. Given the existence of this group of youngsters who are passing through dealing, at times it may be best to let them alone, at least officially, not making growing up any more difficult that it is by adding to it premature labels, fixed negative identities, and coercive strangers—all of which may institutionalize conduct.

14. By now, parents are, to whatever degree, reconciled to the risk of casual drug experimentation at least as part of American life. We counsel no parent or other authority to consider drug-dealing as in any way casual; it is instead a potent sign of interest in being in the center of a drug-using group. Like other folly, it need not be irreversible. It is the button marked "Serious and Continuing Attention," not "PANIC" that parents and others ought to push. What should be done after that is not prescribable according to any formula, nor is it our province or capability to offer a formula as to what steps should be taken. Parents and other authorities these days know that it is well to discuss all such matters with the youngster, once the emotional upset attendant upon the discovery of this combined drug involvement and delinquency is over. Initial inquiries should be directed toward learning what this combination

signifies, how it gratifies, where and to whom it has led. The answer to why a particular child seeks—or drifts in—such directions should be a priority item. Such answers are always incomplete, but that need not hinder reconstructive endeavors, which may, depending on the family and the youth, utilize wise relatives; wholesome neighbor families; straight but admired older youth; a pastor; mental health professionals; a solid work supervisor; an affectionate, understanding, but firm teacher; a manly policeman; a worldly probation officer; or others of such ilk who can provide direction, reflection, affection, a model, and discipline. How parents are to handle their dealing youngster is a personal and narrow concern compared with the broad issues of policy necessarily raised by attention to drug dealing. Nevertheless, nothing is more important to that youngster or to his parents than how that matter proceeds. Indeed, as far as the great world of issues is concerned, that world is composed after all only of an array of similar worried or erring humans and whatever succeeds at the family level in reducing folly and pain might well be taken as a model for large enterprises.

15. Most nations have a heterogeneous population and a partial commitment to pluralism. The Western world is in a period of change and uncertainty in which child-rearing styles and community solidarity have not been adequate to produce, among all offspring, conduct generally approved, that is, conventional and nondelinquent. The clear propensity is for human beings often not to act with the common good in mind. Available for easy use is a variety of mind-altering substances whose novelty or special appeal is such that no communal ethic exists in regard to their employment. Finally, commerce brings profit. Given these facts, we can expect that some people will deal in drugs. Expectations by the many for the control of dealing among a dogged minority should be no greater than for the control of other conduct that has like elements, including pleasure-seeking, escape, pain relief, curiosity, exploitation, easy-living, commitment avoidance, search for meaning or self-definition, and high profits. Whatever expectations do exist for ideal conduct, any that anticipate control by governmental intervention must realize that governments in any but total tyrannies are not able to require total conformity. Those who expect to mold to conformity by means of professional intervention—for ex-

ample, psychiatry, the ministry, social work, probation work—must remain aware of the limitations of the skills of any one man who seeks to shape another after his own image. Those whose expectations rest upon education and the assumption of rationality among men must keep in mind that man is in many ways irrational and that some men appear uneducable. All expectations should include full realization of the need for capacity to endure infinite disappointment.

16. There are those who are tolerant to the point of indifference and who would not intervene at all in conduct that, like drug-dealing, can be shown quite clearly to be correlated with other behaviors that are at best nonconstructive and irresponsible and at worst deadly. They should be reminded that delinquents are not necessarily kind, that drugs are not inevitably beneficent, and that a society without structures and strictures is hardly certain to survive, let alone to be at harmony. Action, then, is required.

17. The evidence indicates clearly that drug trafficking is an international matter. The most popular drug (cannabis) and some with high addiction potential (opiates) cross national boundaries before consumption. Large numbers of young local dealers are international traffickers. All sustaining dealing networks, like any business, rest on an international organization—however tenuous and ephemeral. Sanctuaries (for production, warehousing, transshipment, profit holding, operating centers, offender refuge) do exist, and they provide crucial facilities for traffic. More important than all these essential mechanical matters is the fact that the goals and values that sustain illicit drug use (that is, the styles of life and the orientation of consumers) are an international affair. Young people the world over share backgrounds, values, and drug-using opportunities similar enough to allow the sequential if not simultaneous development of the consumer base that is the international market for psychoactive drugs. Cross-cultural teaching and exchange of drug interests also exist. That market is essential for illicit traffic. No explanations for traffic or attempts to intervene can proceed without acknowledging that the interest in the use of drugs, the willingness to employ them illicitly, and the acceptance of dealers and dealing as part of that quite voluntary life style account for the emergence of trafficking as a service industry. Whatever action is

taken must deal with these two components: the international consumer as the source of demand and the international nature of the services that consumers and others build up to supply that demand. It would follow that whatever international endeavors are undertaken should be coordinated, broadly based, diverse, flexible, and long-term in their design.

As a final note, we should keep in mind that drug-dealing is not the worst problem that the nations of the world face, alarmist journalism to the contrary. We are fortunate that the risks associated with illicit drug use and its correlated dealing are neither so prevalent nor so severe as to rend the fabric of any nation's social life or to threaten the future integrity of any society. Of the severe drug problems, the worst in Western countries (for risks to health in terms of prevalence) are those associated with approved substances such as alcohol and tobacco. Societies that have opted to accept such health risks may also be able to survive the risks associated with illicit substances. What must be weighed is whether accepting one set of risks (alcoholism, for example) compels accepting another (heroin addiction). Insofar as the efforts are not more horrendous than the problem, the endeavors mounted by a society to reduce the real problems and risks as well as perhaps and the pervasive anxieties about the problems can be expected to have some effect, but they will never produce a cure. Insofar as the efforts undertaken to interdict problems associated with illicit drug use and trafficking are partially successful, these should have double value, for they point the way also to constructive responses to those other forms of conduct so closely linked to illicit drugs: the problems of delinquency, of maladjustment, of health care, and of aimless if not wasted lives. Perhaps we can learn through our responses to drug problems better to conduct ourselves in the face of other national and international challenges in the health, criminal, and social spheres. Indeed, to learn to develop helpful international machinery in these areas may be seen as one of the great opportunities arising from the international nature of drug traffic. For nations to share their successes with one another is one of the great hopes that arises from programs underway. This spirit of the construction of collaborative structures and partial solutions capable of being shared ought to motivate future action in the international drug sphere.

Bibliography

ADAMS, R. J., AND STANMEYER, W. S. "Effects of a Closely Supervised Oral Hygiene Program on Oral Cleanliness." *Journal of Periodontology,* 1960, *31,* 242.

AHLSTROM, W. M., AND HAVIGHURST, R. J. *Four Hundred Losers.* San Francisco: Jossey-Bass, 1971.

American Friends Service Committee. *Struggle for Justice: A Report on Crime and Punishment in America.* New York: Hill and Wang, 1971.

"Analysis of Drug Samples Seized by N.Y. Police Shows Much Adulteration." *NAPAN Newsletter,* May 1964, *2*(2).

ANONYMOUS. "On Selling Marijuana." in E. Goode (Ed.), *Marijuana.* Chicago: Aldine-Atherton, 1969.

AUBREY, R. "Drug Education: Can Teachers Really Do the Job?" *Teachers College Record,* 1971, *72,* 417.

BADEN, M. M. "Medical Aspects of Drug Abuse." *New York Medicine,* 1968, *24*(9), 466.

BALINT, M., HUNT, J., JOYCE, C. R. B., MARINKER, M., AND WOODSTOCK, J. *Treatment or Diagnosis: A Study of Repeat Prescriptions in General Practice.* London: Tavistock; Philadelphia: Lippincott, 1970.

BALL, J. C., AND CHAMBERS, C. D. *The Epidemiology of Opiate Addiction in the U.S.* Springfield, Ill.: Thomas, 1970.

BANFIELD, E. C. *The Unheavenly City.* Boston: Little, Brown, 1970.

BARRETT, E. "Police Practice and the Law—From Arrest to Release or Charge." *California Law Review,* 1962, *50,* 11–55.

BENTEL, D. J., AND SMITH, D. E. "The Year of the Middle Class Junkie." *California's Health,* 1971, *28*(10), 1–5.

BERG, D. F. "The Non-Medical Use of Dangerous Drugs in the U.S.A.—A Comprehensive View." *International Journal of the Addictions,* 1970, *5,* 777–834.

BERNE, E. *Transactional Analysis in Psychotherapy.* New York: Grove, 1961.

BIRK. In *Official Report, House of Lords Debates.* Vol. 314, Columns 260–266. London: Her Majesty's Stationery Office, January 14, 1971.

BLUM, E. M., AND BLUM, R. H. *Alcoholism: Modern Psychological Approaches to Treatment.* San Francisco: Jossey-Bass, 1967.

BLUM, R. H. "The Jailer's Revolt: Iron Doors Give Way to Open Doors." *This World, San Francisco Chronicle,* February 3, 1963, 16–19.

BLUM, R. H. (Ed.). *Police Selection.* Springfield, Ill., Thomas, 1964.

BLUM, R. H. *Deceivers and Deceived: Observations on Confidence Men and Their Victims, Informants and Their Quarry, Political and Industrial Spies and Ordinary Citizens.* Springfield, Ill.: Thomas, 1972.

BLUM, R. H., AND ASSOCIATES. *Utopiates: A Study of the Use and Users of LSD-25.* Chicago: Aldine-Atherton, 1964.

BLUM, R. H., AND ASSOCIATES. *Society and Drugs.* San Francisco: Jossey-Bass, 1969a.

BLUM, R. H., AND ASSOCIATES. *Students and Drugs.* San Francisco: Jossey-Bass, 1969b.

BLUM, R. H., AND ASSOCIATES. *The Dream Sellers: Perspectives on Drug Dealers.* San Francisco: Jossey-Bass, 1972a.

BLUM, R. H., AND ASSOCIATES. *Horatio Alger's Children: Role of the Family in the Origin and Prevention of Drug Risk.* San Francisco: Jossey-Bass, 1972b.

BLUM, R. H., AND BLUM, E. M. "Case Identification in Psychiatric Epidemiology." *Millbank Quarterly,* 1962, *15,* 252–288.

BLUM, R. H., AND BLUM, E. M. *The Dangerous Hour: A Sociopsychological Study of the Lore of Crisis and Mystery in Rural*

Greece. London, Chatto and Windus, 1970; New York: Scribner's, 1970.

BLUM, R. H., AND BOVET, D. (Eds.). *Controlling Drugs: An International Handbook for Drug Classification.* San Francisco: Jossey-Bass, in press.

BLUM, R. H., AND DOWNING, J. J. "Staff Response to Innovation in a Mental Health Service." *American Journal of Public Health,* 1964, *54,* 1230–1240.

BLUM, R. H., AND OSTERLOH, W. "Keeping Policemen on the Job: Some Recommendations Arising from a Study of Men and Morale." *Police,* 1966, *10*(5), 28–32.

BLUM, R. H., AND SMITH, J. P. "Intensive Clinical Study." In R. H. Blum and Associates, *Horatio Alger's Children: Role of the Family in the Origin and Prevention of Drug Risk.* San Francisco: Jossey-Bass, 1972.

BLUM, R. H., AND WAHL, J. "Police Views on Drug Use." In R. H. Blum and Associates, *Utopiates: The Use and Users of LSD-25.* Chicago: Aldine-Atherton, 1964.

BLUM, R., WOLFE, J., AND LEWIS, E. "Physicians." In R. H. Blum and Associates, *The Dream Sellers: Perspectives on Drug Dealers.* San Francisco: Jossey-Bass, 1972.

BLUMER, H., SUTTER, A., AHMED, S., AND SMITH, R. *The World of Youthful Drug Use.* Berkeley: School of Criminology, University of California, 1967.

BOWDEN, C. L., AND LANGENAUER, B. J. "Success and Failure in the NARA Addiction Program." *American Journal of Psychiatry,* 1972, *128,* 853–856.

BRILL, A. H. "Regulating and Controlling Marijuana: A First Attempt." *Contemporary Drug Problems,* Winter 1971–1972, *1,* 97–116.

BRILL, L., AND LIEBERMAN, L. *Authority and Addiction.* Boston: Little, Brown, 1969.

BROWN, C. C., AND SAVAGE, C. *The Drug Abuse Controversy.* Baltimore: National Educational Consultants, 1971.

Bureau of Criminal Statistics. *Drug Arrests and Dispositions in California, Reference Tables, 1969.* Sacramento: California State Department of Justice, Division of Law Enforcement, 1969.

Bureau of Criminal Statistics. *Crime and Arrests, Reference Tables, 1970.* Sacramento: California State Department of Justice, Division of Law Enforcement, 1970a.

Bureau of Criminal Statistics. *Drug Arrests and Dispositions in Cali-*

fornia, Reference Tables, 1970. Sacramento: California State Department of Justice, Division of Law Enforcement, 1970b.

Bureau of Narcotics and Dangerous Drugs. *II. Director's Report on Federal Performance Measurements.* Washington, D.C., 1971.

CAHALAN, D. *Problem Drinkers: A National Survey.* San Francisco: Jossey-Bass, 1970.

CAREY, J. T. *The College Drug Scene.* Englewood Cliffs, N.J.: Prentice-Hall, 1968.

CARNEY, F. J. "Evaluation of Psychotherapy in a Maximum Security Prison." *Seminars in Psychiatry,* 1971, *3*(3), 363–375.

CHAMBERS, C. D. *An Assessment of Drug Use in the General Population. Special Report 1, Drug Use in New York State.* n.p.: New York State Narcotic Addiction Control Commission, May 1971.

CHAREN, S., AND PERELMAN, L. "Personality Studies of Marihuana Addicts." *American Journal of Psychiatry,* 1946, *102,* 674–682.

CHEEK, F. E., NEWELL, S., AND JOFFE, M. "Deceptions in the Illicit Market." *Science,* 1970, *167,* 1276.

CHEIN, L., GERARD, D. L., LEE, R. S., AND ROSENFELS, E. *The Road to H: Narcotics, Delinquency and Social Policy.* New York: Basic Books, 1964.

CHERUBIN, C. E. "Investigations of Tetanus in Narcotic Addicts in New York City." *International Journal of the Addictions,* 1967, *2*(2), 253–258.

CHOPRA, R. N. AND CHOPRA, C. S. "The Present Position of Hemp-Drug in India." *Indian Medical Research Memoirs,* 1939, *31,* 1–119.

COLON, J. *Marijuana.* Advisory Task Force Report for the Use of White House Conference on Youth Participants, Drug Task Force Report of the White House Conference on Youth. Washington, D.C., 1971.

COLUMBIS, R. J., ALBANO, E. H., AND LYONS, M. "Drug Detection in Urines of Commercial Blood Bank Donors." *Journal of the American Medical Association,* 1970, *214*(3), 596.

Commission on Marijuana and Drug Abuse. *Marihuana: A Signal of Misunderstanding.* Washington, D.C.: Government Printing Office, 1972.

COOK, S. *Variations in Response to Illegal Drug Use. A Comparative Study of Official Narcotic Drug Policies in Canada, Great Britain, and the United States from 1920 to 1970, Addiction Research Foundations Substudy 1-Co & 11-70.* Ontario: General Publishing, 1970.

CRAFT, M. *Psychopathic Disorder.* Elmsford, N.Y.: Pergamon, 1966.

CRUTCHER, J. A. "Lead Intoxication and Alcoholism: A Diagnostic Dilemma." *Journal of Medical Association of Georgia,* 1967, *56,* 1–4.

CUMMING, E., AND CUMMING, J. *Closed Ranks: An Experiment in Mental Health Education.* Cambridge, Mass.: Harvard, 1957.

DE LONG, J. B. "Treatment and Rehabilitation." In P. Wald and P. Hutt (cochairman), *Dealing with Drug Abuse, A Report to the Ford Foundation, The Drug Abuse Survey Project.* New York: Praeger, 1972.

DEVENYI, P., AND WILSON, M. "Abuse of Barbiturates in an Alcoholic Population." *Canadian Medical Association Journal,* 1971, *104,* 219–221.

DISHOTSKY, N. I., LAUGHMAN, W. D., MOGAR, R. E., AND LIPSCOMB, W. "LSD Use and Genetic Damage: A Critical Review." *Science,* 1971, *172,* 431–440.

DISKIND, M. H., AND KLONSKY, G. *Recent Developments in the Treatment of Paroled Offenders Addicted to Narcotic Drugs.* Albany: New York State Division of Parole, 1964a.

DISKIND, M. H., AND KLONSKY, G. "A Second Look at the New York State Parole Drug Experiment." *Federal Probation,* 1964b, *28,* 34–41.

DOORENBOS, N. J. Personal communication. University: Department of Pharmacognosy, University of Mississippi, 1971.

DREW, L. R. H. "Alcoholism Is a Self-Limiting Disease." *Quarterly Journal of Studies on Alcohol,* 1968, *29,* 956–967.

Drug Research Report, HEW Marijuana Research Plan . . . Outlined to Congress: Chemical and Biological Investigation. Supplement 13 (43) S.20–S.22. Washington, D.C.: U.S. Department of Health, Education and Welfare, 1970.

DUSTER, T. *The Legislation of Morality: Laws, Drugs and Moral Judgments.* New York: Free Press, 1970.

EDWARDS, K. *The Police on the Urban Frontier.* New York: Institute of Human Relations Press, 1968.

EISENBERG, W. V., AND TILLSON, A. "Identification of Counterfeit Drugs, Particularly Barbituates and Amphetamines by Microscopic, Chemical, and Instrumental Techniques." *Journal of Forensic Sciences,* 1966, *11*(4), 529.

EMERSON, A. E. "Social Insects." *Encyclopaedia Britannica,* 1964, *20,* 875–877.

ERIKSON, E. H. *Identity: Youth and Crisis.* New York: Norton, 1968.

FARNSWORTH, D. L. "Drug Dependence Among Physicians." *New England Journal of Medicine*, 1970, *282*, 392–393.

Federal Bureau of Investigation. *Uniform Crime Reports for the United States, 1970*. Washington, D.C.: U.S. Department of Justice, 1971.

FINESTONE, H. "Cars, Kicks and Color." In M. R. Stein and M. White (Eds.), *Identity and Anxiety*. New York: Free Press, 1960.

FOLTZ, R., KINZER, G. W., MITCHELL, R. I., AND TRUITT, E. B. "The Fate of Cannabinoid Components of Marihuana During Smoking." *Marihuana and Health*. Second annual report to Congress from the Secretary of Health, Education and Welfare. Washington, D.C.: Government Printing Office, 1972.

FORD, D. H., AND URBAN, H. B. *Systems of Psychotherapy*. New York: Wiley, 1963.

FREEDMAN, D. X. "Perspectives on the Use and Abuse of Psychedelic Drugs" (personal communication). 1970.

FROEDE, R. C., AND STAHL, C. J. *Fatal Narcotism in Military Personnel*. Presented at the Twenty-Third Annual Meeting of the American Academy of Forensic Sciences, Arizona, February 1971.

FUJII, E. T. *Public Investment in the Rehabilitation of Heroin Addicts* (unpublished manuscript). Feb. 15, 1972.

FULTON, C. "An Analytical Study of Confiscated Samples of Narcotic Drugs." *International Microfilm Journal of Legal Medicine*, 1965, *1*(1), Card 2-G1.

Gallup Opinion Index. Report 80. February 1972.

GARFIELD, E., BOREING, M., AND SMITH, J. P. "Marijuana Use on a Campus: Spring 1969." *International Journal of the Addictions*, 1971, *6*(3), 487–491.

GARFIELD, M., AND GARFIELD, E. "A Longitudinal Study of Drugs on a Campus." *International Journal of the Addictions*, 1973, *8* (3).

GOFFMAN, E. "On the Characteristics of Total Institutions: Staff-Inmate Relations." In D. Cressey (Ed.), *The Prison: Studies in Institutional Organization and Change*. New York: Holt, Rinehart, and Winston, 1961.

GOLDBERG, L. "Drug Abuse in Sweden," Parts I, II. *Bulletin on Narcotics*, 1968, *20*, 9.

GOLDSTEIN, A. "Heroin Addiction and Role of Methadone in Its Treatment." *Archives of General Psychiatry*, 1972, *26*, 291–297.

GOODE, E. "The Marijuana Market." *Columbia Forum*, Winter 1969, *12*(4), 4–8.

GOODE, E. *The Marijuana Smokers.* New York: Basic Books, 1970.

GOODWIN, D. W., CRANE, J. B., AND GUZE, S. B. "Felons Who Drink: An 8-Year Follow-Up." *Quarterly Journal of Studies on Alcohol,* 1971, *32,* 136–147.

GRINSPOON, L. *Marijuana Reconsidered.* Cambridge, Mass.: Harvard University Press, 1971.

GROVES, W. E., ROSSI, P. H., AND GRAFSTEIN, D. *Preliminary Results from National College Study of Life Styles and Campus Communities* (unpublished report). Baltimore: John's Hopkins University, Department of Social Relations, December 1971.

GUZE, S. B., GOODWIN, D. W., AND CRANE, J. B. "Criminality and Psychiatric Disorders." *Archives of General Psychiatry,* 1969, *20,* 583–591.

GUZE, S. B., GOODWIN, D. W., AND CRANE, J. B. "Criminal Recidivism and Psychiatric Illness." *American Journal of Psychiatry,* 1970, *127,* 832–835.

HAINES, L., AND GREEN, W. "Marijuana Use Patterns." *British Journal of Addiction,* 1970, *65,* 347–362.

HARE, R. D. *Psychopathy: Theory and Research.* New York: Wiley, 1970.

HAUSER, R. "Prison Reform and Society." *Prison Service Journal,* 1963, *3*(9), 2–18.

HELPERN, M. "Crime in America—Heroin Importation, Distribution, Packaging and Paraphernalia." *Hearings Before the House Select Committee on Crime, June 27, 1970.* Washington, D.C.: Government Printing Office, 1970.

HOCHMAN, J. L., AND BRILL, N. Q. *Marijuana Use and Psychosocial Adaption.* Paper delivered at American Psychiatric Association meeting in Washington, D.C., May 3, 1971.

"How the FDA Traces Counterfeit Drugs." *American Professional Pharmacist,* December 1964, 32–35.

HUGHES, P. H., CRAWFORD, G. A., AND BARKER, N. W. "Developing an Epidemiologic Field Team for Drug Dependence." *Archives of General Psychiatry,* 1971, *24,* 389–394.

ISBELL, H., GORODETZKY, C. W., JASINSKI, D. R., CLAUSSEN, U., VON SPULEK, F., AND KORTE, F. "Effects of (-) Delta 9-Trans-Tetrahydrocannabinol in Man." *Psychopharmacologia,* 1967, *11,* 184–188.

JAFFE, J. H. "Drug Addiction and Drug Abuse." In L. S. Goodman and A. Gilman (Eds.), *The Pharmacological Basis of Therapeutics.* New York: Macmillan, 1970a.

JAFFE, J. H. "The Implementation and Evaluation of New Treatments for Compulsive Drug Users." In R. T. Harris, W. McIsaac, and C. R. Schuster (Eds.), *Drug Dependence, Advances in Mental Sciences II.* Austin: University of Texas Press, 1970b.

Joint Commission on Mental Health of Children. *Crisis in Child Mental Health: Challenge for the 1970's.* New York: Harper and Row, 1969.

JONES, M. *The Therapeutic Community.* New York: Basic Books, 1953.

JONES, R. T. *Tetrahydrocannabinol and the Marijuana Induced Social "High" or the Effects of the Mind on Marijuana.* Paper presented at the New York Academy of Sciences Conference on Marijuana Chemistry, Pharmacology, and Patterns of Social Usage, New York, May 21, 1971.

JOSEPH, H., AND DOLE, V. P. "Methadone Patients on Probation and Parole." *Federal Probation,* 1970, *34*(2), 42–48.

JOSEPHSON, E., HABERMAN, P., ZANES, A., AND ELISON, J. *Adolescent Marijuana Use: Report on a National Survey.* Paper presented at First International Conference of Student Drug Surveys, Newark, N.J., Sept. 14, 1971.

JOYCE, C. R. B. "Quantitative Estimates of Dependence on the Symbolic Function of Drugs." In H. Steinberg (Ed.), *Scientific Basis of Drug Dependence.* London: Churchill, 1969a.

JOYCE, C. R. B. "Drugs and Society." *World Medicine,* October 1969b, 60–62.

JOYCE, C. R. B. *Basic and Applied Research on Drug Dependence—The Need for Cooperation.* n.p.: International Council on Alcohol and Addictions, Institute on Prevention and Treatment of Drug Dependence, 1970.

KAPLAN, J. *Marijuana: The New Prohibition.* New York: World, 1970.

KAUFMAN, E. "A Psychiatrist's Views and Addict Self-Help Programs." *American Journal of Psychiatry,* 1972, *128,* 846–851.

KRAMER, J. C. "The Place of Civil Commitment in the Management of Drug Abuse." In R. T. Harris, W. McIsaac, and C. R. Schuster (Eds.), *Drug Dependence, Advances in Mental Sciences II.* Austin: University of Texas Press, 1970.

KRAMER, J. C. "The State Versus the Addict: Uncivil Commitment." In M. D. Hershey (Ed.), *Drug Abuse Law Review.* Albany: Sage Hill, 1971.

KRAMER, J. C., BASS, R. A., AND BERECHOCHEA, J. E. "Civil Commitment for Addicts: The California Program." *American Journal of Psychiatry,* 1968, *125,* 816–824.

KRISHNAMOORTHY, E. S. *Report of a Study Tour of the Present Position in Regard to the Licit Production and Consumption of Cannabis (Ganja) in India and the Illicit Traffic Thereinto from Nepal.* International Narcotics Control Board, Fifth Session, Item 12 of the provisional agenda, E/INCB/W.40. New York: United Nations, Oct. 1, 1969.

LANOUETTE, W. "The Use of Information in Drug Legislation, An International Study of Recent Cannabis Law." In R. Blum and D. Bovet (Eds.), *Controlling Drugs: An International Handbook for Drug Classification.* San Francisco: Jossey-Bass, in press.

LENNARD, H. L., EPSTEIN, L. J., AND ROSENTHAL, M. S. "The Methadone Illusion." *Science,* May 1972, *176,* 881–884.

LERMAN, P. "Evaluating the Outcomes of Institutions for Delinquents." *Social Work,* 1968, *13*(3), 55–64.

LERNER, M., AND MILLS, A. "Some Modern Aspects of Heroin Analysis." *United Nations Bulletin on Narcotics,* 1963, *15*(1), 37–42.

LERNER, M., AND ZEFFERT, J. T. "Determination of Tetrahydrocannabinol Isomers in Marijuana and Hashish." *United Nations Bulletin on Narcotics,* 1968, *20,* 53–54.

LEWIN, K. *Field Theory in Social Science.* New York: Harper and Row, 1951.

LILLY, D. M., AND STILLWELL, R. H. "Probiotics: Growth Promoting Factors Produced by Micro-Organisms." *Science,* 1965, *147,* 747–748.

LIND, R. C. "The Benefit-Cost Approach to the Evaluation of Drug Control Programs." In R. H. Blum and D. Bovet (Eds.), *Controlling Drugs: An International Handbook for Drug Classification.* San Francisco: Jossey-Bass, in press.

LINDESMITH, A. R. *The Addict and the Law,* Bloomington: Indiana University Press, 1965.

LIPP, M. R. "Marijuana Use by Medical Students." *American Journal of Psychiatry,* 1971, *128,* 207–212.

LOURIA, D. B. "Drug Abuse: A Current Assessment." *American Family Physician/GP,* 1970, *1,* 74–80.

LYTHGOE, H. C. "Character of Illicit Liquor on the Massachusetts Market." *New England Journal of Medicine,* 1928, *198,* 228–230.

MC COY, A. W. *The Politics of Heroin in Southeast Asia.* New York: Harper and Row, 1972.

MC GLOTHLIN, W. H. *Marijuana: An Analysis of Use, Distribution and*

Control. Monograph SCID-TR-2. Washington, D.C.: Bureau of Narcotics and Dangerous Drugs, June 1970.

MC GLOTHLIN, W. H., ARNOLD, D. O., AND ROWAN, B. K. "Marijuana Use Among Adults." *Psychiatry,* 1970a, *33,* 433–443.

MC GLOTHLIN, W., JAMISON, K., AND ROSENBLATT, S. "Marijuana and the Use of Other Drugs." *Nature,* 1970b, *228,* 1227–1229.

MC GLOTHLIN, W. H., TABBUSH, V. C., CHAMBERS, C. D., AND JAMISON, K. *Alternative Approaches to Opiate Addiction Control: Cost, Benefits, and Potential.* Final report. Washington, D.C.: Bureau of Narcotics and Dangerous Drugs, 1972.

MC GUIRE, W. J. "A Vaccine for Brainwash." *Psychology Today,* February 1970, 36–39; 63–64.

MALABIS, A. L. "Drugs on the Job." *Management Review,* July 1970, 40–42.

MANDEL, J. "Myths and Realities of Marihuana Pushing." In J. L. Simmons (Ed.), *Marihuana Myths and Realities.* Chatsworth, Calif.: Brandon, 1967.

MANHEIMER, D. I., MELLINGER, G. D., AND BALTER, M. B. "Psychotherapeutic Drugs: Use Among Adults in California." *California Medicine,* 1968, *109,* 445–451.

MANHEIMER, D. I., MELLINGER, G. D., AND BALTER, M. B. "Marijuana Use Among Urban Adults." *Science,* 1969, 1544–1545.

MANNO, J., KIPLINGER, G., BENNETT, I., HAYNE, S., AND FORNEY, R., "Comparative Effects of Smoking Marijuana on Motor and Mental Performance in Humans." *Clinical Pharmacology and Therapeutics,* November-December 1970, *11*(6), 808–815.

MARGELTS, S. "The Pot-Smoking Young Executives." *Dun's,* 1970, *95,* 42–43.

Marihuana and Health. First annual report to Congress from the Secretary of Health, Education and Welfare. Washington, D.C.: Government Printing Office, 1971.

Marihuana and Health. Second annual report to Congress from the Secretary of Health, Education and Welfare. Washington, D.C.: Government Printing Office, 1972.

MARSHMAN, J. A., AND GIBBINS, R. J. "The Credibility Gap in the Illicit Drug Market." *Addiction,* 1969, *16,* 4.

MARSHMAN, J. A., AND GIBBINS, R. J. "A Note on the Composition of Illicit Drugs." *Ontario Medical Review,* September 1970, 1.

MARTINSON, R. "The Treatment Evaluation Survey" (personal communication). Albany: Office of Crime Control Planning, State of New York, 1972.

Mayor's Committee on Marijuana. *The Marijuana Problem in the City of New York.* Tempe, Ariz.: Cattell, 1964.

MECHOULAM, R. "Marijuana Chemistry." *Science,* 1970, *168,* 1159–1166.

MESSER, M. "The Predictive Value of Marijuana Use: A Note to Researchers of Student Culture." *Sociology of Education,* 1969, *42,* 91–97.

MILES, W. G. "Present Status of Alcoholism." *Southern Medicine and Surgery,* 1935, *97,* 177–180.

MOORE, R. A. "Alcoholism in Japan." *Quarterly Journal of Studies on Alcohol,* 1964, *25,* 142–150.

MORRIS, N., AND HAWKINS, G. *The Honest Politician's Guide to Crime Control,* Chicago: University of Chicago Press, 1970.

MORTON, A., MUELLER, J., OHLGREN, J., PEARSON, R., AND WEISEL, S. "Marijuana Laws: An Empirical Study of Enforcement and Administration in Los Angeles County." *University of California at Los Angeles Law Review,* 1968, *15,* 1501–1585.

MULVIHILL, D. J., AND TUMIN, M. M., with CURTIS, L. A. *Crimes of Violence—A Staff Report to the National Commission on the Causes and Prevention of Violence.* Vol. 13. Washington, D.C.: Government Printing Office, December 1969.

National Institute of Mental Health. *Alcohol and Alcoholism.* Washington, D.C.: Government Printing Office, 1969.

NILSSON, L., AND LINDROTH, C. H. *Myror.* Stockholm: Forum, 1959.

NISBET, C. T., AND VAKIL, F. "Some Social and Economic Characteristics of U.C.L.A. Marijuana Users." *Social Science Quarterly,* June 1971, *52,* 179–189.

O'DONNELL, J. A. "Lexington Program for Addicts." *Federal Probation,* 1962, *26*(1), 55–60.

O'MALLEY, J. E., ANDERSON, W. H., AND LAZARE, A. "Failure of Out-Patient Treatment of Drug Abuse: 1. Heroin." *American Journal of Psychiatry,* 1972, *128,* 865–868.

O'NEAL, P., ROBINS, L. N., KING, L. J., AND SCHAEFER, J. "Parental Deviance in the Genesis of the Sociopathic Personality." *American Journal of Psychiatry,* 1962, *118,* 1114–1124.

PACKER, H. *The Limits of the Criminal Sanction.* Stanford, Calif.: Stanford University Press, 1969.

PALO ALTO CITIZENS' TASK FORCE. *Palo Alto Drug Use and Abuse Report.* Palo Alto, Calif.: January 1972.

PARRY, H. "The Use of Psychotropic Drugs by U.S. Adults." *Public Health Report,* 1968, *83,* 799–810.

PARRY, H. Unpublished data. Washington, D.C.: Social Research Group, George Washington University, 1971.

PAYNE, J. "No Help for the Young." *Drugs and Society,* 1971, *1*(1), 8–11.

PEPPER, C. "Crime in America—Heroin Importation, Distribution, Packaging, and Paraphernalia." In *Hearings Before the House Select Committee on Crime, June 25, 1970.* Washington, D.C.: Government Printing Office, 1970a.

PEPPER, C. "Crime in America—The Heroin Paraphernalia Trade." In *Hearings Before the House Select Committee on Crime, October 5–6, 1970.* Washington, D.C.: Government Printing Office, 1970b.

PHILLIPS, R., TURK, R., MANNO, J., JAIN, M., FORNEY, R. *Seasonal Variation in Cannabinolic Content of Indiana Marijuana.* Paper presented at the Twenty-Second Annual Meeting of the American Academy of Forensic Sciences, Chicago, Ill., Feb. 27, 1970.

PREBLE, E., AND CASEY, J. J., JR. "Taking Care of Business—the Heroin User's Life on the Street." *International Journal of the Addictions,* 1969, *4*(1), 1–24.

RATHOD, N. H., GREGORY, E., BLOWS, D., AND THOMAS, G. H. "A Two-Year Follow-Up Study of Alcoholic Patients." *British Journal of Psychiatry,* 1966, *112,* 683–692.

REISS, A. A., *The Police and the Public.* New Haven, Conn.: Yale University Press, 1971.

RESNIC, R. B., FINK, M., AND FREEDMAN, A. M. "Cyclazocine Treatment of Opiate Dependence, A Progress Report." *Comprehensive Psychiatry,* 1971, *12,* 491–502.

RINKEL, M. *Specific and Non-Specific Factors in Psychopharmacology.* New York: Philosophical Library, 1963.

ROBINS, L. N. *Deviant Children Grown Up.* Baltimore: Williams and Wilkins, 1966.

ROBINS, L. N. "The Adult Development of the Anti-Social Child." *Seminars in Psychiatry,* 1970, *2,* 420–434.

ROBINS, L. N., AND MURPHY, G. E. "Drug Use in a Normal Population of Young Negro Men." *American Journal of Public Health,* 1967, *57*(9), 1580–1596.

ROBISON, J. *Technical Supplement #2, The California Prison, Parole and Probation System. A Special Report to the Assembly.* Sacramento, Calif.: State of California, 1969.

ROLAND, J. L., AND TESTE, M. "Le cannabisme au Maroc." *Maroc Medical,* June 1958, *387,* 694–703.

ROSENTHAL, R., AND ROSNOW, R. L. (Eds.). *Artifact in Behavioral Research.* New York: Academic Press, 1969.

SAN MATEO COUNTY SCHOOLS. *Five Mind-Altering Drugs: The Use of Alcoholic Beverages, Amphetamines, LSD, Marijuana and Tobacco Reported by High School and Junior High School Students, San Mateo County, California, 1968, 1969, 1970,* plus *Addendum, 1971.* Prepared at the request of the Narcotic Advisory Committee of the Juvenile Justice Commission. San Mateo, Calif.: Department of Public Health and Welfare, Research and Statistics Section, 1968, 1969, 1970, 1971.

SAPOL, E., AND ROFFMAN, R. A. "Marijuana in Viet Nam." *Journal of the American Pharmaceutical Association,* 1969, *9,* 615–618, 630.

SCHLESINGER, E. R., DICKSON, D. G., AND WESTABY, J. "A Controlled Study of Health Education in Accident Prevention." *American Journal of Diseases of Children,* 1966, *3,* 619.

SCHUR, E. *Crimes Without Victims—Deviant Behavior and Public Policy: Abortion, Homosexuality, Drug Addiction.* Englewood Cliffs, N.J.: Prentice-Hall, 1965.

SCHWITZGEBEL, R. K. "Learning Theory Approaches to the Treatment of Criminal Behavior." *Seminars in Psychiatry,* 1971, *3*(3), 328–344.

SHARAF, M. R. "Phoenix House: An Interview with Mitchell S. Rosenthal." *Seminars in Psychiatry,* 1971, *3*(2), 226–244.

SHIN, H. J., AND KERSTETTER, W. A. *Report of the Evaluation of Illinois Drug Abuse Program: Changes in Patient's Arrest Rates.* Chicago: Center for Studies in Criminal Justice, The University of Chicago, June 1971.

SKOLNIK, J. *Justice Without Trial.* New York: Wiley, 1966.

SMITH, J. P. *Addendum to "Final Report."* Bureau of Narcotics and Dangerous Drugs Contract J-68-13, 1971.

South Africa Drug Report. Interdepartmental Committee on the Abuse of Drugs Report. Cape Town: Government Printer, 1952.

STEIN, K. B., SARBIN, T. R., AND KULIK, J. A. "Further Validation of Antisocial Personality Types." *Journal of Consulting and Clinical Psychology,* 1971, *36,* 177–182.

STEVENSON, I. "Physical Symptoms Occurring with Pleasurable Emotional States." *American Journal of Psychiatry,* 1970, *127,* 93–97.

STORER, J. Testimony in *Hearings Before the House Permanent Subcommittee on Investigations: Organized Crime and Illicit Traffic in Narcotics, July 30, 1964.* Washington, D.C.: Government Printing Office, 1964.

SUTTER, A. "Phases of a Ghetto Career." In R. H. Blum and Associates (Eds.), *The Dream Sellers: Perspectives on Drug Dealers.* San Francisco: Jossey-Bass, 1972.

TALBOTT, J. H. "Tetanus in Addicts." *Journal of the American Medical Association,* 1968, *205*(8), 584–585.

TAMERIN, J. S., AND NEUMANN, C. P. *Prognostic Factors in the Evaluation of Addicted Individuals.* Paper presented at 38th Annual Meeting of National Association of Private Psychiatric Hospitals, Key Biscayne, Fla., Jan. 5–28, 1971.

Task force report: Drunkenness. President's Commission on Law Enforcement and Administration of Justice. Washington, D.C.: Government Printing Office, 1967.

Task force report: Narcotics and Drug Abuse. President's Commission on Law Enforcement and Administration of Justice. Washington, D.C.: Government Printing Office, 1967.

TENNANT, F. S., AND PRENDERGAST, T. J. "Medical Manifestation Associated with Hashish." *Journal of the American Medical Association,* 1971, *216,* 1965–1969.

THOMPSON, T. "Drugs as Reinforcers: Experimental Addiction." *International Journal of the Addictions,* 1968, *3,* 199–206.

TRESAN, D. "An Adolescent User's Ward" (unpublished). 1971.

VAILLANT, G. E. "A Twelve-Year Follow-Up of New York Narcotic Addicts: The Relation of Treatment to Outcome." *American Journal of Psychiatry,* 1966, *122,* 727–737.

VAILLANT, G. E., BRIGHTON, J. R., AND MC ARTHUR, C. "Physicians' Use of Mood-Altering Drugs." *New England Journal of Medicine,* 1970, *282,* 365–370.

VAILLANT, G. E., AND RASOR, R. W. "The Role of Compulsory Supervision in Treatment of Addiction." *Federal Probation,* 1966, *30*(2), 53–59.

WALDORF, D. "Life Without Heroin: Some Social Adjustments During Long-Term Periods of Voluntary Abstention." *Social Problems,* 1970, *18*(2), 228–243.

WALLACE, R. K. "Physiological Effects of Transcendental Meditation." *Science,* 1970, *167,* 1751–1754.

WALLER, C. W. "The Chemistry of Marijuana." *Proceedings of the Western Pharmacological Society,* 1971, *14,* 1–3.

WATKINS, C. "Use of Amphetamine by Medical Students." *Southern Medical Journal,* 1970, *63,* 923–929.

WEECH, A., AND BIBB, R. E. "Toward a Rational Approach to Psychedelics: The Controversy over Popular Use from a Clinical Viewpoint." *Comprehensive Psychiatry,* 1970, *11,* 57–68.

WEEKS, C. C. "Hooch Poisoning." *British Medical Journal,* 1942, *1,* 596.

WEIL, A. T. "Altered States of Consciousness." In P. Wald and P. Hutt (cochairmen), *Dealing with Drug Abuse: A Report to the Ford Foundation, The Drug Abuse Survey Project.* New York: Praeger, 1972.

WEIL, A. T., ZINBERG, N. E., AND NELSEN, J. M. "Clinical and Psychological Effects of Marihuana in Man." *Science,* 1968, *162,* 1234–1242.

WERTHMAN, C. AND PILIAVIN, E. "Gang Members and the Police." In D. Bordua (Ed.), *The Police: Six Sociological Essays.* New York: Wiley, 1967.

WIELAND, W. F., AND CHAMBERS, C. D. "Methadone Maintenance: A Comparison of Two Stabilization Techniques." *International Journal of the Addictions,* 1970, *5,* 645–659.

WILSON, J. Q. *Varieties of Police Behavior: The Management of Law and Order in Eight Communities.* Cambridge, Mass.: Harvard University Press, 1968.

WOLFGANG, M. E. *Youth and Violence.* Washington, D.C.: U.S. Department of Health, Education and Welfare, 1970.

WORLD HEALTH ORGANIZATION, EXPERT COMMITTEE ON DRUG DEPENDENCE. *Technical Report Series 460.* Eighteenth report. Geneva, 1970.

ZACUNE, J. "A Comparison of Canadian Narcotic Addicts in Great Britain and in Canada." *Bulletin on Narcotics,* October-December 1971, *23*(4), 41–49.

ZACUNE, J., AND HENSMAN, C. *Drugs, Alcohol and Tobacco in Britain.* London: Heinemann, 1971.

ZAJONC, R. "Brainwash: Familiarity Breeds Comfort." *Psychology Today,* February 1970, 32–35; 60–62.

ZIMRING, F. E. *Perspectives on Deterrence.* Washington, D.C.: NIMH Center for Studies of Crimes and Delinquency, 1971.

ZINBERG, N., AND ROBERTSON, J. *Drugs and the Public.* New York: Simon and Schuster, 1972.

Index

A

Afghanistan: illicit opium market in, 69–71; in narcotics network, 91–92

Alcohol: related to drug education, 278; related to illicit drug use, 2, 7, 9–10, 114, 143, 169, 203, 222–223; related to marijuana use, 39, 54, 58, 60, 208, 209–212; substances in 24–26. *See also* Pruno

Arrest: for marijuana use or sale, 49–50, 56; risk of, 3–5, 107–108, 113, 137–138; risk of in major city, 140–149, 152–159, 160–161

B

Barbiturates: law enforcement priorities regarding, 124; use of in juvenile detention centers, 164, 166, 170

Burma: illicit opium market in, 69–71; in narcotics trading network, 86, 88–89

C

China, People's Republic of, opium markets in, 64, 71

D

Dealers: and arrest, risk of, 3–5, 49–50, 56, 107–108, 113, 137–138, 140–149, 152–159, 160–161; characteristics of 213–215; correction and treatment of, 213–231; evolution of, 2–3, 205; and responsiveness to social controls, 248–249; roles of, 246–248; in student population, 11; subculture of, 244–246; taking action toward, 282–292; transnational research on, 249–250. *See also* Drug dealing

Detention centers, juvenile, illicit drug use in: with minimum security, 163–165, 167–170; in secure facility, 165–170

Drug dealing: effects of on the law, 201–212; problems of, 1–2

309

Drug education: and acceptance of altered states, 277; community center approach to, 277; delinquency approach to, 273–274; focus of, 277–279; health approach to, 272–273; impact of, 263, 269–270, 279–281; impure drugs and, 21–22; moral approach to, 276; and philosophy, 271–272; reasons for, 11; in schools, 267–281; social learning approach to, 274–275; techniques of, 275–276

Drugs, illicit: availability of, 252–253; control of, 98–105, 192–194, 253–256; counterfeiting of, 16–18; dependency model in use of, 256–258; illicit market prices for, 94–98; in prisons, 189–192; social responses to problems of, 232–242; student opinions of purity of, 14–16; substances in, 13–30; traffic in, 7–10, 62–105, 282–283; use of related to tobacco and alcohol, 2, 7, 9–10, 114, 143, 169, 203, 222–223

E

Education. See Drug education

Enforcement of narcotics laws: budget for in college town, 115–116; case costs of in college town, 116–119; case costs of in major city, 159–160; in college town, 114–138; considerations on, 106–113; and dealers, dispositions for, 150–152; effects of, 284–285; effects of in college town, 119–123, 134–136; evidence used for in major city, 149–150; and impure drugs, 19–20; in major city, 139–161; priorities in, 109–113, 123–128, 131–134; sanctuaries from, 128–131, 136–138

F

France, in narcotics network, 78–82, 95

G

Glue-sniffing in prisons, 173, 189, 190

Golden Triangle. See Burma, Laos, Thailand

H

Hallucinogens, substances in, 22–24. See also individual drugs

Hashish: amount of used, 36, 38; distribution of, 43–44; importation of, 42, 58; retail expenditures for, 45–47; seizures of, 47; source of, 41

Heroin: international traffic systems for, 62–105; in juvenile detention centers, 164, 166; law enforcement priorities regarding, 124; menace of users of, 110; in prisons, 173, 176, 179, 189–190, 193, 196–198; quinine's effects in, 20–21; substances in, 28–30

Hong Kong, in narcotics trading network, 86–87, 89–90

I

India: cannabis use in, 52, 53; in narcotics network, 93; opium markets in, 64–71

Informants: use of, 112; use of in college town, 126, 132, 137; use of in major city, 146, 151

Iran: heroin market prices in, 94–95; in narcotics network, 91; opium markets in, 64–68, 71

J

Juvenile detention centers. See Detention centers, juvenile

L

Laos: illicit opium market in, 69–71; in narcotics trading network, 86, 88–89

Latin America: illicit opium market in, 70; in narcotics trading network, 83–85

Law enforcement. See Enforcement of narcotics laws

Laws: as affected by drug dealing, 201–212; criminal, alternatives to,

207–212; criminal, effectiveness of, 202–204

LSD: menace of users of, 110; price of in prisons, 190; research on, 18–19; student opinions of purity of, 15–16; substances in, 22–23; use of in California, 153–154; use of in juvenile detention centers, 163–164, 166, 170

M

Malaysia, as opium market, 88–90
Marijuana: amount of used, 36, 38–40; arrests for use or sale of, 49–50, 56; in California, 153–154; control of by proposed statute, 209–212; control policies for, 54, 56–61; criminal behavior contributed to by, 59; cross-cultural usage patterns of, 52–54; current trends in use of, 50–52; dealers in, evolution of, 204–207; delta-9 THC content of, 26–27, 38; distribution of, 42–45, 48, 56; frequency of use of, 33, 35–36, 37; future policies concerning, 60–61; future use of, 50–54, 55; importation of, 41–42, 57–59; as independent variable, 256; in juvenile detention centers, 163–164, 166, 170; law enforcement concerning, 47–50; market for, 39–47, 56; menace of user of, 110; prevalence and patterns in use of, 31–39, 48; price of in prisons, 190; research on, 18, 256; retail expenditures for, 45–47, 48, 56; sale of, regulated, 59–60; seizures of, 47, 49, 56; source of, 40–41; substances in, 26–28, 44; supply of, suppressed, 57
Mescaline, purity of, 15–16, 23
Mexico: illicit opium market in, 69–70; as source of marijuana, 40–42
Middle East: and South Asia narcotics network, 91–94; and United States narcotics network, 76–86

N

Narcotics. See Drugs, illicit

O

Opium: derivatives from, 72–74; illicit market for, 63–64, 68–76; licit market for, 63, 64–68; processing of, 74–75; trading networks in, 75–94

P

Pakistan: cannabis use in, 52; in narcotics network, 91, 92–93; opium market in, 65, 67, 69–71
Pharmaceutical industry, responsibilities of for drug control, 251–266
Prisons: corruptability of personnel in, 283–284; drug control in, 192–194, 199–200; heroin in, related to folktales, 196–198; illicit drug use in, 171–200; illicit drugs in, obtaining of, 175–187
Pruno, in prisons, 173, 187–189, 193, 198

R

Research: effects of impure drugs on, 18–19; related to future policy action, 243–250

S

Sanctuaries from law enforcement, 128–131, 136–138
Servicemen: cannabis use by, 53; effect of on narcotics network, 86, 90, 97
Singapore, as opium market, 88–90
Social class, law enforcement priorities regarding, 125–128
Society, motivations of concerning drugs, 259–266
South Asia and Middle East narcotics network, 91–94
Southeast Asia: narcotics market prices in, 97–98; narcotics markets in, 70, 87–88; narcotics trading network in, 86–91. See also individual countries
Speed: student opinions of purity of, 15–16; use of in juvenile detention centers, 164, 166, 170

STP, student opinions of purity of, 15–16

T

Thailand: illicit opium market in, 69–71; in narcotics trading network, 86–89
THC: content of in marijuana, 26–27, 38; student opinions of purity of, 15–16
Tobacco: related to drug education, 278; related to drug use, 167, 169
Traffic systems in narcotics, 7–10, 62–105, 282–283
Treatment for drug abuse: assessing approaches in, 215–217, 228–230; communal, 222–223; community-based, 226–228; of dealers, 213–231; effects of impure drugs on, 20–21; legal intervention for, 223–226; medical-psychological, 217–

220; methods of, 217–230; pharmacotherapeutic, 220–222
Turkey: in narcotics network, 76–81, 91; opium markets in, 64–67, 69–71

U

Union of Soviet Socialist Republics, licit opium market in, 64, 66
United Nations: drug control efforts by, 99–103; research of on drug dealers, 250
United States: heroin market prices in, 94–98; and Middle East narcotics trading network, 76–86
User-dealer: responsiveness of to social controls, 248–249; roles of, 246–248; subculture of, 244–246

Y

Yugoslavia, illicit opium market in, 69–70